WORLD EXPLORER

THE UNITED STATES AND CANADA

PRENTICE HALL
Needham, Massachusetts
Upper Saddle River, New Jersey

Program Authors

Heidi Hayes Jacobs

Heidi Hayes Jacobs has served as an educational consultant to more than 500 schools across the nation. Dr. Jacobs is an adjunct professor in the Department of Curriculum on Teaching at Teachers College, Columbia University. She completed her undergraduate studies at the University of Utah in her hometown of Salt Lake City. She received an M.A. from the University of Massachusetts, Amherst, and completed her doctoral work at Columbia University's Teachers College in 1981.

The backbone of Dr. Jacobs' experience comes from her years as a teacher of high school, middle school, and elementary school students. As an educational consultant, she works with K–12 schools and districts on curriculum reform and strategic planning.

Brenda Randolph

Brenda Randolph is the former Director of the Outreach Resource Center at the African Studies Program at Howard University, Washington, D.C. She is the Founder and Director of Africa Access, a bibliographic service on Africa for schools. She received her B.A. in history with high honors from North Carolina Central University, Durham, and her M.A. in African studies with honors from Howard University. She completed further graduate studies at the University of Maryland, College Park, where she was awarded a Graduate Fellowship.

Brenda Randolph has published numerous articles in professional journals and bulletins. She currently serves as library media specialist in Montgomery County Public Schools, Maryland.

Michal L. LeVasseur

Michal LeVasseur is an educational consultant in the field of geography. She is an adjunct professor of geography at the University of Alabama, Birmingham, and serves with the Alabama Geographic Alliance. Her undergraduate and graduate work is in the fields of anthropology (B.A.), geography (M.A.), and science education (Ph.D.).

Dr. LeVasseur's specialization has moved increasingly into the area of geography education. In 1996, she served as Director of the National Geographic Society's Summer Geography Workshop. As an educational consultant, she has worked with the National Geographic Society as well as with schools to develop programs and curricula for geography.

Special Program Consultant

Yvonne S. Gentzler, Ph.D.
School of Education
University of Idaho
Moscow, Idaho

PRENTICE HALL
Simon & Schuster Education Group
A VIACOM COMPANY

Upper Saddle River, New Jersey
Needham, Massachusetts

ISBN 0-13-433709-3

1 2 3 4 5 6 7 8 9 10   01 00 99 98 97

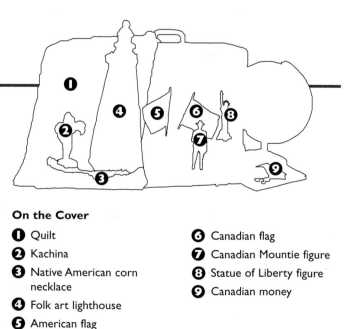

On the Cover

❶ Quilt
❷ Kachina
❸ Native American corn necklace
❹ Folk art lighthouse
❺ American flag
❻ Canadian flag
❼ Canadian Mountie figure
❽ Statue of Liberty figure
❾ Canadian money

Content Consultants for the World Explorer Program

Teacher Advisory Board

The World Explorer Team

TABLE OF CONTENTS

THE UNITED STATES AND CANADA   1

OF SPECIAL INTEREST

MAPS

CHARTS, GRAPHS, AND TABLES

READ ACTIVELY

How can I get the most out of my social studies book?
How does my reading relate to my world? Answering questions like these means that you are an active reader, an involved reader. As an active reader, you are in charge of the reading situation!

The following strategies tell how to think and read as an active reader. You don't need to use all of these strategies all the time. Feel free to choose the ones that work best in each reading situation. You might use several at a time, or you might go back and forth among them. They can be used in any order.

BEFORE YOU READ

Give yourself a purpose

The sections in this book begin with a list called "Questions to Explore." These questions focus on key ideas presented in the section. They give you a purpose for reading. You can create your own purpose by asking questions like these: How does the topic relate to your life? How might you use what you learn at school or at home?

Preview

To preview a reading selection, first read its title. Then look at the pictures and read the captions. Also read any headings in the selection. Then ask yourself: What is the reading selection about? What do the pictures and headings tell about the selection?

Reach into your background

What do you already know about the topic of the selection? How can you use what you know to help you understand what you are going to read?

Ask questions

Suppose you are reading about the continent of South America. Some questions you might ask are: Where is South America? What countries are found there? Why are some of the countries large and others small? Asking questions like these can help you gather evidence and gain knowledge.

Predict

As you read, make a prediction about what will happen and why. Or predict how one fact might affect another fact. Suppose you are reading about South America's climate. You might make a prediction about how the climate affects where people live. You can change your mind as you gain new information.

Connect

Connect your reading to your own life. Are the people discussed in the selection like you or someone you know? What would you do in similar situations? Connect your reading to something you have already read. Suppose you have already read about the ancient Greeks. Now you are reading about the ancient Romans. How are they alike? How are they different?

Visualize

What would places, people, and events look like in a movie or a picture? As you read about India, you could visualize the country's heavy rains. What do they look like? How do they sound? As you read about geography, you could visualize a volcanic eruption.

Respond

Talk about what you have read. What did you think? Share your ideas with your classmates.

Assess yourself

What did you find out? Were your predictions on target? Did you find answers to your questions?

Follow up

Show what you know. Use what you have learned to do a project. When you do projects, you continue to learn.

THE UNITED STATES AND CANADA

Spreading "from sea to shining sea," the United States and Canada take up nearly seven-eighths of North America. From the groups who migrated to these areas before the dawn of history to later settlers from around the world, a wide variety of people have flocked to North America. Out of the region's natural riches and varied cultures have grown successful nations. In this book, you'll see how the United States and Canada are working to create a good life for every citizen.

Guiding Questions

The readings and activities in this book will help you discover answers to these Guiding Questions.

- ☛ How has physical geography affected the cultures of the United States and Canada?

- ☛ How have historical events affected the cultures of the United States and Canada?

- ☛ How has the variety of peoples in the United States and Canada benefited and challenged the two nations?

- ☛ How has modern technology benefited and challenged the United States and Canada?

- ☛ How did the United States and Canada become two of the wealthiest nations in the world?

Project Preview

You can also discover answers to the Guiding Questions by working on projects. Preview the following projects and choose one that you might like to do. For more details, see page 140.

Write a Children's Book Write a short book for young students about a topic in the United States and Canada.

Make a Time Line of Local History Make an illustrated time line of the history of your community.

Set Up a Weather Station Keep a log of local weather conditions. Compare your weather to other parts of the country.

Create a Diorama Sculpt the physical features of a geographic region in the United States and Canada with clay or dough. Add details to the landscape.

Football is a popular sport in the United States. Top left, a football team congratulates a fellow team member. Middle, this child in Canada is taking part in a favorite national sport—sledding. Left, a couple in California enjoys their garden.

EXPLORER'S JOURNAL

A journal can be your personal book of discovery. As you explore the United States and Canada, you can use your journal to keep track of things you learn and do. You can also record thoughts about your journey. For your first entry, write your thoughts on where in the United States and Canada you would like to go and what you would want to see there.

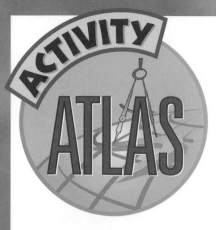

ACTIVITY ATLAS

The United States and Canada

Learning about Canada and the United States means being an explorer and a geographer. No explorer would start out without first checking some facts. Begin by exploring the maps of the United States and Canada on the following pages.

Relative Location

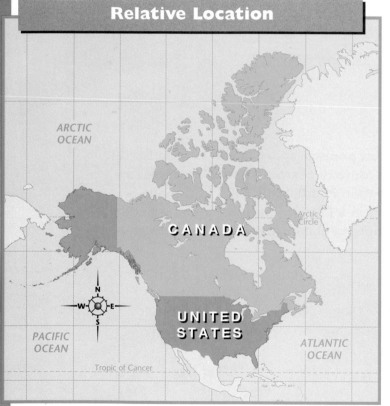

LOCATION

1. Explore the Location of the United States and Canada Look at the map at left. In this book you will read about the United States, which is colored orange on the map, and Canada, which is green. Which country extends farther north? If you were on the east coast of the United States, which direction would you travel to get to the Pacific Ocean? Why do Canadians think of the United States as their neighbor to the south?

Relative Size

REGIONS

2. Compare the Sizes of the United States and Canada Look at the map to the right. Compare it to the map above. Notice that not all of the United States is shown on the map at right. Which country do you think is bigger, the United States mainland or Canada? Check your estimate by looking up both of the countries in the World View at the back of this book.

3. Explore the United States and Canada
The United States and Canada together take up most of the continent of North America. Look at the map. What other country is on the same continent? What country borders Canada? What countries border the United States? Name the cities that are the national capitals of the United States and Canada. Which 2 of the 50 United States do not share a border with any other state? Which of the Canadian cities on the map is the farthest south? North?

4. Locate Bodies of Water Important to the United States and Canada What three oceans surround the United States and Canada? Find the Great Lakes on the map. How many are there? Which one lies entirely within the United States? What river connects the Great Lakes to the Atlantic Ocean? The largest bay in the world is located in Canada. What is its name? Would you enter the bay from the Pacific Ocean or from the Atlantic Ocean?

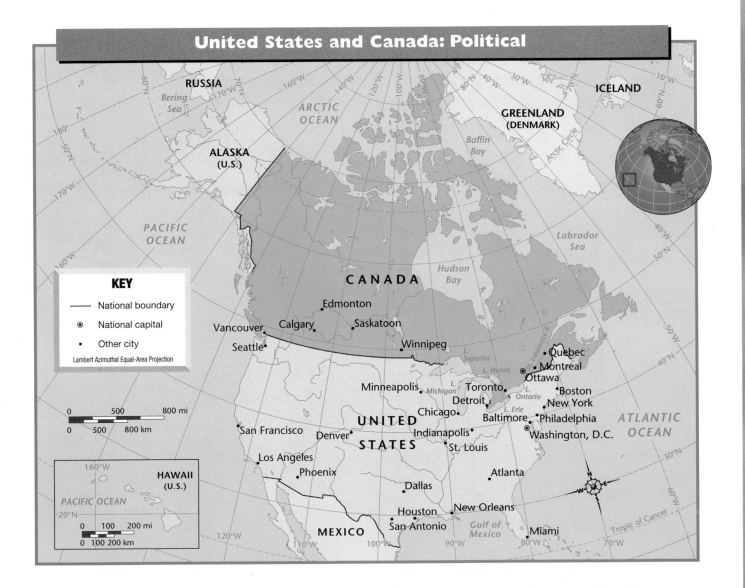

United States and Canada: Political

PLACE

5. Find Geo Cleo Geo Cleo is traveling through the United States and Canada. Use her clues and the map below to answer her questions about where she has been on her tour of the United States and Canada.

A. Whew! I've been hiking through the Rocky Mountains! Right now I'm heading south. I just crossed the Colorado River. What country am I in?

B. Today, I crossed the border of the United States, and I'm flying to Victoria Island in Canada. Which direction am I going?

C. Now I'm on a ship. We're heading from the Gulf of St. Lawrence to the Great Lakes. What river will we travel on?

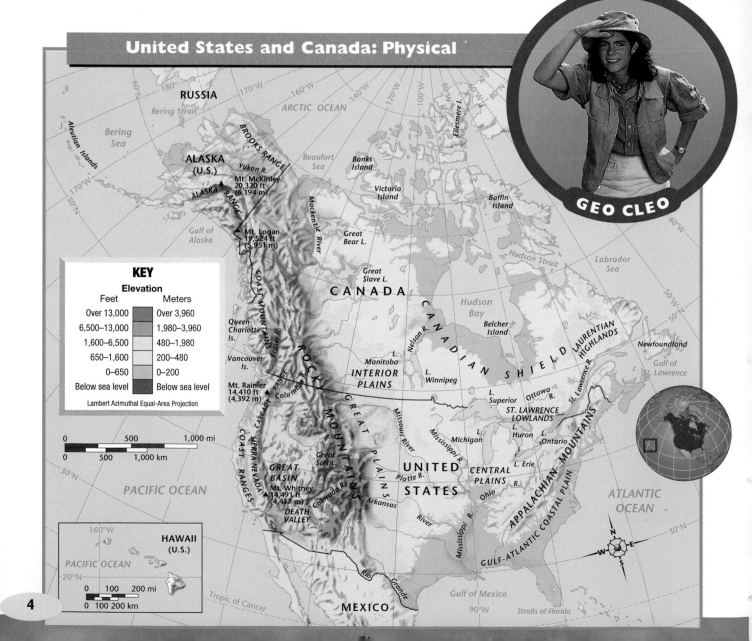

GEO CLEO

United States and Canada: Physical

KEY

Elevation

Feet	Meters
Over 13,000	Over 3,960
6,500–13,000	1,980–3,960
1,600–6,500	480–1,980
650–1,600	200–480
0–650	0–200
Below sea level	Below sea level

Lambert Azimuthal Equal-Area Projection

0   500   1,000 mi
0   500   1,000 km

HAWAII (U.S.)

PACIFIC OCEAN

0   100   200 mi
0   100 200 km

6. Investigate Land Use in the United States and Canada The use of land is one of the main features of a place. How many different types of land use are identified on the map? Which is the most common use of the land in Canada? In the United States? Compare the use of land in the eastern half of the United States to the western half. What are the main differences?

7. Compare Land Use to Physical Features Look at the physical map on the opposite page. Compare it to the land use map on this page. What relationship do you see between physical features and the way people use the land? How do people use the land in mountainous regions? What type of land seems to be good for farming? Look at the manufacturing areas. What physical feature is close to most of them?

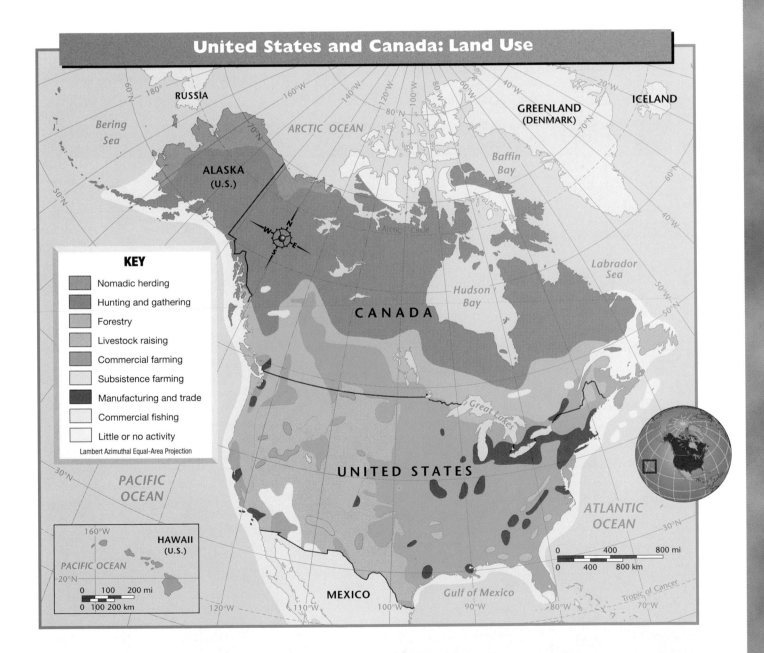

United States and Canada: Land Use

KEY
- Nomadic herding
- Hunting and gathering
- Forestry
- Livestock raising
- Commercial farming
- Subsistence farming
- Manufacturing and trade
- Commercial fishing
- Little or no activity

Lambert Azimuthal Equal-Area Projection

RUSSIA
Bering Sea
ALASKA (U.S.)
ARCTIC OCEAN
GREENLAND (DENMARK)
ICELAND
Baffin Bay
Labrador Sea
Hudson Bay
CANADA
Arctic Circle
Great Lakes
UNITED STATES
PACIFIC OCEAN
ATLANTIC OCEAN
HAWAII (U.S.)
PACIFIC OCEAN
MEXICO
Gulf of Mexico
Tropic of Cancer

0   100   200 mi
0 100 200 km

0   400   800 mi
0   400   800 km

8. Investigate the Climates of the United States and Canada

You already know that climate affects the way people live. For example, you don't find snowplows on the beach or skis in the desert! Look at the map below. How many different types of climate regions are there in the United States and Canada? Do the climates seem to change more from east to west or from north to south? Which of the two countries has a region of humid subtropical climate? Which has the biggest area of subarctic climate?

9. Investigate How Climate Affects the Way People Live

Look at the climate map below. What city fits each of these descriptions?

• In this area of marine west coast climate, winds blowing from the ocean help keep the climate very damp. People in this Canadian city are used to a climate with lots of rain.

• People who live here are in a tropical wet and dry climate. They do not own winter coats or boots, and many have never seen snow.

• The humid continental climate region includes some major cities of both countries. People here usually need clothes for all four seasons. Their houses must have good heating systems. Many are also air conditioned in the summer. This city is on Lake Michigan.

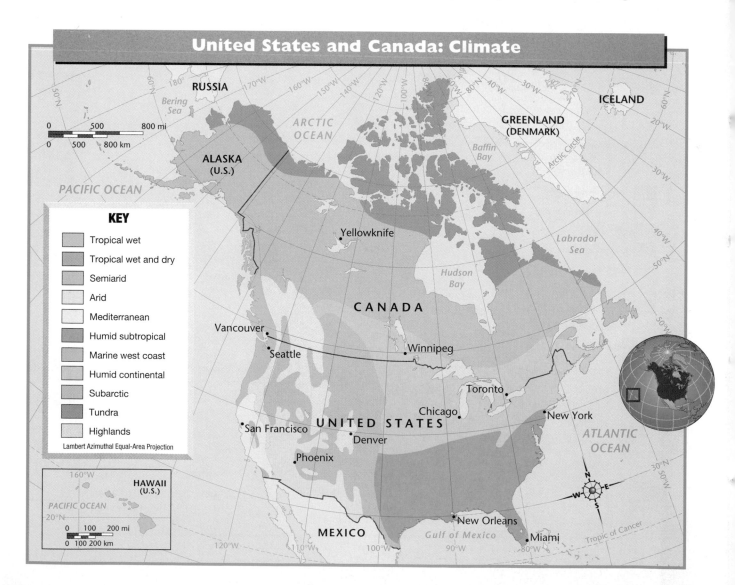

United States and Canada: Climate

KEY
- Tropical wet
- Tropical wet and dry
- Semiarid
- Arid
- Mediterranean
- Humid subtropical
- Marine west coast
- Humid continental
- Subarctic
- Tundra
- Highlands

Lambert Azimuthal Equal-Area Projection

10. **Analyze the Populations of the United States and Canada** The United States and Canada are often referred to as "countries of immigrants." Through the years, people have moved to both of these countries from other places around the world. The chart below lists the percentages of the populations of the United States and Canada whose ancestors came from some other places. (Only the places of ancestry for the highest percentages of people are listed in the table.) Which are the three most common places of ancestry for people in the United States? How does this compare to the most common places of ancestry for people in Canada? Both Canada and the United States belonged to England in the early part of their histories. What effect has this had on the populations of Canada and the United States?

Most Common Sources of Ancestry		
Source	Percent of United States Population	Percent of Canadian Population
Africa	9.6 percent	0.8 percent
China	0.6 percent	2.2 percent
England	13.1 percent	14.6 percent
France	4.1 percent	22.7 percent
Germany	23.3 percent	3.4 percent
Ireland	15.6 percent	2.6 percent
Italy	5.9 percent	2.7 percent
Mexico	4.7 percent	less than 1 percent
The Netherlands	2.5 percent	1.3 percent
North America	3.5 percent	1.4 percent
Poland	3.8 percent	1.0 percent
Scotland	2.2 percent	3.3 percent
Ukraine	less than 1 percent	1.5 percent

◀▲ **A New Home** Many immigrants from Caribbean countries settle in Miami (above left) because its climate is similar to that of their homelands. Vancouver (left), on Canada's Pacific Coast, has a large Asian population.

THE UNITED STATES AND CANADA

Physical Geography

PICTURE ACTIVITIES

These scenic peaks are part of a huge mountain system called the Rocky Mountains. They stretch across parts of the United States and Canada. To get to know this mountain system, do the following activities.

Study the picture
What do you think the weather is like in the Rocky Mountains? Based on what you see in the photograph, what kind of vegetation probably grows here?

Tour the Rockies
Why do you think tourists visit national parks in the Rocky Mountains? What sports or other activities might they enjoy in the parks? What effect do you think tourism has on the economies of the Rocky Mountain states and provinces?

Land and Water

BEFORE YOU READ

Reach Into Your Background

Have you ever climbed a hill or mountain—or been to the top of a skyscraper? What could you see from such a high place that you could not see from the ground? You probably saw the landscape and how places related to each other. Keep that idea in mind as you read this section.

Questions to Explore

1. What are the main physical features of the United States and Canada?

2. How do the physical environments of the United States and Canada affect the way people live?

Key Terms

glacier
tributary
Continental Divide

Key Places

Rocky Mountains
Appalachian Mountains
Death Valley
Great Lakes
St. Lawrence River
Mississippi River

Alaska's Mount McKinley is the highest mountain in North America and attracts thousands of visitors every year. In 1992, Ruth Kocour joined a team of climbers to scale the 20,320-foot (6,194-m) peak. After the team had set up camp at 9,500 feet (2,896 m), the first storm arrived. The team quickly built walls of packed snow to shield their tents from the wind. They dug a snow cave to house their kitchen and waited for the storm to blow itself out. Kocour recalls, "Someone on another team went outside for a few minutes, came back, and had a hot drink. His teeth cracked."

Maybe camping in the cold mountains is not for you. Perhaps you would prefer the sunny beaches of Florida or the giant forests of the Northwest. Maybe you would like to see the Arizona desert or the vast plains of central Canada. The landscape of the United States and Canada varies greatly.

▼ Dressed for warmth and carrying heavy backpacks, hikers stride across Mount McKinley's Kahiltna Glacier.

Where in the World Are We?

The United States and Canada are located in North America. To the east is the Atlantic Ocean, to the west, the Pacific. To the north, Canada borders the Arctic Ocean, while to the south, the United States touches Mexico and the Gulf of Mexico. The United States also includes Alaska and Hawaii.

Which is bigger, the United States or Canada? Canada has more land—it is the second-largest country in the world. The United States is the fourth largest. But the United States has more people—almost 10 times more people—than Canada. The United States has the third-largest population in the world, after China and India.

Landforms of the United States and Canada

From outer space, the United States and Canada appear as one landmass, with mountain ranges and vast plains running from north to south. Locate these mountains and plains on the physical map in the Activity Atlas at the front of your textbook.

Extending about 3,000 miles (4,827 km) along the western section of the continent, the Rocky Mountains are the largest mountain system in North America. In the east, the Appalachian (ap uh LAY chun) Mountains are the second largest. They stretch about 2,000 miles (3,200 km). In Canada, the Appalachians become the Laurentian (loh REN shun) Highlands. Tourists visit these mountain ranges year round.

READ ACTIVELY

Predict What are the major landforms of the United States and Canada?

▼ White-water rafters splash their way down a mountain stream in the Appalachians in West Virginia.

Kilauea Ready to Erupt

Visitors to Volcanoes National Park in Hawaii can marvel at the natural fireworks provided by one of the state's active volcanoes, Kilauea. The 122 islands that make up Hawaii, like many other islands in the Pacific Ocean, were created by volcanoes long ago. **Critical Thinking** How do you think volcanic eruptions affect the people who live in Hawaii?

Between the Rockies and the Appalachians lies a huge plains area. In Canada, these lowlands are called the Interior Plains. In the United States, they are called the Great Plains and the Central Plains. Much of this region has rich soil. In the wetter eastern area, farmers grow crops like corn and soybeans. In the drier western area, farmers grow wheat, and ranchers raise livestock.

Special Features of the United States The United States has several unique features. A plains area runs along its eastern and southern coasts. In the Northeast, this plain is narrow; it broadens as it spreads south and west. Flat, fertile land and access to the sea attracted many settlers to this area. Large cities developed here.

West of the Rockies lies a region of plateaus and basins. Perhaps the most notable feature of this area is the Great Basin. In the northeast section of this bowl-shaped valley is the Great Salt Lake. Death Valley is in the southwest section. Much of Death Valley lies below sea level. It is also the hottest place in North America. Summer temperatures here regularly climb to 120°F (50°C).

To the west of this region of plateaus and basins lie two more mountain ranges. These are the Sierra Nevada in California and the Cascades in Washington and Oregon. The Cascades were formed by volcanoes. One of these volcanoes—Mount St. Helens—erupted in 1980. People over 1,000 miles (1,609 km) away, in Denver, had to scrape volcanic ash from the eruption off of their cars.

LINKS TO SCIENCE

The Next Hawaiian Island Loihi, off the southern tip of Hawaii, is the world's most active volcano. But no one has seen it erupt. Its peak is 3,000 feet (914 m) below the ocean's surface. Years of continuous eruption have produced layer after layer of molten lava. Scientists predict that in 100,000 years Loihi will rise above the surface of the ocean and become the next Hawaiian Island.

Far to the north, snow and ice cover Alaska's many mountains. **Glaciers,** huge, slow-moving sheets of ice, fill many of the valleys between these mountains. Most of Alaska's people live along the warmer southern coast.

Special Features of Canada Canada, too, has a number of unique features. East of Alaska lies the Yukon (YOO kahn) Territory of Canada. Mount Logan, Canada's highest peak, is here. It is part of the Coast Mountains, which stretch south along the Pacific almost to the United States border.

Further east, beyond the Interior Plains, lies the Canadian Shield. This huge region of ancient rock covers about half of Canada. The land on the shield is rugged. As a result, few people live here.

Southeast of the shield are the St. Lawrence Lowlands. Located along the St. Lawrence River, these lowlands are Canada's smallest land region. However, they are home to more than half of the country's population. The region is also Canada's manufacturing center. And because the lowlands have fertile soil, farmers in this region produce about one third of the country's crops.

Major Bodies of Water

Both the United States and Canada have important lakes and rivers. People use these bodies of water for transportation, recreation, and industry. Many American and Canadian cities developed near these bodies of water. As you read, find these water bodies on the physical map in the Activity Atlas.

▶ French Canadians own this farmland in Canada's fertile St. Lawrence Lowlands. Unlike English Canadian farmers, who favor square fields, French Canadians prefer farming long strips of land.

A Ship on the St. Lawrence Seaway

This picture shows a ship passing through the Welland Canal on the St. Lawrence Seaway. The canal, which connects lakes Erie and Ontario, is wide enough to fit ocean-going ships up to 230 feet (70 m) long. **Critical Thinking** Why do you think that people sometimes call the St. Lawrence Seaway "Canada's highway to the sea"?

The Great Lakes   Lakes Superior, Michigan, Huron, Erie, and Ontario make up the Great Lakes, the world's largest group of freshwater lakes. Of the five, only Lake Michigan lies entirely in the United States. The other four lakes are part of the border between the United States and Canada.

During an ice age long ago, glaciers formed the Great Lakes. As the glaciers moved, they dug deep trenches in the land. Water from the melting glaciers filled these trenches to produce the Great Lakes and many other lakes. Today, the Great Lakes are important waterways in both the United States and Canada. Shipping on the Great Lakes helped industry to develop in the two countries.

Mighty Rivers   Canada has two major rivers. The Mackenzie River, the country's longest, forms in the Rockies and flows north into the Arctic Ocean. The St. Lawrence River connects the Great Lakes to the Atlantic Ocean. A system of locks and canals enables large ships to navigate the river. As a result, the St. Lawrence is one of North America's most important transportation routes.

In Canada, the St. Lawrence is called the "Mother of Canada." In the United States, America's largest river has an equally grand title.

Visualize Picture the Great Lakes region during the Ice Age. How is the scene different today?

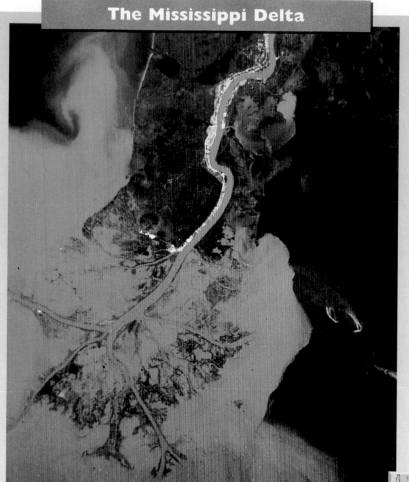

The Mississippi Delta

As the Mississippi River flows into the Gulf of Mexico, it dumps silt, forming a huge triangular plain called a delta. This satellite image shows the size of the delta. The waters of the Mississippi are shown as light blue, the land is shown in shades of black.

Native Americans call the Mississippi River the "Father of Waters." It has its headwaters, or starting point, in Minnesota. From here, the river flows through the Central Plains to the Gulf of Mexico. Two other major rivers, the Ohio and the Missouri, are tributaries of the Mississippi. A **tributary** (TRIB yoo ter ee) is a stream that flows into a larger river.

Look again at the physical map in the Activity Atlas and find the Rocky Mountains. Notice that the Fraser, Columbia, and Colorado rivers form in the Rockies and flow west. Now find the Platte and Missouri rivers. They flow east from the Rockies. This is because the Rockies form the **Continental Divide,** the boundary that separates rivers flowing toward opposite sides of the continent.

SECTION 1 REVIEW

1. **Define** (a) glacier, (b) tributary, (c) Continental Divide.

2. **Identify** (a) Rocky Mountains, (b) Appalachian Mountains, (c) Death Valley, (d) Great Lakes, (e) St. Lawrence River, (f) Mississippi River.

3. (a) Which lakes lie on the border between the United States and Canada? (b) Why are these bodies of water important?

4. Give two examples of ways in which physical features have affected life in the United States and Canada.

Critical Thinking

5. **Drawing Conclusions** Hundreds of years ago, many people coming to the United States and Canada settled along coastal plains and rivers. Why do you think these areas attracted settlers?

Activity

6. **Writing to Learn** Suppose that you are planning a vacation. If you had your choice, what physical features of the United States and Canada would you like to see? Write a paragraph describing the places you would like to visit and why.

Climate and Vegetation

Reach Into Your Background

Would you like to go snow skiing in summer? Or how about taking a dip in an open-air pool at the height of winter? The climates of the United States and Canada are so varied that you can do these things!

Questions to Explore

1. What kinds of climates and vegetation do the United States and Canada have?

2. How do climate and vegetation affect where and how the people of the United States and Canada live?

Key Terms

rain shadow
tropics
tundra
permafrost
prairie
province

Key Places

Vancouver
Winnipeg

▼ Whatever the weather outside, it is always pleasant in climate-controlled Eaton Center, a shopping mall in Toronto, Ontario.

On a hot and sunny February morning, a reporter left his home in Miami Beach, Florida, and headed for the airport. Wearing lightweight trousers and a short-sleeved shirt, he boarded a plane to snowy Toronto. Was he forgetting something? Surely he knew that the temperature would be below freezing in Toronto.

He did, indeed, know all about the bitter cold that would greet him when he got off the plane. But he was going to research an article on Toronto's tunnels and underground malls. He wanted to find out whether people could really visit hotels, restaurants, and shops without having to go outside and brave the harsh Canadian winter.

Climate Zones

As the reporter well knew, Toronto and Miami Beach have very different climates. Climate zones in the United States and Canada range from the polar climate of the northern reaches of Canada to the desert climate of the southwestern United States. What accounts for this great variety in climates? The size of the region, first of all. Also, such factors as latitude, mountains, and oceans affect the kinds of climates found in the region.

Predict How do you think the ocean affects Canada's climate?

Canada's Climates—Braving the Cold Generally, the farther a location is from the Equator, the colder its climate. Look at the climate regions map in the Activity Atlas at the front of your textbook. Notice that much of Canada lies well to the north of the 40° line of latitude, a long way from the Equator. Therefore, much of Canada is very cold!

The ocean affects Canada's climates, too. Water heats up and cools down more slowly than land. Winds blowing across water tend to warm the land in winter and cool the land in summer. Therefore, areas that are near an ocean generally have fairly mild climates year round. Also, winds blowing across the ocean pick up moisture. When these winds blow over land, they drop the moisture in the form of rain or snow.

The climate regions map shows how oceans influence climate. Notice that much of the northwestern coast of Canada has a marine west coast climate. The waters of the Pacific Ocean help make the climate mild all year. And moisture-carrying winds blowing from the Pacific make the northwestern coast rainy, especially during winter. If you are planning a vacation in the west coast city of Vancouver, take an umbrella and a raincoat. It rains year round.

Being a great distance from the ocean also affects climate. Inland areas often have climate extremes. Find Winnipeg, in Canada's Interior Plains, on the map. Winter temperatures here are very cold, averaging around 0°F (–18°C). Yet summer temperatures run between 70°F and 90°F (20°C and 32°C).

One final factor—mountains—influences climate, especially rainfall. Winds blowing from the Pacific Ocean rise as they meet the various mountain ranges in the west. As they rise, they cool and drop their moisture. The air is dry by the time it reaches the other side of the

▼ In Canada's humid continental climate zone, moist air and hot summer temperatures can combine to produce heavy rainstorms. People in Winnipeg (below) shelter under the first thing to hand—garbage bags. In winter, temperatures can be so cold that rivers and canals freeze. People in Ottawa, Ontario (below right), skate on a frozen canal.

16

mountains. The area on the side of the mountains away from the wind is in a rain shadow. A **rain shadow** is an area on the dry, sheltered side of a mountain that receives little rainfall.

Climates of the United States   Latitude also influences climate in the United States. On the climate map in the Activity Atlas, you will see that Alaska lies north of the 60°N line of latitude. Far from the Equator, Alaska is cold for a good part of the year. Now find the southern tip of Florida and Hawaii. They lie near or within the **tropics,** the area between the $23\frac{1}{2}$°N and $23\frac{1}{2}$°S lines of latitude. Here, it is almost always hot.

The Pacific Ocean and mountains affect climate in the western United States. Wet winds from the ocean drop their moisture before they cross the mountains. As a result, the eastern sections of California, Nevada, and Arizona are semiarid or desert. Death Valley, which is located here, has the lowest average rainfall in the country—about 2 inches (5 cm) a year.

East of the Great Plains, the country has continental climates. In the north, summers are warm and winters are cold and snowy. In the south, summers tend to be long and hot, while winters are mild. The coastal regions of these areas sometimes experience violent weather. In

Predict How do you think the mountains affect climate in the western United States?

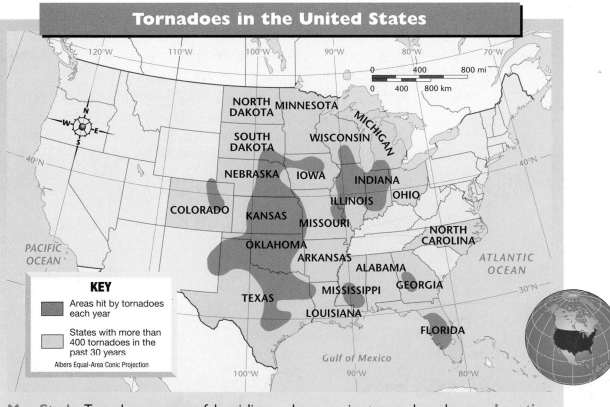

Tornadoes in the United States

KEY

Areas hit by tornadoes each year

States with more than 400 tornadoes in the past 30 years

Albers Equal-Area Conic Projection

Map Study Tornadoes, or powerful, swirling windstorms, sometimes strike inland areas of the United States. The winds of a tornado may reach speeds of 200 miles (320 km) an hour, causing tremendous damage. **Location** The area from north central Texas through Kansas is sometimes called "Tornado Alley." Why do you think this is so?

summer and fall, hurricanes and tropical storms develop in the Atlantic Ocean. These storms sometimes hit the coasts of the southeastern and eastern United States. Bringing winds of more than 75 miles (121 km) per hour, the storms can do incredible damage.

Natural Vegetation Zones

Climate in the United States and Canada helps produce four major kinds of natural vegetation or plant life. As you can see on the map below, these are tundra, grassland, desert scrub, and forest.

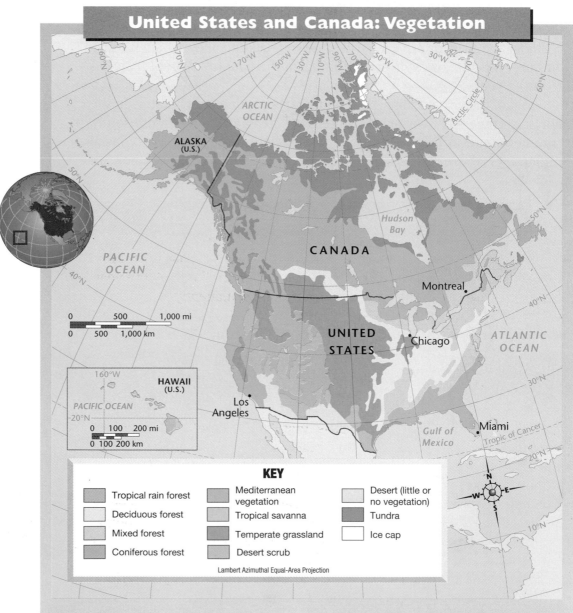

United States and Canada: Vegetation

KEY

- Tropical rain forest
- Deciduous forest
- Mixed forest
- Coniferous forest
- Mediterranean vegetation
- Tropical savanna
- Temperate grassland
- Desert scrub
- Desert (little or no vegetation)
- Tundra
- Ice cap

Lambert Azimuthal Equal-Area Projection

Map Study Natural vegetation is much more varied in the United States than it is in Canada. **Place** In terms of natural vegetation, what part of the United States has the most in common with Canada?

Cattle Raising in the West

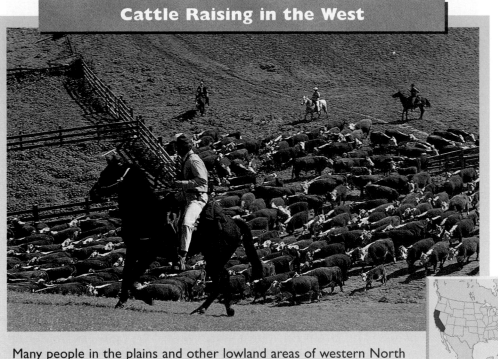

Many people in the plains and other lowland areas of western North America make a living by raising cattle. These cowhands in California are rounding up cattle and bringing them into a fenced area. **Critical Thinking** Why do you think that areas of flat or rolling land are better for raising cattle than mountainous areas?

Northern Tundras The **tundra** is found in the far north. It is a cold, dry region that is covered with snow for more than half the year. The Arctic tundra contains **permafrost,** or permanently frozen soil. During the short, cool summer, the surface of the permafrost thaws. Mosses, grasses, and bright wildflowers grow. Few people live in the tundra. However, some Inuits (IN oo wits), a native people of Canada and Alaska, live here. They make a living by fishing and hunting.

Prairies **Prairies** are regions of flat or rolling land covered with grasses. They are located in areas that have humid climates. The world's largest prairie lies in the plains of North America. It covers much of the American central states and stretches into the Canadian provinces of Alberta, Saskatchewan (suh SKACH uh wun), and Manitoba. These three provinces are sometimes called the Prairie Provinces. A **province** is a political division of Canada, much like our states. Look at the physical map in the Activity Atlas to locate the prairies, or plains areas, of the United States and Canada.

When pioneers first saw the prairies of the Midwest, they described the land as "a sea of grass." Today, farmers grow fields of corn and soybeans here. Further west, the Great Plains receive less rainfall. Therefore, only short grasses will grow. These grasses are ideal for grazing cattle. And the land is suitable for growing wheat. The Prairie Provinces, too, have many wheat farms and cattle ranches.

LINKS ACROSS TIME

Hundreds of Years of Storms Between 1493 and 1870, 400 hurricanes struck the Gulf of Mexico and Florida. Residents suffered because they did not know that the storms were coming. Things improved when sailing became more common and radios were invented. Sailors, therefore, could warn that storms were coming. Today, high-tech weather satellites provide the warning people on land require.

► The forests of the United States and Canada are ideal places for many kinds of outdoor activities. These people are bird watching in the forests of Quebec (kwih BEK) province, Canada.

Desert Scrub   With little rainfall, desert and semiarid regions have few plants. The Great Basin is a large, very dry region between the Rocky Mountains and the Sierras in the United States. The land cannot support large numbers of people, but many sheep graze on the area's short grasses and shrubs.

Forests   Forests cover nearly one third of the United States and almost one half of Canada. The mild climate of the northern Pacific Coast encourages great forests of coniferous (koh NIF ur us) trees, such as fir and spruce. Coniferous trees have cones that carry and protect their seeds. The Rockies and the Appalachians, too, are blanketed with coniferous forests. From the Great Lakes across southeastern Canada and New England and down to the southeastern United States, you will find forests of coniferous trees mixed with deciduous (dee SIJ oo us) trees. The latter shed their leaves in the fall.

SECTION 2 REVIEW

1. **Define**   (a) rain shadow, (b) tropics, (c) tundra, (d) permafrost, (e) prairie, (f) province.

2. **Identify**   (a) Vancouver, (b) Winnipeg.

3. (a) Describe the climate and vegetation of the American prairie. (b) What are the climate and vegetation of Canada's Pacific Coast?

4. What geographic features might lead someone to settle in Vancouver, rather than in Winnipeg?

Critical Thinking

5. **Making Comparisons** Contrast the climate and vegetation of the tundra with the climate and vegetation of the area around the Great Lakes.

Activity

6. **Writing to Learn**   You are taking a journey from north-western Canada to the south-eastern United States. Describe some of the climate zones you pass through.

Natural Resources

BEFORE YOU READ

Reach Into Your Background

Jot down four or five activities that you do in a typical day— take a shower, eat lunch, ride the bus to school, and so on. As you read this section, think about how natural resources play a part in these activities.

Questions to Explore

1. What are the major resources of the United States and Canada?

2. How do these resources affect the economies of these countries?

Key Terms
alluvial
agribusiness
hydroelectricity

Key Places
Imperial Valley
Grand Coulee Dam
St. Lawrence Lowlands

Surrounded by redwood forests, Carlotta, California, has little more than a gas station and a general store. Yet on one day in September 1996, police arrested more than 1,000 people here. Was Carlotta filled with outlaws like some old Wild West town? No, but it was the scene of a showdown. A logging company wanted to cut down some of the oldest redwood trees in the world. Protesters wanted to preserve the forest and the animals that live there. Both sides believed in the importance of natural resources. But they disagreed strongly about how to use them.

As in Carlotta, people all over North America use their natural resources for recreation, industry, and energy. In this section, you will read about the natural resources of the United States and Canada. You will also learn how people use them.

Natural Resources of the United States

Native Americans, pioneers, and explorers in North America knew it was a land of plenty. Fertile soil, water, forests, and minerals were abundant. These resources helped to build two of the leading economies in the world.

▼ These redwood trees are part of Muir Woods, a national park just northwest of San Francisco, California.

Predict Why is soil an important resource in the United States?

Soil The United States has vast expanses of fertile soil. Two soil types are especially important. The Midwest and the South have rich, dark soils. Along the Mississippi and other river valleys are **alluvial** (uh LOO vee ul) soils. These are deposited by water; they are the fertile topsoil left by rivers after a flood. Areas that have good soil are suitable for farming. Until the 1900s, most American farms were owned by families. Since then, large companies have bought more and more family farms across the country. For example, southern California's Imperial Valley has vast vegetable fields operated by **agribusinesses.** These are large companies that run huge farms.

Water Water is a vital resource all over the United States. People need water to drink. And they need it to grow crops. Factories rely on water for many industrial processes, including cooling moving parts. And both industry and farmers transport goods on rivers. Canada's St. Lawrence and Mackenzie rivers serve as shipping routes. The same is true of the Mississippi, Ohio, and Missouri rivers in the United States.

A Modern Irrigation System

Where rainfall averages less than 10 inches (25 cm) a year, as in the southwestern United States, irrigation supplies the water that crops need to thrive. However, the Southwest's limited supply of river water must be carefully rationed. This photograph shows a high-technology irrigation system watering several fields on a California farm. **Critical Thinking** Look back at the photograph of French-Canadian farmland in Section 1. How do the shapes of fields in that photograph compare with the shapes of fields here?

United States and Canada: Natural Resources

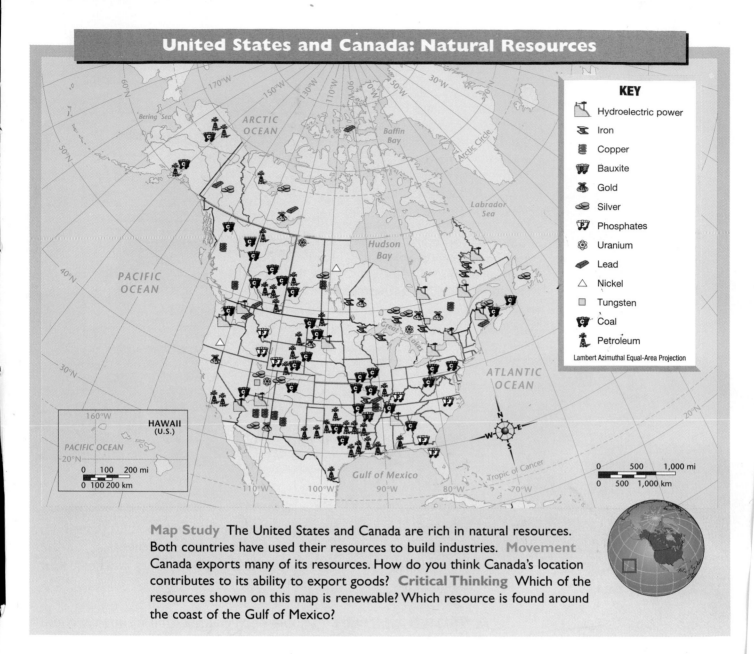

KEY

- Hydroelectric power
- Iron
- Copper
- Bauxite
- Gold
- Silver
- Phosphates
- Uranium
- Lead
- Nickel
- Tungsten
- Coal
- Petroleum

Lambert Azimuthal Equal-Area Projection

Map Study The United States and Canada are rich in natural resources. Both countries have used their resources to build industries. **Movement** Canada exports many of its resources. How do you think Canada's location contributes to its ability to export goods? **Critical Thinking** Which of the resources shown on this map is renewable? Which resource is found around the coast of the Gulf of Mexico?

Water is used for other purposes, too. Dams along many rivers generate **hydroelectricity** (hy dro ee lek TRIS ih tee), or power generated by moving water. The Grand Coulee (KOO lee) Dam on the Columbia River in the state of Washington produces more hydroelectricity than any other dam in the United States.

Abundant Energy and Mineral Resources The United States is the second-largest producer of coal, petroleum, and natural gas in the world. North America's biggest oil reserves are along the northern coast of Alaska. A pipeline carries crude oil south from the wells to the port of Valdez. From here, giant tankers carry the oil to the south to be refined. Abundant energy resources have fueled industrial expansion. They have also helped to provide Americans with one of the world's highest standards of living.

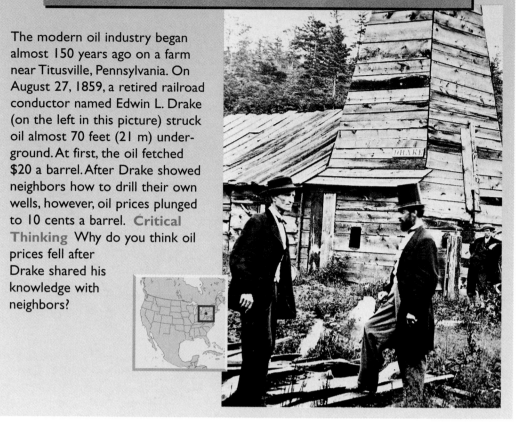

The modern oil industry began almost 150 years ago on a farm near Titusville, Pennsylvania. On August 27, 1859, a retired railroad conductor named Edwin L. Drake (on the left in this picture) struck oil almost 70 feet (21 m) underground. At first, the oil fetched $20 a barrel. After Drake showed neighbors how to drill their own wells, however, oil prices plunged to 10 cents a barrel. **Critical Thinking** Why do you think oil prices fell after Drake shared his knowledge with neighbors?

The United States also has valuable deposits of copper, gold, granite, iron ore, and lead. Mining accounts for a small percentage of the country's economy and employs about 1 percent of its workers. But these minerals are very important to other industries.

A Wealth of Trees People once claimed that a squirrel could leap from one tree to another all the way from the Atlantic Coast to the Mississippi River. That is no longer true, but America's forests are still an important resource. In the Pacific Northwest, the South, the Appalachians, and areas around the Great Lakes, forests produce lumber, wood pulp for paper, and fine hardwoods for furniture.

Natural Resources of Canada

Canada's first European settlers earned their living as fur trappers, loggers, fishers, and farmers. Today, the economic picture has changed. Less than 5 percent of Canada's workers earn their living in these ways.

Farmland About 12 percent of Canada's land is suitable for farming. Most is located in the Prairie Provinces. This region produces most of Canada's wheat and beef. The St. Lawrence Lowlands are another major agricultural region. This area produces grains, milk, vegetables, and fruits.

Predict What resources do the United States and Canada share?

◀ Powerful tugboats tow huge booms of logs harvested from Canada's forests.

Minerals and Energy Resources The Canadian Shield contains much of Canada's mineral wealth. About 85 percent of the nation's iron ore comes from mines near the Quebec-Newfoundland border. The region also has large deposits of gold, silver, zinc, copper, and uranium. The Prairie Provinces, particularly Alberta, have large oil and natural gas deposits.

Canada harnesses the rivers of Quebec Province to make hydroelectricity. These rivers generate enough hydroelectric power that some can be exported to the northeastern United States.

Forests With almost half its land covered in forests, Canada is a leading producer of timber products. These products include lumber, paper, plywood, and wood pulp. The major timber-producing provinces include British Columbia, Quebec, and Ontario.

SECTION 3 REVIEW

1. **Define** (a) alluvial, (b) agribusiness, (c) hydroelectricity.

2. **Identify** (a) Imperial Valley, (b) Grand Coulee Dam, (c) St. Lawrence Lowlands.

3. Describe the major natural resources in the United States and Canada.

4. Why is water an important resource? Give two examples of how it is used in the United States and Canada.

Critical Thinking

5. **Making Comparisons** Based on what you know about the physical geography of the two countries, why do you think their resources are similar?

Activity

6. **Writing to Learn** What do you think is the most important resource in the United States and Canada? Write a paragraph explaining your choice.

Using Distribution Maps

Your weekend adventure includes hiking alone in a deep, dark forest. You carry everything you need—tent, sleeping bag, stove, food, and water—in a backpack. Tree branches creak in the wind, and a hawk calls in the distance. You hear the rustle of a small animal scurrying through the leaves.

You soon realize there are sounds you do not hear—the sounds of people. You do not hear traffic, or the hum of a washing machine, or anyone talking.

Where can you go to have such a wonderful experience? There are many wilderness areas in the United States and Canada. Some are forested, others are desert areas, and still others are in mountain regions. What they all have in common, however, is that few people live there.

You can find these places by looking at a special kind of map called a population distribution map. Such a map will also show you a lot more about people and where they live.

Get Ready

A population distribution map is a map that shows the areas in which people live as well as the areas in which people do not live.

You can use a population distribution map to better understand a country or region you are learning about. But a population distribution map also provides clues to why people live where they do. This information is basic to understanding human life on the Earth.

Try It Out

Knowing how population distribution maps are made will help you understand how to use one. Make a population distribution map of your school. A model of such a map is shown below.

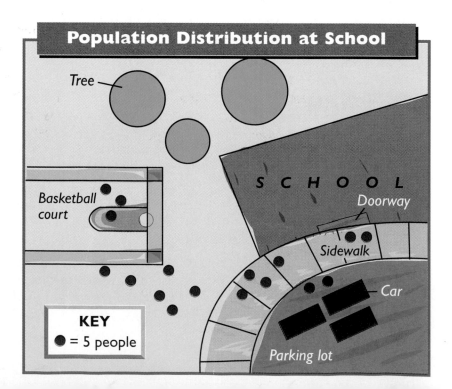

Population Distribution at School

Tree

Basketball court

SCHOOL

Doorway

Sidewalk

Car

Parking lot

KEY
● = 5 people

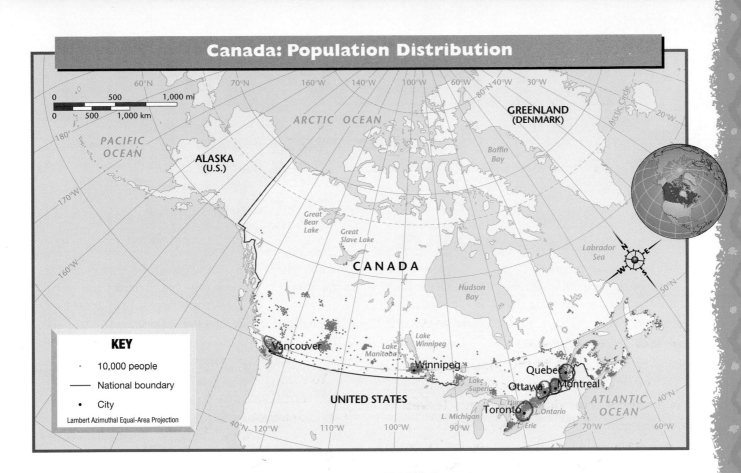

Canada: Population Distribution

KEY
- · 10,000 people
- — National boundary
- • City

Lambert Azimuthal Equal-Area Projection

A. Draw a map of your schoolyard or playground. It does not have to be perfect, but it should show the area around the school, the entrances to the school and the sidewalks leading to the school's doorways, and the school parking lot.

B. Make a key for your map. Have each dot represent five people.

C. Add dots to your map to represent how the population of your school is distributed. Choose a specific time of day, such as 11:00 A.M. Place the dots in the places where people are at 11:00 A.M. on an average day. Remember to draw the right number of dots to show how many people are in the area around the school.

D. Give your map a title. Now study your population distribution map. Your map answers the same two questions that any population distribution map answers: Where are the people? How many people are in each place? Your map also provides clues about another question: Why is the population distributed in the way that it is?

Apply the Skill

Now you know how population distribution maps are made and what questions they answer. Try looking at one that shows a whole country. Use the map to follow the steps below.

1 **Familiarize yourself with the map.** Look it over to get a sense of what it is about. What country is shown? How is population represented? How many people does each dot stand for?

2 **Answer the "where" and "how many" questions that population distribution maps address.**
- Where do the people of Canada live?
- Where do *most* of the people live?

3 **Answer the "why" question that this population distribution map addresses.** Write a paragraph to answer this question.
- Why do you think the population of Canada is distributed the way it is? Consider geographic reasons such as climate and landforms.

Review and Activities

Reviewing Main Ideas

1. List two major geographic features of the United States and Canada and describe their importance.
2. Why do relatively few people live in the deserts of the United States or in the Canadian Shield region in Canada?

3. How does the climate in the Great Basin affect the area's vegetation?
4. (a) What is Canada's smallest land region? (b) Why do most Canadians live there?

5. Of which three energy sources is the United States the world's second-largest producer?
6. Which natural resources help support the economy of Canada's Prairie Provinces?

Reviewing Key Terms

Match the definitions in Column I with the key terms in Column II.

Column I

1. an area on the dry, sheltered side of a mountain that receives little rainfall
2. a region of flat or hilly land covered with tall grasses
3. a large mass of ice that flows slowly over land
4. relating to soil deposited by a river or stream
5. a river that flows into a larger river
6. a cold, dry region that is covered with snow for more than half the year

Column II

a. tributary

b. glacier

c. rain shadow

d. tundra

e. prairie

f. alluvial

Critical Thinking

1. **Drawing Conclusions** If you were going to build a new city in the United States or Canada, where would you locate it? What geographic features would influence your decision?
2. **Recognizing Cause and Effect** How does climate affect the growth of vegetation in the United States and Canada? Give two examples.

Graphic Organizer

Copy this web on a sheet of paper and complete it. You may choose any region in the United States or Canada.

Physical Features

Canada — Pacific Coast — Climate

Natural Resources

Map Activity

United States and Canada

For each place listed below, write the letter from the map that shows its location. Use the maps in the Activity Atlas to help you.

1. Canadian Shield
2. Great Basin
3. Great Plains
4. Rocky Mountains
5. Appalachian Mountains
6. Pacific Ocean
7. Atlantic Ocean
8. Great Lakes

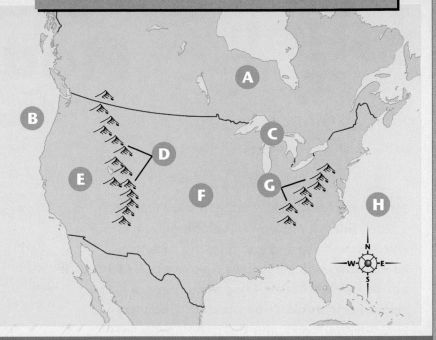

Writing Activity

Write a Poem

Write a poem describing some aspect of the geography of the region where you live. Choose from landforms, bodies of water, climate, vegetation, or other natural resources.

Internet Activity

Use a search engine to find **Natural Resources Research Information Pages.** Click on **Canada.** Choose **Natural Resources Canada** and then click on **For Kids Only.** Create your own natural resources interactive map. Click on **United States** then choose **State Level.** Research a natural resources program in your state.

Skills Review

Turn to the Skills Activity.
Review the parts of a population distribution map. Then list the three questions a distribution map answers.

How Am I Doing?

Answer these questions to help you check your progress.

1. Can I describe the main physical features of the United States and Canada?

2. Do I understand how geography and climate affect the way people live in the United States and Canada?

3. Can I identify some of the natural resources of the United States and Canada?

4. What information from this chapter can I use in my book project?

Making a Model River

Charles Kuralt, a famous traveler and journalist, knows how important rivers are. "I started out thinking of America as highways and state lines," he wrote. "As I got to know it better, I began to think of it as rivers. . . . It wouldn't be much of a country without the rivers, and the people who have figured out a way to make a living beside them. . . . America is a great story, and there is a river on every page of it."

People of both the United States and Canada have long depended on their rivers. Native Americans and immigrants alike built their villages and towns on the banks of rivers, where they could fish and hunt and water their crops. These natural highways have carried boats through rugged land from the earliest times. Recently, they have become sources of hydroelectric power. Even today, most major cities stand on riverbanks.

Purpose

Rivers have an important place in both the geography and history of the United States and Canada. This activity will help you understand the growth and behavior of rivers.

Materials

- a plastic or flexible 12-by-9-inch aluminum tray with sides at least 4 inches high
- sand
- scissors
- a bucket or pan
- a pitcher of water
- a ruler
- duct tape
- a plastic or rubber hose about 3 feet long
- a brick or square object
- a funnel small enough to fit inside the hose

◀ The Chenoga River meanders through eastern New York state.

Procedure

STEP ONE

Predict how your river will flow. You will make the model river in a box of sand. What do you think it will look like? Will it flow in a straight line, or will it wind back and forth? Will the channel of the river be shallow or deep? Will the channel be the same along the whole length of the river, or will it change? Draw a sketch of how you think your river will look.

STEP TWO

Construct a river box. First, fill the tray with sand, leaving 1 inch at the top of the tray. Then use the scissors to cut a 1-inch V-shaped notch into the center of one end of the tray. This notch will allow the "river" water to drain away. Arrange the tray so that the water will drain into a pan or a bucket.

STEP THREE

Create a landscape for the river's flow. With a pitcher of water, wet the sand evenly until it is damp and packed, but not soupy. With the scissors, poke a small hole below the notch to drain excess water from the sand. Drag the ruler across the sand to make it level. Use duct tape to secure the hose at the end of the tray opposite the notch. Prop the tray up on the brick so that the landscape slopes toward the notch.

STEP FOUR

Let the river run! Put the funnel into the end of the hose. Use the pitcher to slowly pour a stream of water into the funnel. The water will start to make a river in the landscape. Then watch. You'll see a river form before your very eyes!

Observations

1. How did the shape and size of your river compare with the way you predicted it would look in Step One?

2. What happened to the sand in the river's channel?

3. Sediment is material picked up, carried, and deposited by a river. Describe the shape made in the sand as your river deposited its sediment near the drainage notch.

ANALYSIS AND CONCLUSION

1. What factors influenced the form your river took?

2. Increase the flow of water in your river. How does this affect the size and shape of your river?

3. Explain why knowledge of how rivers behave is important to each of the following groups of people: city planners, farmers, people who live near rivers, and boaters.

THE UNITED STATES AND CANADA
Shaped by History

Labrador Sea

Hudson Bay

Saskatchewan River
Lake Winnipeg
Columbia River
Snake River
Colorado River
Rio Grande
Missouri River
Platte River
Arkansas River
Mississippi River
Ohio River
Great Lakes
St. Lawrence River
Hudson River

NEW FRANCE

CLAIMED BY SPAIN

LOUISIANA

BRITISH COLONIES

ATLANTIC OCEAN

FLORIDA

NEW SPAIN

Gulf of Mexico

PACIFIC OCEAN

KEY
Britain
Spain
France
Lambert Azimuthal Equal-Area Projection

0   300   600 mi
0   300   600 km

MAP ACTIVITIES

As you can see, three different European countries influenced North America in the 1700s. To help you identify which country influenced which areas, do the following activities.

Look at the map
Find the area in which you live. In 1753, what country controlled that area?

Compare and contrast
Which European country held the largest territory? Which European country had the territory farthest north?

The First Americans and the Arrival of the Europeans

BEFORE YOU READ

Reach Into Your Background

Suppose you go on a world trip. You land on an isolated island and meet the inhabitants. How do you react? Are you suspicious and frightened because the inhabitants' culture and yours are so different? Or are you excited and eager to learn from them and teach them about your culture?

Questions to Explore

1. Who were the first Americans?
2. What effect did the arrival of Europeans have on Native Americans?
3. How did the United States win its independence from Great Britain?

Key Terms

indigenous
missionary
indentured servant
plantation
boycott
Revolutionary War

Key People and Places

Christopher Columbus
William Penn
Thomas Jefferson
George Washington
Jamestown
Pennsylvania Colony

Perhaps as early as 30,000 years ago, small family groups of hunters and food gatherers reached North America from Asia. This migration took place during the last ice age. At that time, so much water froze into thick ice sheets that the sea level dropped. As a result, a land bridge was exposed between Siberia and Alaska. Hunters followed herds of bison and mammoths across this land bridge. Other migrating people may have paddled small boats and fished along the coasts.

Over time, the first Americans spread throughout North and South America. They developed different ways of life to suit the environment of the places where they settled.

▼ These bone tools were found near the area where scientists think a land bridge once connected Asia and North America.

A Southwestern Pueblo

Some Native American groups in the Southwest—the modern-day states of New Mexico, Arizona, Utah, and Colorado—used very distinctive building styles. Around A.D. 700, they began building their villages into the sides of steep cliffs or on top of flat-topped hills called mesas. These villages, or pueblos, were a lot like our high-rise apartment buildings. As many as 1,200 people might live in one village. Below is a diagram of a room in a pueblo.

The thick (4–6 in, or 10–15 cm) walls were made of adobe, a clay mixture. It was poured into special molds to make bricks, which dried in the sun. After a wall was built, it was coated with a layer of adobe similar to paint.

Pueblos were also designed for defense. In case of an attack, someone could pull away the ladder from the rooftop "door." This made it hard for intruders to enter the house.

In one corner of the room were the *metates*, specially shaped stones for grinding corn for cooking.

Who Were the First Americans?

Louise Erdrich is an American writer. She is also part Native American. In her novel *The Crown of Columbus,* she describes the variety of Native American cultures before the Europeans arrived:

“[T]hey] had hundreds of societies, millions of people, whose experience had told them that the world was a pretty diverse place. Walk for a day in any direction and what do you find: A tribe with a whole new set of gods, a language as distinct from your own as Tibetan is from Dutch—very little, in fact, that's even slightly familiar.”

The Europeans Arrive

Some scientists think that Native Americans migrated from Asia. But many Native Americans disagree. They believe they are **indigenous** (in DIJ uh nus) people. That means they originated in this place. One thing is clear, however. Native Americans' ways of life began to change after 1492. That year, Christopher Columbus, a sea captain sailing from Spain, explored islands in the Caribbean Sea. Later, Europeans changed North America forever.

Spanish and French Claims to the Americas Spanish settlers spread out across the Americas. Some went to today's southwestern United States and Mexico. Others went to Florida and the Caribbean islands. Still others went to South America. These colonists often enslaved Native Americans. The colonists forced Native Americans to work in mines or on farms. Working conditions were so harsh that thousands died. Spanish missionaries tried to make Native Americans more like Europeans, often by force. **Missionaries** are religious people who want to convert others to their religion.

Spain gained great wealth from her American colonies. Seeing this, other countries soon also wanted colonies in the Americas. French explorers claimed land along the St. Lawrence and Mississippi rivers. Unlike the Spanish, the French were more interested in furs than gold. French traders and missionaries often lived among the Native Americans and learned their ways. The French did not take over Native American land.

The English Colonists Grow Powerful
English settlers established 13 colonies along the Atlantic Coast. These settlers came to start a new life. Some wanted to be free from debt. Others wanted to own land. Still others wanted to practice their religions in their own ways. Some came as **indentured servants,** or people who had to work for a period of years to gain freedom.

Migrating Plants When Columbus returned from the Americas to Spain, he brought gold. But he carried something else that may have been even more valuable—corn. In the next hundred years, European travelers brought back beans, squash, potatoes, peppers, and tomatoes. These foods changed European diets forever.

▼ Explorers used compasses like this one, which dates from 1580, to help them find their way to the Americas.

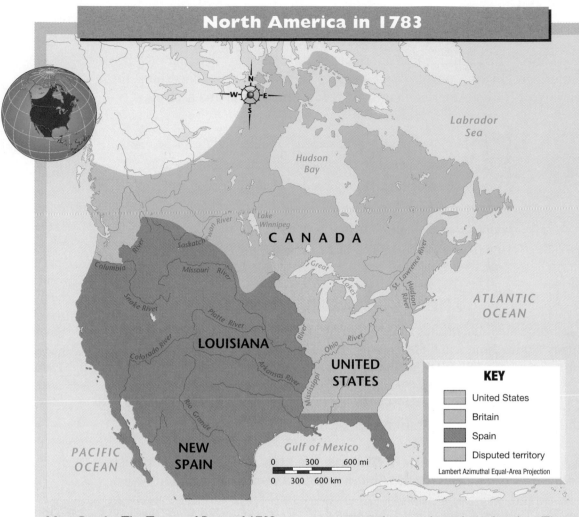

North America in 1783

Labrador Sea

Hudson Bay

CANADA

Lake Winnipeg

Saskatch... River

Columbia River

Snake River

Missouri River

Platte River

Colorado River

Arkansas River

LOUISIANA

Great Lakes

St. Lawrence River

Hudson River

Ohio River

ATLANTIC OCEAN

UNITED STATES

Mississippi

Rio Grande

PACIFIC OCEAN

NEW SPAIN

Gulf of Mexico

0	300 600 mi
0	300 600 km

KEY

United States
Britain
Spain
Disputed territory

Lambert Azimuthal Equal-Area Projection

Map Study The Treaty of Paris of 1783 set the western border of the United States at the Mississippi River. The United States claimed, but did not have possession of, areas on its northern and southern borders. These areas are shown in purple on the map.
Location With which countries did the United States have disputes over territory?

The first permanent English settlement was Jamestown, Virginia, founded in 1607. By 1619, it had the beginnings of self-government. In the same year, the first Africans arrived here as indentured servants. Later, about 1640, Africans were brought as slaves. Many were forced to work on the **plantations.** These were large farms in the South.

In 1620, the Pilgrims arrived in Massachusetts from England. They wanted to worship God in their own way and to govern themselves. They named their settlement Plymouth. About 60 years later, William Penn founded the Pennsylvania Colony. He wanted a place where all people, regardless of race or religion, were treated fairly. Penn was unusual because he paid Native Americans for their land. Before Penn—and after—most settlers took land, then fought Native Americans to control it.

In 1754, Britain and France went to war over land in North America. Americans call this war the French and Indian War. (At this time, Native

READ ACTIVELY

Visualize Visualize a meeting between William Penn and Native American groups. What issues do you think were discussed?

Americans were called "Indians," because early European explorers thought that they had found India.) With the colonists' help, the British were victorious.

The Break With Britain

The war with France had been very expensive. And, despite the victory over France, the British felt they needed an army in North America to protect the colonists. The British thought the colonists should help pay for the war and for their defense. Therefore, the British put taxes on many goods the colonists bought from Britain. No one represented the colonists in the British Parliament. The colonists demanded, "no taxation without representation." They also **boycotted,** or refused to buy, British goods.

Patriots such as Samuel Adams, Thomas Paine, and Patrick Henry encouraged colonists to rebel against British rule. The **Revolutionary War** began in 1775. In July 1776, representatives from each colony voted for independence. Thomas Jefferson wrote the official Declaration of Independence. His powerful words *liberty, equality,* and *justice* inspired many colonists to fight. George Washington led the American forces to victory in 1781. The Treaty of Paris, signed in 1783, made American independence official.

After the war, the 13 new states agreed to work together. But they had no strong central government. To form one, leaders from each state except Rhode Island met in Philadelphia in 1787 and wrote the Constitution. It set up the framework of our federal government. The Constitution was approved in 1789. It is still the highest law of the United States.

▲ Great Britain imposed several different kinds of taxes on the colonies. Many colonists especially hated the tax which required them to buy stamps, like this one, for legal documents and almost every other type of printed matter.

SECTION 1 REVIEW

1. **Define** (a) indigenous, (b) missionary, (c) indentured servant, (d) plantation, (e) boycott, (f) Revolutionary War.

2. **Identify** (a) Christopher Columbus, (b) William Penn, (c) Thomas Jefferson, (d) George Washington, (e) Jamestown, (f) Pennsylvania Colony.

3. Where do many scholars think the first Americans came from?

4. What was a major conflict between Native Americans and the European colonists?

Critical Thinking

5. **Recognizing Cause and Effect** Why did the colonists object to the taxes placed on them by the British?

Activity

6. **Writing to Learn** How were Native Americans involved with the people who arrived from Europe? Do some research about one Native American group. Write a report telling what happened as its people met the Europeans.

Growth, Settlement, and Civil War in the United States

BEFORE YOU READ

Reach Into Your Background

Have you ever gone camping? As you lay in your sleeping bag surrounded by trees and stars, what thoughts did you have about the wilderness? Did you think of keeping it just the way it was, or did you picture it as it might look if people lived there?

Questions to Explore

1. What were the effects of westward movement in the United States?
2. What were the causes and effects of the United States Civil War?

Key Terms

Louisiana Purchase
Manifest Destiny

immigrant
Industrial Revolution
abolitionist
Civil War
Reconstruction
segregate

Key Places

Meriwether Lewis
William Clark
Thomas Jefferson
Andrew Jackson
Harriet Beecher Stowe
Abraham Lincoln
Andrew Johnson

▼ It took Meriwether Lewis (left) and William Clark (right) three years to complete their exploration of the lands west of the Mississippi River.

In 1803, President Thomas Jefferson sent Meriwether Lewis and William Clark to explore land west of the Mississippi River. They traveled all the way to the Pacific Coast. As they journeyed up the Missouri River, Lewis and Clark found plants and animals completely new to them. They also created accurate, highly valuable maps of the region. Much of the information was new. Lewis and Clark also met Native American groups along the way. During these meetings, the two men tried to learn about the region and set up trading alliances. Few of those Native Americans had any idea how the visit would change their way of life.

A Growing Nation

In 1803, President Jefferson had a great piece of luck. France offered to sell to the United States all the land between the Mississippi River and the eastern slopes of the Rocky Mountains—for only $15 million. This sale of land, called the **Louisiana Purchase,** doubled the size of the United States.

Before this new land could be settled, the United States faced another challenge from Great Britain. The War of 1812 lasted two years. Again, the United States was victorious.

The Nation Prospers

Peace and prosperity followed the War of 1812. As the country grew, so did the meaning of democracy. In the 13 original states, only white males who owned property could vote. New states passed laws giving the vote to all white men 21 years old or older, whether they owned property or not. Soon, all states gave every adult white male the right to vote. Women and African Americans, however, could not vote.

In 1828, voters elected Andrew Jackson as President. He looked after the interests of poor farmers, laborers, and settlers who wanted Native American lands in the Southeast. In 1830, President Jackson persuaded Congress to pass the Indian Removal Act. It required the

▲ In the 1820s, a Cherokee leader named Sequoyah developed a system of writing that enabled his people to read and write in their own language.

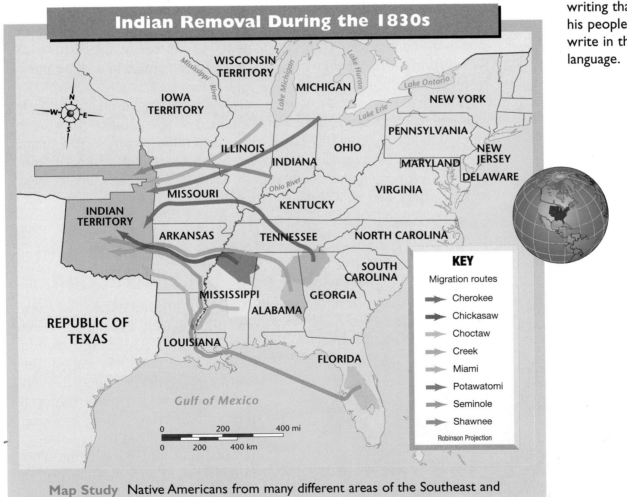

Indian Removal During the 1830s

KEY

Migration routes

➡ Cherokee
➡ Chickasaw
➡ Choctaw
➡ Creek
➡ Miami
➡ Potawatomi
➡ Seminole
➡ Shawnee

Robinson Projection

Map Study Native Americans from many different areas of the Southeast and Midwest were forced to leave their lands. **Movement** Which Native Americans crossed the Gulf of Mexico on their journey west?

Cherokee and other Native Americans in the area to leave their homelands. They were sent to live on new land in Oklahoma. So many Cherokee died on the journey that the route they followed is known as the Trail of Tears.

More Room to Grow The United States continued to gain land. In 1836, American settlers in the Mexican territory of Texas rebelled against Mexican rule. The Texans then set up the Lone Star Republic. In 1845, Texas became part of the United States. Only a year later, the United States went to war with Mexico. The U.S. won the war and gained from Mexico much of what is now the Southwest region.

Many Americans believed that it was the United States' **Manifest Destiny** to "own" all the land from the Atlantic to the Pacific. By this they meant the United States had a right to it. They also meant that it was America's fate to rule it. In the 1840s, American wagon trains began to cross the continent heading for the West.

The Industrial Revolution At the same time, thousands of people were pouring into cities in the Northeast. Some had left farms to work in factories. Others were **immigrants,** or people who move from one country to another. These people came from Europe in search of jobs in the United States. This movement was spurred by the **Industrial Revolution,** or the change from making goods by hand to making them by machine.

The first industry to change was clothmaking, or textiles. New spinning machines and power looms enabled people to make cloth more quickly than they could by hand. Other inventions, such as the steam engine, made travel easier and faster. Steamboats and steam locomotives moved people and goods rapidly. By 1860, railroads linked most major Eastern and Southeastern cities.

READ ACTIVELY

Predict How did the cotton gin and new lands affect slavery in the United States?

▼ Settlers heading west moved their belongings in covered wagons like this one. Some people called the wagon a *prairie schooner* because, from a distance, its white canvas cover looked like a ship's sail.

The Civil War and Reconstruction

In the mid-1800s, a new invention set off a chain of events that deeply divided the young nation. The machine, called the cotton gin, quickly removed seeds from cotton, which made the crop more profitable. But growing cotton still required many laborers for planting and harvesting. This is one reason why slaves were an important part of plantation life. Cotton wore out the soil, though. Plantation owners wanted to expand into new western lands. But that meant that slavery would spread into the new territories. Some people did not want this. The debate began. Should the states or the federal government decide about slavery in the new territories?

Causes of Conflict   Until 1850, there were equal numbers of slave and free states in the United States. Then California asked to be admitted to the union as a free state. After a heated debate, Congress granted the request. The Southern states were not pleased. To gain their support, Congress also passed the Fugitive Slave Act. It said people anywhere in the country must return runaway slaves to their owners. This action only increased the argument over slavery. In 1852, Harriet Beecher Stowe published *Uncle Tom's Cabin,* a novel about the evils of slavery.

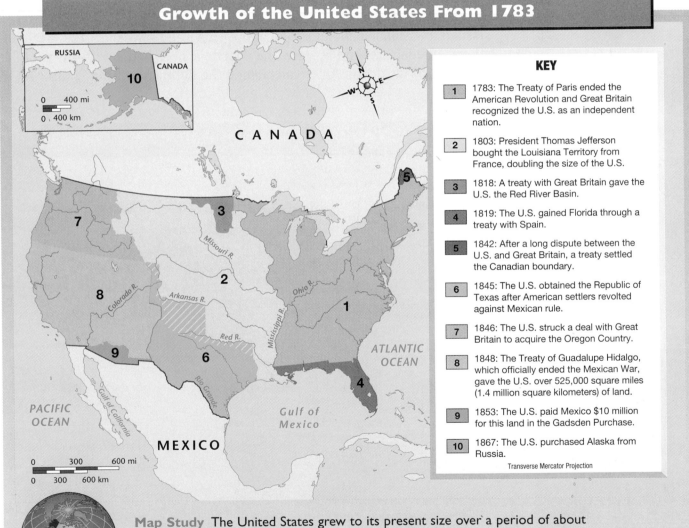

Growth of the United States From 1783

KEY

1 1783: The Treaty of Paris ended the American Revolution and Great Britain recognized the U.S. as an independent nation.

2 1803: President Thomas Jefferson bought the Louisiana Territory from France, doubling the size of the U.S.

3 1818: A treaty with Great Britain gave the U.S. the Red River Basin.

4 1819: The U.S. gained Florida through a treaty with Spain.

5 1842: After a long dispute between the U.S. and Great Britain, a treaty settled the Canadian boundary.

6 1845: The U.S. obtained the Republic of Texas after American settlers revolted against Mexican rule.

7 1846: The U.S. struck a deal with Great Britain to acquire the Oregon Country.

8 1848: The Treaty of Guadalupe Hidalgo, which officially ended the Mexican War, gave the U.S. over 525,000 square miles (1.4 million square kilometers) of land.

9 1853: The U.S. paid Mexico $10 million for this land in the Gadsden Purchase.

10 1867: The U.S. purchased Alaska from Russia.

Transverse Mercator Projection

Map Study The United States grew to its present size over a period of about 100 years. **Regions** What parts of the United States once were claimed by Great Britain? **Critical Thinking** The United States made agreements with many countries in order to gain land. How did the United States gain the Louisiana Territory? How did the United States gain Alaska?

CITIZEN HEROES

After reading this book, thousands of Northerners became **abolitionists** (ab uh LISH un ists). These people wanted to end slavery. Many helped slaves escape to Canada. There, slavery was illegal. Most Southerners, however, felt that abolitionists were robbing them of their property.

The debate over slavery raged. When Abraham Lincoln, a Northerner, was elected President in 1860, many Southerners feared they would have little say in the government. As a result, some Southern states seceded, or withdrew, from the United States. They founded a new country—the Confederate States of America, or the Confederacy.

Conflict Erupts Into War In 1861, the Civil War between the Northern states and the Confederacy erupted. It lasted four years. The North, known as the Union, had more industry, wealth, and soldiers. The Confederacy had experienced military officers. They also had cotton. Many foreign countries bought southern cotton. Southerners hoped that they would help supply the Confederacy.

Despite the North's advantages, the war dragged on. In 1863, Lincoln issued the Emancipation Proclamation. This freed slaves in areas loyal to the Confederacy. And it gave the North a new battle cry—freedom! Thousands of African Americans joined the fight against the South.

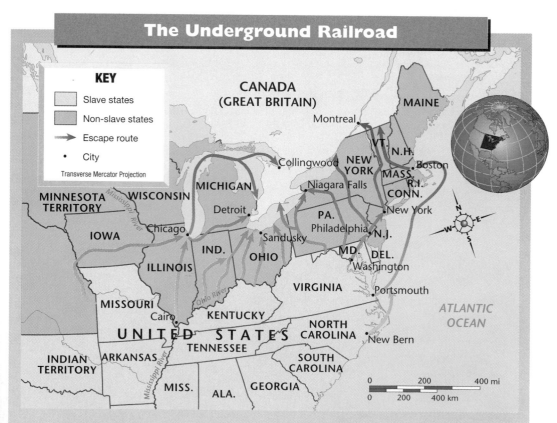

The Underground Railroad

Map Study The Underground Railroad (above) was a series of routes that escaped slaves used to travel secretly to the North or to Canada. Slaves relied on "conductors," like Harriet Tubman (left), to guide them on their journey.
Location What slave states bordered nonslave states?

Fighting for Their Cause

The picture to the left shows African American soldiers outside their barracks at Fort Lincoln, Washington, D.C., in early 1865. Twenty-one African Americans received the Congressional Medal of Honor (below), the country's highest award for bravery. **Critical Thinking** Why do you think African Americans were willing to fight for the Union?

The Civil War ended in 1865. Lincoln wanted the Southern states to return willingly to the Union. This was the first step in his plan for the **Reconstruction,** or rebuilding, of the nation.

Reconstructing the Union   Less than a week after the end of the war, Lincoln was killed. Vice President Andrew Johnson tried to carry out Lincoln's plan. But Congress resisted his efforts. Finally, Congress took complete control of Reconstruction. The Union Army governed the South until new state officials were elected.

That happened in 1877. But as soon as the Union Army withdrew, Southern lawmakers voted to **segregate,** or separate, blacks from whites. Segregation affected all aspects of life. The difficult struggle to preserve the United States had succeeded. But the long struggle to guarantee equality to all Americans still lay ahead.

SECTION 2 REVIEW

1. **Define** (a) Louisiana Purchase, (b) Manifest Destiny, (c) immigrant, (d) Industrial Revolution, (e) abolitionist, (f) Civil War, (g) Reconstruction, (h) segregate.

2. **Identify** (a) Meriwether Lewis, (b) William Clark, (c) Thomas Jefferson, (d) Andrew Jackson, (e) Harriet Beecher Stowe, (f) Abraham Lincoln, (g) Andrew Johnson.

3. (a) What was the Indian Removal Act? (b) How did it affect Native Americans?

4. How did the Industrial Revolution affect the United States?

5. Why did the Southern states withdraw from the Union?

Critical Thinking

6. **Expressing Problems Clearly**   How did the issue of slavery become a cause of the Civil War?

Activity

7. **Writing to Learn**   Write an entry that Lincoln might have made in his diary on his plan for Reconstruction.

The United States Becomes a World Power

Reach Into Your Background

Have you ever wondered about the contrast between rich and poor neighborhoods in a city? Such contrasts have always been part of city life, where rich, middle-class, and poor people live near each other but live very different lives.

Questions to Explore

1. How did the United States become a world power?

2. How did the citizens of the United States gain more equality from the 1950s to the present?

Key Terms

labor force
settlement house
Homestead Act
communism
Cold War
civil rights movement

Key People

Jacob Riis
Jane Addams
Woodrow Wilson
Franklin D. Roosevelt
Harry S. Truman
Martin Luther King, Jr.

▼ Jacob Riis argued that tenements like these in New York City, which crowded as many as 10 people to a room, bred misery, disease, and crime.

Jacob Riis was an angry man. In his book *How the Other Half Lives,* he took his readers on tours of slum life in the late 1800s. He wanted other people to be angry, too—angry enough to change things.

"**C**ome over here. Step carefully over this baby—it is a baby, in spite of its rags and dirt—under these iron bridges called fire escapes, but loaded down . . . with broken household goods, with washtubs and barrels, over which no man could climb from a fire . . . That baby's parents live in the rear tenement [slum] here. . . . There are plenty of houses with half a hundred such in."

The United States From 1865 to 1914

The Industrial Revolution made life easier for the rich and the middle class. By the late 1800s, a handful of people had made millions of dollars in industry. But life did not improve for the poor. City slums were crowded with poor immigrants. Many could not speak English. These newcomers were a huge **labor force,** or supply of workers. Employers paid them very little. Even small children had to work so that families could make ends meet.

Reformers like Jacob Riis began to protest such poverty. In Chicago, Jane Addams set up a **settlement house,** or community center, for poor immigrants. Mary Harris Jones helped miners organize for better wages. Because of her work to end child labor, people called her "Mother Jones."

One way for people to leave poverty behind was to move to the open plains and prairies of the Midwest. To attract settlers to this region, the United States government passed the **Homestead Act** in 1862. It gave 160 acres (65 hectares) of land to any adult willing to farm it and live on it for five years. Life on the plains was not easy. Trees and water were in short supply. And settlers faced swarms of insects, wild prairie fires, and temperatures that were very hot in summer and cold in winter. Still, most homesteaders held on for the five years. Railroads helped connect the East Coast with the West, which speeded up settlement.

READ ACTIVELY

Visualize Visualize life on a homestead farm on the prairie.

Life in the West, 1900s

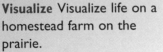

New technology helped settlers turn vast areas of the West into productive farmland. Above, a huge combine harvester cuts wheat on a farm in Washington State. Shown at right is a settler's suitcase packed with treasured belongings for the trip to the West. **Critical Thinking** Why was the development of new farming technology important to the settling of the Plains region?

The United States Expands Beyond Its Shores   The United States also expanded beyond its continental borders. Russia owned the territory of Alaska. In 1867, Secretary of State William Seward arranged for the United States to buy it. In 1898, the United States took control of Hawaii, another territory. The same year, the United States fought and won the Spanish-American War. The victory gave the United States control of the Spanish lands of Cuba, Puerto Rico, Guam, and the Philippines. America had a strong economy, military might, and overseas territory.

The World at War

Now the United States was a player in world affairs. As a result, the country was drawn into international conflicts. In 1914, World War I broke out in Europe. President Woodrow Wilson did not want America to take part. But when Germany began sinking American ships, Wilson had no choice. He declared war. The United States joined the Allied Powers of Great Britain and France. They fought against the Central Powers, which included Germany, Austria-Hungary, and Turkey. In 1917, thousands of American soldiers sailed to Europe. With this added strength, the Allies won the war in 1918. The terms of peace in the Treaty of Versailles punished Germany severely. Its harshness led to another worldwide conflict 20 years later.

▲ During World War I, the United States government paid for the war effort by selling bonds. These were certificates that included a promise to pay back the face amount plus interest. Posters like this urged Americans to buy bonds to win the war.

Fighting World War I

American troops in World War I and World War II served with great bravery. Here, a United States Army soldier in World War I rests during a pause in the shooting. More than 4 million Americans served in World War I. About 15 million Americans served in World War II.

Charles Lindbergh, a 25-year-old stunt flier and airmail pilot from Minnesota, made the world's first nonstop flight between the Americas and Europe in 1927. Lindbergh and his plane, *Spirit of St. Louis,* became a symbol of a daring, adventuresome spirit.

In the United States, during the 10 years after World War I, the economy boomed. Women enjoyed new freedoms and the hard-won right to vote. More and more people bought cars, refrigerators, radios, and other modern marvels.

In 1929, however, the world was grabbed by an economic disaster called the Great Depression. In America, factories closed, people lost their jobs, and farmers lost their farms. Many banks closed, and people lost their life's savings. By 1933, people were losing hope. But that year, President Franklin D. Roosevelt took office. He created a plan called the New Deal. This was a series of government programs to help people get jobs and to restore the economy. Some of these programs, like Social Security, are still in place today. Social Security provides income to people who are retired or disabled.

The Great Depression was very hard on Germany. Its people also lost hope. In 1933, they responded by turning to Adolf Hitler. Soon he had become dictator of Germany. Hitler convinced Germans that their nation would become wealthy and powerful by taking over other countries. Also, he claimed that Germans were a superior ethnic group—and should lead Europe. In 1939, Hitler's armies invaded Poland. This started World War II.

By the end of the war in 1945, Europe was in ruins. People around the world learned that Hitler had forced countless Jews, Gypsies, Slavs, and others into brutal prison camps. Millions of people, including some six million Jews, were murdered in these camps. This horrible mass murder is called the Holocaust (HAHL uh kawst).

READ ACTIVELY

Connect Why is it important that women, as well as men, can vote?

A New Home During the Cold War, the United States built underground "silos" for missiles. As new missiles were built, the Air Force removed the old ones and sold the silos. Some were used to store crops and other materials. One Kansas county turned a silo into a school. In 1984, a family bought a silo and built a home inside. The family paid $40,000 for the silo. Originally, it had cost the American people $4 million to build.

▼ Which of the wars shown on this time line did not involve open warfare?

As with World War I, the United States tried to stay out of the conflict. But in 1941, Japan attacked the United States naval base at Pearl Harbor, Hawaii. The Japanese were allied with the Germans, so the United States declared war on both nations. The United States sent armed forces to fight in Europe and in the Pacific. President Roosevelt, who led the nation in war, did not live to see peace. He died in April 1945. Vice President Harry S. Truman became President.

In May, the Allies defeated the Germans. During the summer, President Truman decided to drop two atomic bombs on Japan. That convinced Japan to give up. Finally, World War II was over.

Postwar Responsibilities

After World War II, the United States took on new international responsibilities. During World War I, the Soviet Union had been created. It adopted a form of government called **communism.** Under this system, the state owns all industries. In theory, the people share work and its rewards equally. After World War II, the communist Soviet Union took control of many Eastern European countries. The United States feared that the Soviets were trying to spread communism throughout the world. As a result, the United States and the Soviet Union entered the **Cold War.** This was a period of great tension, although the two countries never faced each other in an actual war. Two wars grew out of this tension. One was the Korean War, and the other was the Vietnam War. The Cold War lasted more than 40 years.

The economy of the United States boomed after World War II. But not all citizens shared in the benefits. In the South, segregation was a way of life. Many people began the **civil rights movement** to fight this injustice. People like Martin Luther King, Jr., led the movement to end segregation and win rights for African Americans. This success inspired others who felt they were treated unequally. Mexican American farmworkers, women, and disabled people also made gains in civil rights.

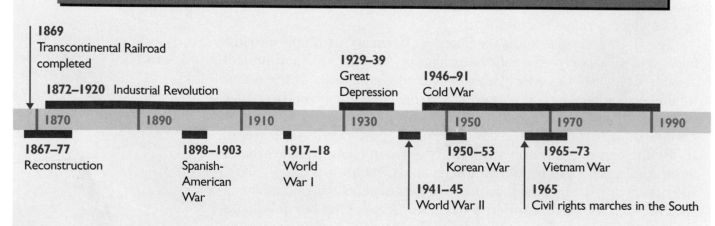

United States From the 1860s to 1990s

1869 Transcontinental Railroad completed

1872–1920 Industrial Revolution

1929–39 Great Depression

1946–91 Cold War

1870 1890 1910 1930 1950 1970 1990

1867–77 Reconstruction

1898–1903 Spanish-American War

1917–18 World War I

1950–53 Korean War

1941–45 World War II

1965–73 Vietnam War

1965 Civil rights marches in the South

A Birthday Celebration

On July 4, 1976, the United States celebrated its bicentennial, or two hundredth birthday. One of the most spectacular events of the celebration was a review of a huge fleet of sailing ships sent by foreign countries. Here, one of the ships sails into New York Harbor. **Critical Thinking** What events do you think would be appropriate for a country's two hundredth birthday? Why?

Many challenges remain, however. There are problems of homelessness and hunger, of low wages and pollution. But Americans have faced such problems before. Once, children worked in factories and mines for 12 hours a day, 6 days a week. Americans met that challenge and conquered it. During the Great Depression, hundreds of thousands of people were out of work. Droughts destroyed farms all through the Plains states. Again, Americans found ways to solve these problems. They did it by harnessing their energy, creativity, and willingness to work hard in the face of any challenge.

SECTION 3 REVIEW

1. **Define** (a) labor force, (b) settlement house, (c) Homestead Act, (d) communism, (e) Cold War, (f) civil rights movement.

2. **Identify** (a) Jacob Riis, (b) Jane Addams, (c) Woodrow Wilson, (d) Franklin D. Roosevelt, (e) Harry S. Truman, (f) Martin Luther King, Jr.

3. List three events that helped make the United States a world power.

4. What gains in equality did African Americans make after World War II?

Critical Thinking

5. **Recognizing Cause and Effect** How did the Homestead Act help settle the Plains of the Midwest?

Activity

6. **Writing to Learn** People who stay home during a war also find ways to help the country. Do research in the library about such things as rationing and volunteer work during World War II. You can also interview friends or family members about that period. Then write a report about what life was like at home during the war.

Growth, Settlement, and Independence in Canada

BEFORE YOU READ

Reach Into Your Background

Have you ever seen a commercial for a product—or talked to a friend about some item—then rushed out immediately to buy it? Fads like this can make a company rich. The same thing happened back in the 1600s and 1700s. French businessmen got rich by selling American beaver skins. Many Europeans wanted hats made from the beaver's thick, glossy fur.

Questions to Explore

1. Why were France and Britain rivals in Canada?
2. How did Canada become an independent nation?
3. How did Canada become a world power?

Key Terms
dominion
bilingual

Key People and Places
Louis Papineau
William Mackenzie
Earl of Durham
Ontario
Quebec
Yukon

The Haida people of British Columbia tell this tale. As in many Native American tales, nature plays an important role.

▼ The trade in beaver furs was so profitable during the 1700s and 1800s because beaver hats like this were the height of fashion in Europe.

"While he was crying and singing his dirge [sad song], a figure emerged from the lake. It was a strange animal, in its mouth a stick that it was gnawing. On each side of the animal were two smaller ones also gnawing sticks. Then the largest figure . . . spoke, 'Don't be so sad! It is I, your wife, and your two children. We have returned to our home in the water. . . . Call me the Beaver woman."

To the Haida and other native peoples in Canada, beavers were especially important. Imagine how they felt when European trappers killed almost all of the beavers to make fur hats.

The Battle of Quebec was a turning point in the Seven Years' War. This painting illustrates how British troops found a path through the cliffs that protected Quebec. **Critical Thinking** Do you think that Quebec would have fallen to the British if troops had not found a path in? Why or why not?

The French and the British in Canada

The profitable fur trade in Canada brought two European powers—France and Great Britain—into conflict there. Actually, the two rivals fought wars all over the world. In 1713, they signed a peace treaty. The treaty gave Great Britain the Hudson Bay region and the southeastern corner of Canada, called Acadia.

The peace was uneasy. Against their will, French Catholics in Acadia came under the rule of British Protestants. The French controlled the lowlands south of Hudson Bay and around the St. Lawrence River. Both countries wanted to control the Ohio River Valley, farther to the south. The French wanted its beavers for furs. The British wanted its land for settlement.

The contest for this region was so intense that in 1754, it erupted into the Seven Years' War. In the United States, this conflict is called the French and Indian War. The British won the decisive Battle of Quebec in 1759. The Treaty of Paris, signed four years later, gave Great Britain complete control over Canada. Some French settlers returned to France. Those who stayed resisted English culture. The first two British governors of Canada were sympathetic. They gained passage of the Quebec Act. It gave the French people in Quebec the right to speak their own language, practice their own religion, and follow their own customs.

LINKS ACROSS THE WORLD

Acadia Until 1763, France and Britain claimed land that today is Nova Scotia, New Brunswick, and part of Maine. The French called this region Acadia. When the British took over, Acadians who refused to pledge loyalty to Great Britain were driven from their homes. Some formed a colony in Louisiana. The name *Acadian* came to sound like "cajun." Now the Cajun culture is an important part of life in Louisiana.

British Loyalists in Canada

Some British Loyalists remained in the United States after the American Revolution. Many, however, moved to Canada. In Canada, the British government gave the Loyalists land to make up for the homes they had left behind. This painting shows Loyalists drawing lots for land.

During the American Revolution, some Americans did not want independence. They were called British Loyalists. After the war, many Loyalists moved to Canada. But most did not want to live in a French culture. To avoid problems, Great Britain divided the land into two colonies, Upper and Lower Canada. Most Loyalists moved into Upper Canada. It is now called Ontario. French Canadians remained in Lower Canada. It is now Quebec.

During the War of 1812, the French and British groups worked together. This was crucial when the United States tried to invade Canada. The United States had troops on the border between the two countries. The French, British, and native peoples forced the Americans back.

Canada Seeks Self-Rule

Once the war ended, however, Canadians again could not cooperate. Both French Canadians and British Canadians hated British rule. Many felt Britain was too far away to understand their needs. But the two groups did not join in rebellion. In 1837, a French Canadian named Louis Papineau (pah pee NOH) organized a revolt in Lower Canada. His goal was to establish the region as a separate country. The British easily defeated the rebels. The same thing happened in Upper Canada. William Mackenzie led the people against British rule. Again, the British easily defeated the rebels.

READ ACTIVELY

Ask Questions What do you want to know about how Canada became independent from Britain without going to war?

Still, British leaders were afraid more trouble was coming. They sent the Earl of Durham to learn what was wrong. When Durham returned, he had many suggestions. First, he suggested that the Canadians be given more control of their government. He also thought all the Canadian provinces should be united. But the British government united only Upper and Lower Canada to form the Province of Canada. Nova Scotia, Newfoundland, Prince Edward Island, and New Brunswick were not included in this union. If Canada were completely united, the British feared, the Canadians might make a successful rebellion.

But Canadians felt that all provinces should be represented in their government. Otherwise it could not be effective. In 1864, leaders from every province met. Together they worked out a plan to form a union. On July 1, 1867, the British Parliament accepted the plan. It passed the British North American Act. This made Canada "one Dominion under the name of Canada." A **dominion** is a self-governing area. Canada was still subject to Great Britain. But now a central government would run the country. Canadians would solve their own problems. Without a war, Canadians had won the right to control their own government.

After its "peaceful revolution," Canada saw years of growth and change. Skilled European farmers settled Canada's western plains. The region filled with productive farms. Gold and other valuable minerals were discovered in the Yukon in the 1890s. That brought miners to the far northwest. Canada was becoming rich and important.

CITIZEN HEROES

A Voice of Protest In 1869, the Canadian government wanted to finish the cross-country railroad across the flat plains region. Louis Riel, leader of the *métis* (may TEE)—mixed European and Native American people—objected to the plan. The *métis* said the railroad would bring new settlers, who would take away their land. The government refused to stop, so Riel led an armed revolt. It failed, and Riel was executed for treason, but the government did set aside land for the *métis*. Today, French Canadians consider Riel a hero.

▼ On November 7, 1885, Canada's far-flung provinces were tied together as the last spike was driven in, completing the Canadian Pacific Railway.

Canada Takes Its Place in the World When Britain entered World War I, Canadians were still British subjects. Canada, therefore, entered the war, too. Canada willingly sent soldiers and resources overseas. Canada contributed so much to the Allied victory that the young country became a world power. Great Britain recognized Canada's new strength and granted it more independence. During the Great Depression, Canada focused on solving problems at home. But when World War II began in 1939, Canada took part. Once again, Canadian efforts helped win the war.

Canada: Postwar to the Present

During the war, Canadians built factories. They made war supplies and goods like clothes and shoes. Because of the war, people could not get such products from Europe. After the war, Canadian goods found a ready market in Europe.

Also during the postwar years, immigrants poured into Canada. They came from Asia, Europe, Africa, and the Caribbean. The newcomers filled jobs in new factories and other businesses. Soon, Canada became the world's fourth-largest industrial nation.

STUDENT ART

Rebecca Bond
age 10
Ajax, Ontario, Canada

The CN Tower is a communications and observation tower in downtown Toronto. "I painted the CN Tower," the artist said, "because its my favorite place in Toronto. You can see the whole city from the top." **Critical Thinking** If you were asked to paint a picture of one of your area's landmarks, which one would you choose? Why?

Toronto and the CN Tower

Industrialization brought back old arguments. British Canadians built new factories in Quebec. That alarmed French Canadians. By 1976, some French Canadians were tired of being part of Canada. Quebec, they argued, should be independent. Instead, in 1982, the Canadians wrote a new constitution. Special sections spelled out ways to respect French Canadian culture and concerns. New laws made Canada a **bilingual** country. That is, Canada had two official languages—English and French. In addition Canadians could now change their constitution without Great Britain's permission. Canada was completely independent.

Canada's government is modeled on the British parliamentary system. It is called a constitutional monarchy. It is also called a parliamentary democracy because the group of representatives that makes its laws is modeled on the English parliament. Another thing ties Canada to Great Britain. Canada belongs to the Commonwealth of Nations. All member countries were once British colonies. Great Britain gives members financial aid, advice, and military support.

Fort York, Toronto

During the War of 1812, United States forces crossed Lake Ontario and occupied York, then Canada's capital, for four days. American soldiers burned government buildings and looted private houses. Today York is called Toronto. Here, in the shadow of Toronto's modern skyline, militia dressed in British uniforms of the period parade at historic Fort York.

SECTION 4 REVIEW

1. **Define** (a) dominion, (b) bilingual.

2. **Identify** (a) Louis Papineau, (b) William Mackenzie, (c) Earl of Durham, (d) Ontario, (e) Quebec, (f) Yukon.

3. (a) Why was the Ohio River Valley important to the French? (b) Why was it important to the English?

4. How did Canada become an industrial power after World War II?

Critical Thinking

5. **Making Comparisons** Compare the ways in which Canada and the United States became independent nations.

Activity

6. **Writing to Learn** Write a few reasons that a French Canadian might give for separating from British Canada.

Partners and Friends

THE UNITED STATES AND CANADA TODAY

Reach Into Your Background

Think about the land on which your community is built. What do you think it looked like 300 years ago? What natural resources did it have? How have people changed it? Which changes are improvements and which are not? If you had the job of protecting the environment of your community, what would you do?

Questions to Explore

1. What environmental concerns do the United States and Canada share today?

2. What economic ties do the United States and Canada have to each other and to the world?

Key Terms

fossil fuel
acid rain
clear-cut
interdependent
tariff
free trade
NAFTA

Key Places

Cuyahoga River
Lake Erie
Niagara Falls
St. Lawrence Seaway

▼ The United States and Canada worked together to construct several buildings astride the border between the two countries at Derby Line, Vermont.

A minke whale swam northward in the Atlantic Ocean. She was very large—weighing four tons and about as long as a classroom—but still she swam gracefully. Every few minutes she dived for fish and came back up for air. The sight was breathtaking.

But there were people on the ocean that day. They wanted to do more than watch the whale. They were whale hunters from Norway, where whale meat is still part of people's diets.

A hundred years ago, Canadians, Americans, and others from all over the world also hunted whales. These animals were valued for their meat, oil, and bones. Then people began to realize that whales were disappearing. Today, the United States and Canada are members of the International Whaling Commission. Members work together to protect whales. This is just one of the ways the United States and Canada have become cooperative neighbors.

Environmental Issues

Protecting whales is one of many environmental issues that concern both the United States and Canada. Both countries share many geographic features—the coasts of the Atlantic and Pacific oceans, the Great Lakes, and the Rocky Mountains, for example. Both countries use natural resources in similar ways. And both have used technology to meet their needs. But technology has left its mark on their water, air, forests, and futures.

Solving Water Problems   Can you picture a river on fire? Impossible, you say? In 1969, a fire started on the Cuyahoga (KY uh hoh guh) River. That river flows past Cleveland, Ohio, and then empties into Lake Erie. Along the way, Cleveland's factories had poured waste, garbage, and oil into the river. The layer of pollutants was so thick that it burned without being put out by the water beneath it.

The Cuyahoga was typical of the rivers that empty into Lake Erie. So much pollution had been dumped into the lake that most of the fish had died. Swimming in the river was unthinkable. But the fire on the Cuyahoga was a wake-up call. The United States and Canada signed a treaty promising to cooperate in cleaning up the lake. Such treaties as this have greatly reduced freshwater pollution in the United States. Today, people again enjoy fishing and boating on the Cuyahoga.

The Cuyahoga River, Yesterday and Today

On August 22, 1969, a fireboat hosed down a burning pier that had been set on fire by flames from the Cuyahoga River (above right). Today, after a huge cleanup campaign, the view is different. Waterfront attractions such as restaurants and cruise boats (above left) offer visitors and residents a chance to enjoy the river views.

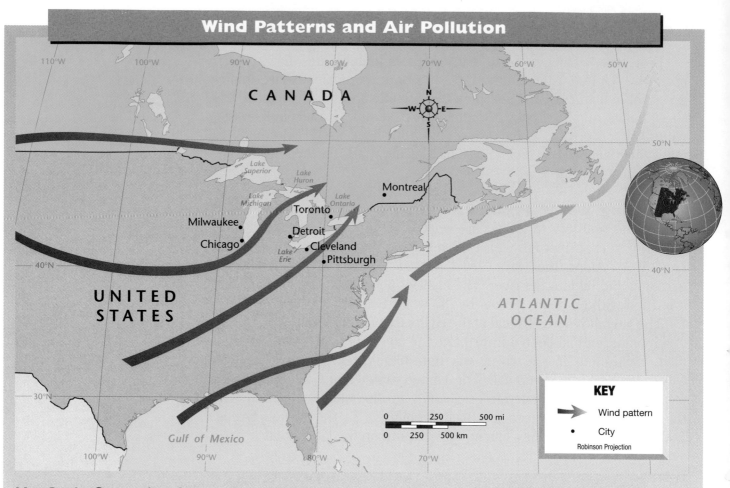

Wind Patterns and Air Pollution

CANADA

Lake Superior
Lake Huron
Lake Michigan
Lake Ontario
Lake Erie

Montreal
Toronto
Milwaukee
Detroit
Chicago
Cleveland
Pittsburgh

UNITED STATES

ATLANTIC OCEAN

Gulf of Mexico

KEY
➔ Wind pattern
• City
Robinson Projection

0 250 500 mi
0 250 500 km

Map Study Cities such as Chicago, Cleveland, and Pittsburgh have been centers of industry since the late 1800s. Factories in these and other Great Lakes cities were powered by burning coal. The wind carried much of the pollution from these factories away from United States cities—and straight into Canada. Today, Canada and the United States cooperate to keep air pollution under control. **Location** What Canadian cities marked on the map lie in the path of winds from industrial cities in the United States?

READ ACTIVELY

Predict What happens to the air pollution created in the Northeast or in Great Lakes areas of the United States?

Improving Air Quality On many days, you can look around most big cities and see that the air is filled with a brown haze. This pollution is caused by cars and factories burning **fossil fuels,** such as gasoline and coal. Not only is this air unhealthy for people to breathe, but it can also create other serious problems hundreds of miles away. Wind picks up pollutants in the air, where they combine with moisture to form an acid. When the moisture turns into rain, it is **acid rain.** Acid rain kills plants and trees. When enough acid rain falls on lakes, it kills fish and water plants. Coal-burning power plants in the Northeast and in Great Lakes areas have created this situation.

But polluted winds do not stop at international borders. Acid rain caused by United States power plants has affected forests and lakes in Canada, from Ontario to Newfoundland. When the Canadian government protested the situation in the 1980s, the two countries signed agreements to control air quality.

Renewing Forests   "I'm like a tree—you'll have to cut me down," cried Kim McElroy in 1993. The other demonstrators with her agreed. They were blocking the path of logging trucks trying to enter the forest of Clayoquot Sound on Vancouver Island, British Columbia. The protesters believed that cutting down the trees would damage the environment. In similar forests throughout the United States and Canada, logging companies practiced **clear-cutting,** or cutting down all the trees in an area. Without trees, soil washes away, other plants die, and animals lose their homes.

On the other hand, people need lumber for houses. Paper companies need wood pulp to make their products. People who work for logging companies need their jobs.

The Canadian and American governments want to maintain both the forests and the timber industry. They are working to develop ideas that will do that. For example, British Columbia passed a law that sets aside parts of the Clayoquot Sound's forests for logging. The law also imposes new rules on loggers to prevent damage in the areas where cutting is allowed.

"Economics Has Made Us Partners"

Not all next-door neighbors get along as well as the United States and Canada. President John F. Kennedy once described the relationship this way: "Geography has made us neighbors. History made us friends. And economics has made us partners." With 3,000 miles (4,827 km) of border between the two countries, economic cooperation has benefited both. Part of this cooperation has been in transportation between the countries, particularly around the Great Lakes.

▼ Clear-cutting in Oregon's Mount Hood National Forest scars the land with large bare patches.

Ask Questions What would you like to know about the economic relationship between the United States and Canada?

The St. Lawrence Seaway Have you ever heard of someone going over Niagara Falls in a barrel? The barrel would drop about 190 feet (58 m)—a pretty crazy stunt! But suppose you had a cargo of manufactured goods in Cleveland to send to Montreal. You decide to ship by water, because it is the cheapest and most direct means of transportation. Now what do you do? Niagara Falls lies between lakes Erie and Ontario. After that, your cargo would have to travel down a total drop of another 250 feet (76 m) in the St. Lawrence River before it reached Montreal. And once your cargo was unloaded, how would you get the ship back to Cleveland?

To solve this problem, the United States and Canada built the St. Lawrence Seaway. Completed in 1959, it is a system of locks, canals, and dams that allows ships to move from one water level to another. Now, ships can travel from Duluth, Minnesota, on Lake Superior, all the way to the Atlantic Ocean. The St. Lawrence Seaway makes it much easier for the United States and Canada to trade with each other and with Europe.

Trade What country is the biggest trading partner of the United States? It is Canada. And the United States is Canada's largest trading partner, too. About three fourths of all of Canada's foreign trade—both exports and imports—is with the United States. Our economies are **interdependent**. That means that in order to be successful, each country needs to do business with the other.

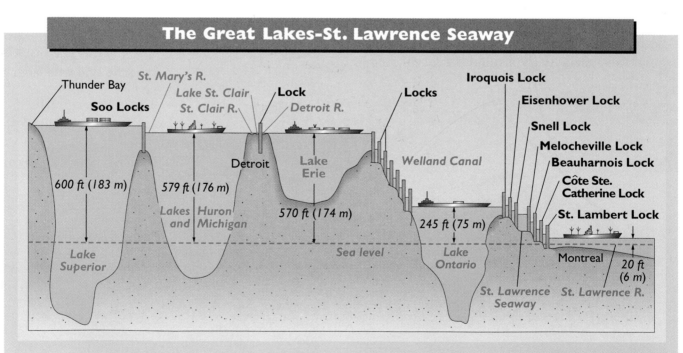

The Great Lakes-St. Lawrence Seaway

Chart Study Ships traveling from Lake Superior to the Atlantic Ocean must go through a series of locks. A lock is an enclosed part of a canal with a watertight gate at each end. Letting water into the lock raises ships. Letting water out lowers them. This diagram shows the location of locks along the St. Lawrence Seaway. **Critical Thinking** How do you think building the St. Lawrence Seaway affected the economies of the United States and Canada?

The Grain Industry in Alberta

This train is taking on a load of wheat from the nearby grain elevator. A grain elevator is a tall building where grain is stored. The train takes the wheat west to the Pacific Coast or east to the Great Lakes. The wheat then is loaded on ships for export. Wheat is one of Canada's most important exports. In fact, Canada is the world's second leading grain exporter. The United States leads the world in grain exports.

Before 1989, both countries charged fees called **tariffs** on many things they imported from each other. Tariffs raise the cost of goods, so they can limit the amount of trade. In 1989, Canada and the United States agreed to eliminate tariffs and have **free trade.** Since then, trade between them has increased. And in 1994, the United States and Canada joined Mexico to sign the North American Free Trade Agreement, or **NAFTA.** The goal of this agreement is to encourage trade and economic growth in all three countries.

SECTION 5 REVIEW

1. Define (a) fossil fuel, (b) acid rain, (c) clear-cut, (d) interdependent, (e) tariff, (f) free trade, (g) NAFTA.

2. Identify (a) Cuyahoga River, (b) Lake Erie, (c) Niagara Falls, (d) St. Lawrence Seaway.

3. Why is there disagreement about logging in some forests?

4. Why is acid rain from the United States a problem in Canada?

5. How has geography contributed to the trade partnership between Canada and the United States?

Critical Thinking

6. Expressing Problems Clearly Explain briefly why the United States and Canada cooperated to build the St. Lawrence Seaway.

Activity

7. Writing to Learn Write a paragraph that explains the main reasons why Canada and the United States are important to each other.

Interpreting Diagrams

Suppose that your pen pal in Canada wants to know what your school looks like. Which would you rather do, write her a letter describing your school, or send her a photograph?

Many people would probably choose to send the photograph. A photograph would show her in an instant what your school looks like. But writing a letter also has its benefits. You can describe details a photograph might not show.

Which should you do—send a letter or send a photograph? The best solution would be to send both. The photograph would show your pen pal what your school looks like, and the letter would tell her about it. In a way, you would be playing a long-distance game of show-and-tell with your pen pal!

Get Ready

You can also have show-and-tell with a diagram. As you know, a diagram is a picture that shows how something works or is made. It usually includes labels that tell about certain parts of the picture. It is like a combination of the letter and the photograph you would send to your pen pal. A diagram can both show things through a picture and tell about them through labels.

A diagram is like a game of "show-and-tell"—the picture *shows,* and the labels *tell.*

Try It Out

To understand how diagrams are made—and how to learn more from them—make one yourself. Complete these steps:

A. Find a photograph of a bicycle. You can cut one out of an old catalog or a magazine. Look for a photograph that is about the same size as the diagram on the next page.

B. Write a description of the bicycle. Describe in words the bicycle for someone who has never seen one before. Be sure to describe what it looks like, what its different parts are, and how the parts work.

C. Draw a diagram of the bicycle. Using the picture and your paragraph as a reference, draw a diagram of the bicycle. Be sure to label each part and explain how it works.

D. Compare the picture, the paragraph, and the diagram. Which of the three does the best job of showing and explaining what a bicycle is, what its parts are, and how it works?

As you can see, both pictures and words are useful. But nothing works as well as the combination of pictures and words you find in a diagram.

Apply the Skill

Now that you see how a simple diagram can "show and tell," you are ready to see how a more complicated diagram does the same thing. Use the diagram to complete the steps that follow.

1. **Read and look at the diagram below.** Look it over to get a sense of what it is about. What does this diagram illustrate? What do the labels tell?

2. **Study the picture.** What does the picture tell you about how a locomotive works?

3. **Study the words.** What path does the steam take through the engine?

4. **Think about diagrams.** Write a few sentences that explain how this diagram helps you understand locomotives.

How a Locomotive Works

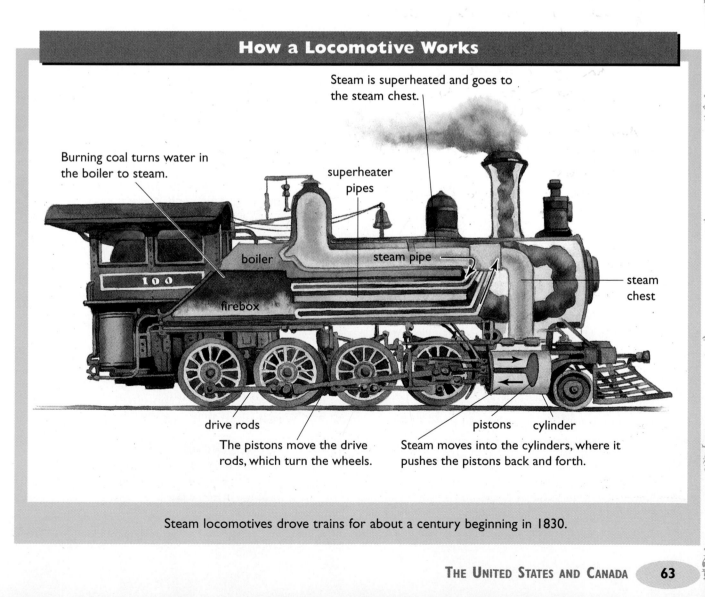

Steam is superheated and goes to the steam chest.

Burning coal turns water in the boiler to steam.

superheater pipes

boiler

steam pipe

firebox

steam chest

drive rods

The pistons move the drive rods, which turn the wheels.

pistons   cylinder

Steam moves into the cylinders, where it pushes the pistons back and forth.

Steam locomotives drove trains for about a century beginning in 1830.

Review and Activities

Reviewing Main Ideas

1. Some scholars say that the first people in North America were not indigenous. According to this theory, how did the first people get here?
2. How did Europeans change Native American ways of life?
3. Name two reasons why early colonists wanted to break away from Great Britain.
4. How did westward expansion affect voting laws?
5. How did the United States become a world power?
6. Besides African Americans, which groups campaigned for civil rights after the 1950s?
7. Why did Canada become more independent from Britain after World War I?
8. After World War II, Canada's influence on the rest of the world increased. Why?
9. How is acid rain produced?
10. What is the value of the St. Lawrence Seaway?

Reviewing Key Terms

Use each key term in a sentence that shows the meaning of the term.

1. indigenous
2. Manifest Destiny
3. immigrant
4. Industrial Revolution
5. abolitionist
6. Reconstruction
7. Cold War
8. civil rights movement
9. dominion
10. bilingual
11. fossil fuel
12. acid rain
13. interdependent
14. tariff
15. free trade

Critical Thinking

1. **Identifying Central Issues** Explain why Southern colonists believed that they needed slaves.
2. **Making Comparisons** Compare the ways in which the United States and Canada gained their independence from Great Britain.

Graphic Organizer

On a sheet of paper, copy this chart and fill in the empty ovals with forces that made the United States a world power.

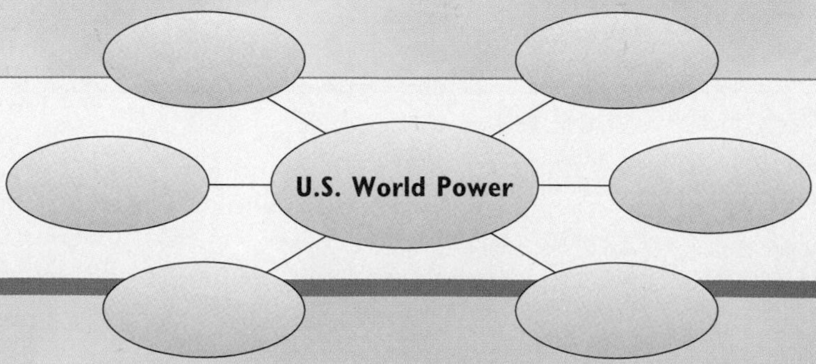

U.S. World Power

Map Activity

Canada

For each place listed below, write the letter from the map that shows its location.

1. Ontario

2. Quebec

3. Yukon

4. Lake Erie

5. St. Lawrence Seaway

Place Location

Writing Activity

Writing Activity

Think about ways in which the United States and Canada are similar. How are they different? Write a summary comparing the two countries.

Internet Activity

Use a search engine to find and browse **Selected Civil War Photographs.** Use a search engine to fine **Civil War Slang.** Print out the sheet then use the search engine again to find **Civil War Letters of Galutia York.** Use the slang sheet to help you read the letters. Give a presentation on the daily life of a Civil War soldier.

Skills Review

Turn to the **Skills Activity.**

Review the four steps for reading a diagram. Then write a few sentences explaining why a diagram is more effective than a paragraph of a picture in providing information.

How Am I Doing?

Answer these questions to help you check your progress.

1. Do I understand how differences between the North and South led to the Civil War?

2. Can I describe how the United States became a world power?

3. Can I recognize the differences between the ways in which the United States and Canada gained their independence?

4. What information from this chapter can I use in my book project?

ACTIVITY SHOP

Transportation

By foot and in flight, in horse-drawn wagons and in locomotives, the people of Canada and the United States have always been on the move.

Transportation has played an important role in the histories of both countries. Early Native Americans spread across the continent on foot, on horseback, and in canoes. European colonists arrived in sailing ships, and settlers traveled west in covered wagons. History has always been affected by the ways in which people have traveled.

Purpose

In this activity, you will conduct an investigation of the ways in which people have crossed the rugged land and vast distances of the United States and Canada.

Find the Routes

Some of the roads in Canada and the United States have existed since Native Americans followed animal trails through the wilderness. Others have only existed since town or city planners decided to build them. Many roads change over time. Footpaths became cement sidewalks or paved highways. Look for different roads and paths in your community. Make a note of even the largest highway or the smallest path across the corner of someone's lawn. How old do you think the different routes are? Make a map of all the routes you take on your way to school.

◀▼ From trails to highways, transportation routes come in many forms.

Do a Sailboat Study

Ships with great sails brought the first Europeans to this continent. Read about sailboats and sailing ships to see how they work. Then make a model sailboat. Draw a plan for your sailboat and choose your materials very carefully. Test your sailboat by floating it in water and blowing on it to create wind. Make any changes you need to improve the boat.

Calculate Travel Times

As the United States and Canada have grown older, travel times have become shorter and shorter. The chart below shows how long it has taken to travel from New York to St. Louis, the "Gateway to the West," in various years between 1800 and today.

New York to St. Louis		
Year	**Method**	**Approximate Travel Time**
1800	stagecoach and horseback	5 weeks
1860	passenger train	3 days
1930	passenger train	1 day
1950	automobile	24 hours
Today	passenger jet	3 hours

Use the chart to see how much travel speeds have improved. First, calculate the average speed in miles per hour of each method of transportation shown in the chart (distance in miles ÷ time in hours = speed in miles per hour). Then, draw a line graph of your results.

Links to Other Subjects

Finding routes .... **Geography**

Doing a sailboat study .... **Science**

Calculating travel times .... **Math**

Singing transportation songs .... **Music**

Telling a travel tale .... **Language Arts**

Sing Some Transportation Songs

"I've been workin' on the railroad, all the livelong day. . . ." Sound familiar? People have written many folk songs about trains, cars, boats, and other ways of getting around. What other transportation songs can you think of? Find the words and music to a few, and perform them with your classmates.

Tell a Travel Tale

You may not be a world traveler yet, but you have traveled. You've walked, ridden in cars and buses, and perhaps you've even ridden a train, boat, or plane. Write the story of your most exciting journey. Explain how you traveled, and what made the voyage exciting.

ANALYSIS AND CONCLUSION

Write a summary of your investigation. Describe the steps you followed and consider the following questions in your summary.

1. Why is transportation so important?

2. How has transportation affected the histories of the United States and Canada?

3. People are continually trying to make transportation faster and more efficient. Why do you think this is so?

Cultures of the United States and Canada

In addition to official U.S. holidays, like the Fourth of July, Americans celebrate many ethnic holidays. These people in New York City are enjoying the Puerto Rican Day Parade, which is held every June. To help you think about the mixture of people in the United States, do the following activities.

Take a poll

Ask students in your class where their great-grandparents are from. Many will be from the United States, of course. What other countries are represented?

Study restaurant listings

Use a telephone book to list the kinds of food served in restaurants in your community. How many countries are represented?

The United States

A NATION OF IMMIGRANTS

SECTION

1

BEFORE YOU READ

Reach Into Your Background

"So what'll it be tonight? Italian, Mexican, Chinese?" Does someone ask this question when your family is trying to decide on a restaurant or where to get take-out food? A wide variety, or diversity, of food is just one advantage of living in a society made up of different cultures. What else do you like about cultural diversity?

Questions to Explore

1. What influences have made the United States a culturally diverse nation?

2. How does this diversity affect life in the United States?

Key Terms

cultural diversity
cultural exchange
ethnic group

This view of **cultural diversity,** or a wide variety of cultures, comes from Tito, a teenager from Mexico. What do you think of it?

"My parents say, 'You have to learn the American culture.' I listen to them, but then I think about an ideal society where there's a little bit of every culture and it goes together just right. Say there's a part of the United States that's very hot. The problem to solve: What can we do to keep these people from overheating? The people who came here from the tropics have certain secrets of surviving in hot climates. Well, they come along and would say, 'When I lived in the tropics . . . we made our buildings with thick walls and a lot of windows. The buildings were white to reflect away the sun.' And the others would say, 'Hey, what a great idea. It works!' Different ideas would come together and make everything a whole lot better."

▼ A family enjoys dinner at a Mexican restaurant in San Antonio, Texas.

Diverse Cultures in the United States

The United States has always been culturally diverse. The country is geographically diverse, too—that is, it has a variety of landforms, climates, and vegetation. The cultures of the first Americans reflected their environments. Native Americans near the ocean ate a great deal of fish and told stories about the sea. Native Americans in forests learned how to trap and hunt forest animals. Native American groups also traded with each other. When groups trade, they get more than just goods. They also get involved in **cultural exchange.** In this process, different cultures share ideas and ways of doing things.

Cultural Exchange When Europeans came to North America, they changed Native American life. Some changes came from things that Europeans brought with them. For example, there were no horses in the New World when the Spanish explorers came. Once horses arrived, they changed the way that many Native Americans lived and became an important part of Native American culture.

Predict What kinds of things do you think the Europeans learned from Native Americans?

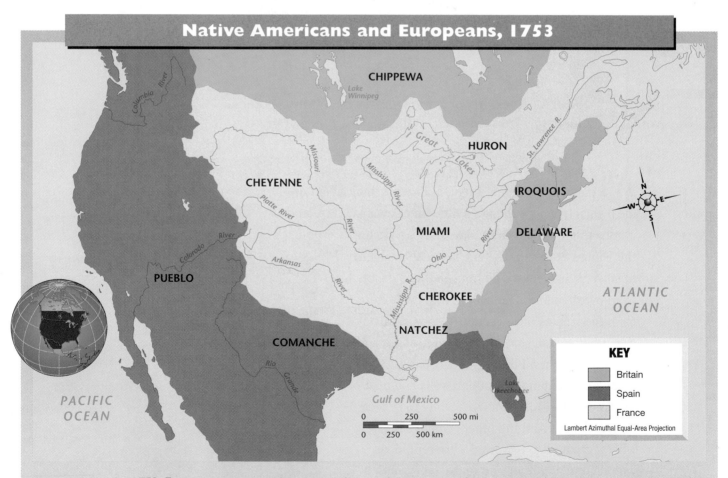

Native Americans and Europeans, 1753

CHIPPEWA

Lake Winnipeg

Columbia River

Great Lakes

HURON

St. Lawrence R.

Missouri River

Mississippi River

CHEYENNE

IROQUOIS

Platte River

River

MIAMI

River

DELAWARE

Colorado River

Arkansas

Ohio

PUEBLO

River

CHEROKEE

ATLANTIC OCEAN

NATCHEZ

Mississippi R.

COMANCHE

Rio Grande

Lake Okeechobee

PACIFIC OCEAN

Gulf of Mexico

0   250   500 mi

0   250   500 km

KEY

Britain

Spain

France

Lambert Azimuthal Equal-Area Projection

N E W S

Map Study By 1753, European countries had claimed all the land in North America. However, most of North America was still populated by Native Americans. This map shows some of the largest Native American groups who lived in European-claimed areas. **Regions** What European country claimed the land where the Cheyenne lived?

Immigration to the United States, 1940–1990

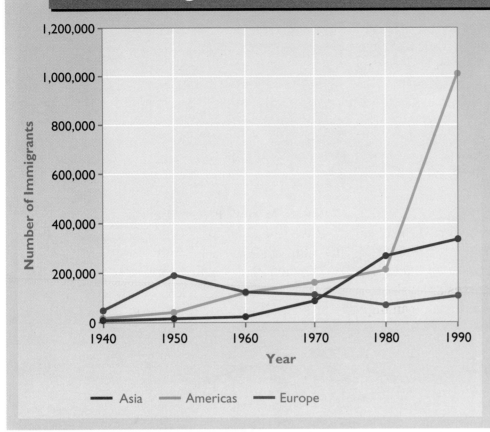

Chart Study This chart shows how many immigrants came to the United States from Asia, the Americas, and Europe between 1940 and 1990. **Critical Thinking** In 1940, roughly equal numbers of immigrants moved to the United States from each region. By 1950, most immigrants to the United States were European. How had things changed by 1990?

Cultural exchange occurred in two ways. Native Americans contributed many things to European culture. The French learned how to trap and to survive in the forest. English families learned to grow local foods such as corn and pumpkins. Cultural exchange also took place between enslaved Africans and their owners. The Africans learned English and used European tools. African music and foods entered the daily lives of slave owners.

This give-and-take happens every time immigrants come to a country. When Russian settlers came to the Midwest, they brought a kind of hardy wheat from their home country. Farmers soon learned that this tough wheat grew well in the Midwestern climate. These immigrants helped the Midwest become the leading wheat-growing area in the country today. In fact, so much wheat is grown here that it is called "America's breadbasket." Members of other ethnic groups have made important contributions to American culture, too. An **ethnic group** is a group of people who share a language, history, and culture.

What to Keep and What to Change? When immigrants move from one country to another, they must make difficult decisions. For instance, what things in their original culture should they keep, and what should they change? They must learn the language, laws, and manners of the people in their new home. For some, this is difficult. Others, however, want to forget the life they lived before.

Using Your Fingers and Toes Native Americans created the first number systems north of the Mexican border. The San Gabrielino in California used "all my hand finished" to mean 10. "All my hand finished and one my foot" was 15. The Chukchee used their fingers to count. Their word for "five" is *hand,* for "ten" *both hands,* and for "twenty" *man*— meaning both hands and both feet.

►Chinese American boy scouts in San Francisco proudly show off a dragon, which symbolizes Chinese New Year. Do you have to be Chinese to observe this holiday? Of course not—Americans of all ethnic backgrounds join in the joyous celebration.

For instance, Florence Benjamin, a third-generation American, asked her grandfather to teach her Russian. He replied, "From the time I came to this country, America has been my home and English my language. It is the only country that has been good to me and to the Jews. It is the one that is best for you. You don't need Russian." This man was grateful because American laws protected him. To him, being an American meant having the freedom *not* to use his native language.

On the other hand, some newcomers have difficulty adjusting to new ways. The United States is so different from their home country. Adults are sometimes afraid that the differences will come between them and their children. Anna, a teenager from Greece, describes the tensions that can grow among family members:

    ❝Once I understood English, once I started to see a whole American world out there that I never knew existed, a world that you don't see in Greece, I felt a little distant from [my parents]. The distance grew. They would be proud of me, but they also began to feel threatened. My new knowledge had no meaning for them. This has been hard and sad for all of us.❞

Almost all immigrants cling to things that remind them of their former homes. Think about your family or your friends' families. Does someone play an instrument special to your heritage? Do they use special phrases from the language they learned from their parents or grandparents? These customs give people a sense of identity. They also enrich American life.

Connect What traditions do you think reflect your ethnic heritage?

United States Culture

Have you ever listened to music at a Caribbean carnival or watched a dragon parade amid bursting firecrackers at Chinese New Year? Although these traditions came from other countries, they are now a part of the diverse culture of the United States.

Regions of the United States also have cultural differences. Some things make all places seem alike, such as television and radio. But regional differences remain, in foods, accents, and pastimes. Consider musical styles. There is Cajun zydeco from Louisiana and bluegrass music from the Southeast. These styles "belong" to particular regions. However, people everywhere in the country enjoy them. Exchanging such things helps us appreciate the diversity of American life.

American culture also includes ordinary, everyday items. They often appear in the work of American artists. Composer Aaron Copland used cowboy songs in his ballet *Billy the Kid.* Andrew Wyeth painted haunting pictures of ordinary people in humble country surroundings. In

▼ In small towns—like Elm Grove, Wisconsin—and large cities, people celebrate the Fourth of July with big parades.

**Joseph Andereasen
age 11**
United States

Sport is very much a part of a nation's culture. Baseball has been called the national pastime of the United States. Perhaps as many as 50 million people attend major league baseball games each season. **Critical Thinking** Who do you think the artist feels is the most important player? Why?

John Steinbeck's novel, *The Grapes of Wrath,* a poor farm family escapes dust storms of the 1930s. The African American poet Langston Hughes described life in Harlem, New York City in the early 1900s.

Cultures around the world also influence America's art. Musicians borrow from Asia, South America, Africa, and Eastern Europe. Painters use techniques and images from Europe, Africa, and Asia. Writers use themes from the world's folk tales. Like Tito, the boy from Mexico, American artists all believe in different ideas coming together to "make everything a whole lot better."

SECTION 1 REVIEW

1. **Define** (a) cultural diversity, (b) cultural exchange, (c) ethnic group.

2. How has the arrival of immigrants affected the culture of the United States?

3. Why are the cultures in different environments so different from each other?

4. Describe the cultural exchange that occurred between Native Americans and Europeans.

Critical Thinking

5. **Recognizing Cause and Effect** Why do you think Anna's parents felt uneasy and threatened when she began to feel a part of American society?

Activity

6. **Writing to Learn** Write a brief poem about a custom that is important to your family or the family of a friend.

Canada
A MOSAIC

BEFORE YOU READ

Reach Into Your Background

Have you ever made a mosaic, or a picture from tiles, beads, or other small bits of material? If you have, you know how satisfying it is to create a single pattern from many different shapes and colors. Canadians are proud of their "mosaic" society. It is the product of different cultures that keep their own identities while contributing to the whole nation.

Questions to Explore

1. Why do Canadians consider their society a mosaic?

2. How have the indigenous peoples of Canada worked to preserve their cultures?

Key Term
reserve

Key People and Places
Gordon Lightfoot
Nunavut

Channel-surf Canadian radio or television, and you may be surprised at the different languages you hear. Journalist Andrew H. Malcolm describes the variety of languages in Canada this way:

“**O**ne Toronto radio station broadcasts in thirty languages, including announcements of arrival delays for flights from 'back home.' In many Vancouver neighborhoods the street signs are in . . . English and Chinese. One Toronto television station survived simply by broadcasting programs in many languages aimed at many different ethnic communities, including [Pakistani] movies in Urdu with English subtitles. Toronto's city government routinely prepares its annual property tax notices in six languages: English, French, Chinese, Italian, Greek, and Portuguese.”

▼ For people across the world, the Royal Canadian Mounted Police, or Mounties, are a symbol of Canada.

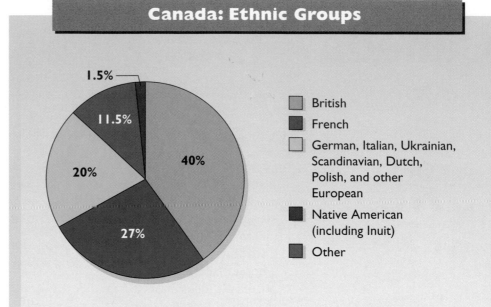

Canada: Ethnic Groups

- British
- French
- German, Italian, Ukrainian, Scandinavian, Dutch, Polish, and other European
- Native American (including Inuit)
- Other

1.5%
11.5%
20%
40%
27%

Chart Study Like the United States, Canada is very ethnically diverse.
Critical Thinking Hundreds of years ago, Native Americans were the largest ethnic group in Canada. What group is largest today? What percentage of Canada's people are of European descent?

Forming an Identity
Until the 1830s, no French-Canadian poets or novelists had any of their work published in Canada. The Quebec Movement of 1860 was the first attempt to preserve French culture. In the 1960s, Quebec poets worked to create a French-Canadian identity. One example is Paul Chamberland. In his book called *Terre Québec,* which means "the land of Quebec," he uses language to encourage pride in the province's French roots.

▼ Some French-Canadian drivers have license plates that refer to Quebec as *la belle province,* or "the beautiful province."

The People of Canada

The people who speak these languages came to Canada in search of better lives. Since Canada is the second-largest country in the world, it was attractive to newcomers in search of land and new opportunities. From the beginning, Canada's leaders made immigration easy. At first, they preferred European settlers. Laws set limits on immigrants who were Jews, Asians, or Africans. But that has changed. Today, people of all ethnic groups may move to Canada as long as they can support themselves.

Sometimes the ties among Canadians are not as strong as those among Americans. People in the United States may disagree with one another. But they rarely talk about forming independent states or countries. Some Canadian groups do.

For instance, the French Canadians of Quebec are very concerned about preserving their heritage. They are glad that Canada is a bilingual country. It has two official languages—English and French. In Quebec, special laws promote French culture and language. For instance, all street and advertising signs are written in French. An English translation of the sign appears below the French. But many French Canadians want more. They want Quebec to become a separate country. To show their determination, they have license plates that read *Je me souviens,* or "I remember." This refers to remembering their French heritage.

Canada's indigenous peoples also want to preserve their culture. Most, however, do not want to be independent. Instead, they are trying to fix problems from the past. In Canada, as in the United States, early European settlers took over the indigenous peoples' lands. Many indigenous peoples were sent to **reserves.** These were areas that the government set aside for them. Others were denied equal rights and facilities. In Canada, new laws allow the indigenous peoples to use their own languages in their schools. Now, people want their own languages on the street signs in their communities.

The Chippewa have a special problem. During World War II, the Canadian army took over Chippewa land for a military base. The Chippewa were sent to a reserve. The government said it would return the land after the war. Although the war ended in 1945, the land was not returned until 1994. The Chippewa sued the government for breaking its promise. They will use the money awarded to them for many projects. One big project is cleaning up dangerous waste that the military left behind. Chippewa chief Thomas M. Bressette feels his people deserved better treatment from the government:

Connect How is the history of Canada's indigenous peoples similar to that of Native Americans in the United States?

Remembering Canada's History

The community of Chemainus, British Columbia, is famous for its collection of 32 historical murals. The murals are huge, and the people depicted in them are larger than life. This mural honors the role that the country's first peoples, the Inuits and the Indians, have played in Canada's history.

▼ An Inuit artist uses a drill to put the finishing touches on a soapstone carving. Creating such traditional artwork is one way the Inuits retain their identity.

Ask Questions What do you want to know about the ways in which Canadians have encouraged artists to express Canadian ideals?

"While our people were giving their lives [in the war] in Europe, the Government here in Canada was taking their land away from them and putting us on postage-stamp [size] reserves. We're asking for a share in the resources. We don't want to appear as beggars dependent on the government handouts, but we are now being denied the resources that we so willingly gave up to support this nation."

Canada's Inuits are also trying to improve their lives. For centuries, these nomadic hunters lived in the Arctic. They had great survival skills and were fine craftworkers and artists. They made everything they needed. Modern technology, however, allows them to buy the clothes, tools, and weapons they once used to make. Many Inuits have lost their traditional skills. As a result, some feel they are losing their identity as Inuits. In the early 1990s, the Inuits convinced the Canadian government to grant them a huge section of land. It is located in the Northwest Territory. At the turn of the century, they will move into their new homeland. They call it *Nunavut,* or "Our Land."

Canadian Culture—The Mosaic

Canada has made a special effort "to recognize all Canadians as full and equal participants in Canadian society." This means that people can be Canadian and express their ethnic heritage at the same time. There is one cultural issue that unites most Canadians. They feel that the United States has too much influence on their culture. This worry is not new. As early as 1939, Canada established the National Film Board. Its job is to support movies with Canadian national themes and concerns.

Canadians still search for ways to express their unique culture. Painters have played a role. In the 1920s and 1930s, several painters formed the "Group of Seven." These artists developed bold new techniques for their paintings of Canada's landscape. The group inspired other Canadian artists to experiment. Many are still doing this today. Some ethnic artists follow other paths. For instance, Inuit print-makers and sculptors give new life to the images and ideas of their ancestors.

Many Canadian writers and musicians are famous for their work. American writer Mark Twain highly praised Lucy Maud Montgomery's *Anne of Green Gables.* The heroine, Anne, was "the dearest and most moving and delightful child since Alice in Wonderland," Twain said. Today, writers such as Margaret Atwood and Alice Munro are praised for their work. "The Wreck of the Edmund FitzGerald" is a well-known

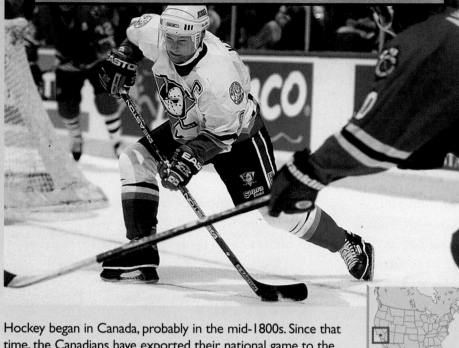

Hockey began in Canada, probably in the mid-1800s. Since that time, the Canadians have exported their national game to the United States. Twenty of the 26 teams in the National Hockey League are located in U.S. cities. Also, some 60 percent of players in the NHL are Canadians. Above, Canadian Paul Kariya of the Anaheim Mighty Ducks prepares to move forward with the puck.

CITIZEN HEROES

Overcoming Obstacles Terry Fox never earned millions a year or had an athletic shoe named after him. But he was one of the greatest Canadian athletes. In 1980, for 143 days in a row, he ran a daily marathon, which is 26 miles (42 km) long! Through snow, hail, and intense heat, he ran 3,339 miles (5,374 km). But why? When Terry was 19, his right leg was amputated because of bone cancer. He ran to raise money to help others with the disease. When his "Marathon of Hope" was over, he had raised $25 million for cancer research.

folk song about a ship that sank in a storm on Lake Superior. Most people think the song is old. Actually, it was written in the 1970s by Canadian folksinger Gordon Lightfoot.

In sports, Canada has turned the tables. It has influenced the United States. Ice hockey and lacrosse are two of Canada's athletic exports. Every year, hockey teams from the United States and Canada compete for the Stanley Cup, a Canadian prize.

SECTION 2 REVIEW

1. **Define** reserve.

2. **Identify** (a) Gordon Lightfoot, (b) Nunavut.

3. How does Canadian society seem like a mosaic?

4. How have Canada and Quebec tried to protect French culture?

5. What have the Inuits done to protect their culture?

Critical Thinking

6. **Making Predictions** Think about the Inuits moving into a new homeland. What do you think might happen to their culture? Why?

Activity

7. **Writing to Learn** Write a brief paragraph explaining why you think ice hockey developed in Canada.

Organizing Information

What tools do you use to help you study? You certainly use your books, and you probably use a pencil and paper. Perhaps you use a dictionary or note cards. What about maps? You can make a map of the material you want to learn and not just for your geography class.

When you think of a map, you might picture a map from your textbook of a country or a continent. Perhaps you think of a globe or of a street map. There are dozens—maybe even hundreds—of different kinds of maps. But there is an entirely different kind of map that you may not know of. It does not show the land or the water or even the sky.

This kind of map is called a concept map. As you read about a new topic, you can draw a concept map of the information. When you take notes, a concept map can help you organize information in a way that can be easier to understand and remember.

Get Ready

A concept map shows how concepts, or ideas, are related to one another. You can make a concept map about almost anything. Look at the concept map below.

The *subject* of this concept map, "lamps," is in the middle. Two important *features* of this subject are identified in the circles. Lines connect the features to the subject to show that they are related.

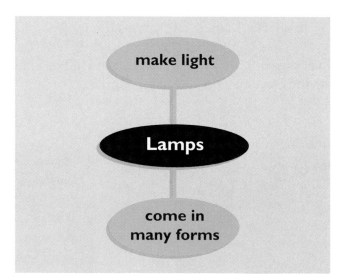

Now look below at how this concept map can grow. Can you see where *details* have been added to each of the features of lamps? Lines connect the details to each feature to show that they are related.

The subject of the concept map is in the middle. The features of the subject are identified at the next level. The final level identifies details of the features. As you get farther away from the middle of a concept map, it becomes more specific.

This type of concept map is sometimes called a "web." Can you see how its shape is similar to that of a spider web?

How do the concept maps show a great deal of information in a simple way? Notice that they show how all the ideas are related to each other. That is what makes concept maps so useful.

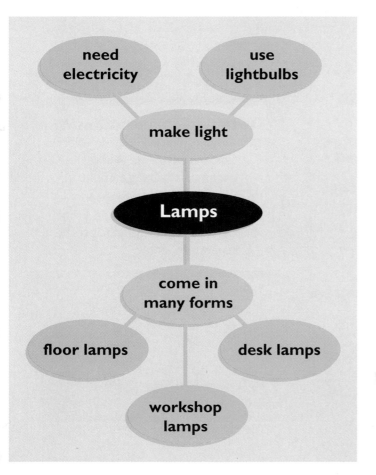

Try It Out

Try drawing your own concept maps. Draw a web for each of the subjects below.
- cars
- school
- music

Start with the subject in the center of the web. Then add features in circles connected to the subject with lines. Next add details of each feature. Some information you could include in a web about cars is shown in the chart.

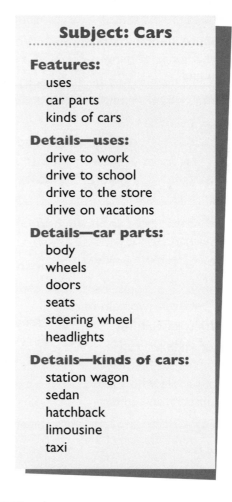

Subject: Cars

Features:
 uses
 car parts
 kinds of cars

Details—uses:
 drive to work
 drive to school
 drive to the store
 drive on vacations

Details—car parts:
 body
 wheels
 doors
 seats
 steering wheel
 headlights

Details—kinds of cars:
 station wagon
 sedan
 hatchback
 limousine
 taxi

Apply the Skill

Concept maps can be especially useful when you use them in your schoolwork. Reread Chapter 3 and create a web for each of the subjects below.
- Nunavut
- immigration
- traditions

Review and Activities

Reviewing Main Ideas

1. What contributions have Native Americans made to American culture?

2. If you went to an ethnic street festival, what kinds of things might you find?

3. What challenges face immigrants who move to the United States?

4. Why did the Chippewa sue the Canadian government?

5. How is Canadian culture similar to a mosaic?

Reviewing Key Terms

Match the definitions in Column I with the key terms in Column II.

Column I

1. the exchange of customs, ideas, or things between two cultures

2. a wide variety of cultures

3. an area set aside for native peoples

4. a group of people who share a language, history, and culture

Column II

a. cultural diversity

b. cultural exchange

c. ethnic group

d. reserve

Critical Thinking

1. **Drawing Conclusions** What do you think will be the effect on Canada if Quebec eventually becomes a separate country?

2. **Expressing Problems Clearly** Why do some French Canadians want Quebec to be a separate country?

Graphic Organizer

Immigrants have contributed much to the cultures of the United States and Canada. Copy the chart onto a sheet of paper. Then fill in the empty boxes with examples of regions from which immigrants to the United States and Canada came.

	United States	Canada
Regions from which immigrants came		

Map Activity

Native American Groups

For each Native American group listed below, write the letter from the map that shows its location.

1. Miami

2. Chippewa

3. Cherokee

4. Iroquois

5. Pueblo

6. Cheyenne

7. Comanche

8. Huron

Place Location

Writing Activity

Writing a Letter

Suppose that Anna and Tito are pen pals. Write a letter from Tito to Anna, suggesting ways she might get her parents more involved in American culture. Remember, Tito believes problems can be solved when different ideas come together. Perhaps he might suggest that her parents contribute ideas to a community project. What kind of project could they participate in? How could participation make Anna's parents feel like they are part of their new society?

Internet Activity

Use a search engine to find the **Canadian Heritage** page. Choose English or French and explore the various links. Make a travel brochure for Canada including national historic sites, official languages, and cultures. Include text, photos, and illustrations in your brochure.

Skills Review

Turn to the Skills Activity. Review how concept maps are used to organize information. Then answer the following questions: (a) What three levels of information are shown on a concept map? (b) What is another name for a concept map?

How Am I Doing?

Answer the following questions to check your progress.

1. Can I identify the important contributions immigrants have made to the United States?

2. Do I understand why Canadian culture is described as a mosaic?

3. Can I describe some challenges faced by immigrants to a country such as the United States or Canada?

4. What information from this chapter can I use in my book project?

Western Wagons

BY STEPHEN VINCENT BENÉT

BEFORE YOU READ

Reach Into Your Background

What are some of the stories that explain something about your culture's beginnings? Why do people in your neighborhood live in your city instead of another one?

Many stories tell about such beginnings. Every culture has stories about its own beginnings and the beginnings of human life. Here is a poem by an American poet who wrote about a special kind of beginning in the United States.

Questions to Explore

1. What kind of beginning does "Western Wagons" describe?
2. As you read the poem, think how its rhythm echoes a wagon ride.

prairie-schooner a covered wagon used by American pioneers to travel across the country

Ask Questions What questions would you like to ask someone who went West in the wagons?

They went with axe and rifle, when the trail was still to blaze,
They went with wife and children, in the prairie-schooner days,
With banjo and with frying pan—Susanna, don't you cry!
For I'm off to California to get rich out there or die!

We've broken land and cleared it, but we're tired of where we are.
They say that wild Nebraska is a better place by far.
There's gold in far Wyoming, there's black earth in Ioway,
So pack up the kids and blankets, for we're moving out today!

The cowards never started and the weak died on the road,
And all across the continent the endless campfires glowed.
We'd taken land and settled—but a traveler passed by—
And we're going West tomorrow—Lordy, never ask us why!

◀ This photograph was taken in 1866. The colors were hand painted on the photograph. It shows a wagon train on its way through the Strawberry Valley in the Sierra Nevada, a mountain range in California.

We're going West tomorrow, where the promises can't fail.
O'er the hills in legions, boys, and crowd the dusty trail!
We shall starve and freeze and suffer. We shall die, and tame the
    lands.
But we're going West tomorrow, with our fortune in our hands.

EXPLORING YOUR READING

Look Back

1. In "Western Wagons," what hopes do the people have for their future?

Think It Over

2. What is the mood of the travelers in "Western Wagons"?

Go Beyond

3. This poem mentions men and boys but barely refers to women or girls. Why do you think that is so? How could the poem be changed to include the women and girls who were part of these beginnings?

Ideas for Writing: Poem

4. Think of some important or unusual element of your family, community, or some other group to which you belong. It could be a special custom or a more general way of living. Write a poem that explains how this began, using historical facts or inventing a story.

CHAPTER 4

Exploring the United States

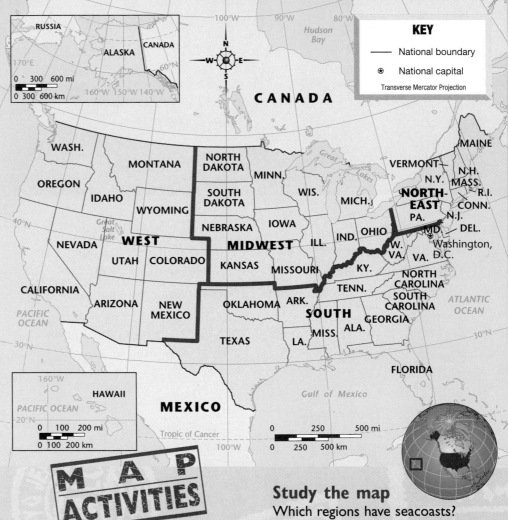

KEY
— National boundary
⊗ National capital
Transverse Mercator Projection

MAP ACTIVITIES

The United States can be divided into distinct regions. These are the Northeast, the South, the Midwest, and the West. To learn more about these regions, do the following activities.

Study the map
Which regions have seacoasts? Which region has the largest states, and which has the smallest?

Look for clues
Think about what it would be like to live in each region. What has attracted people to different parts of the United States? What kinds of work do you think people in different regions do?

The Northeast

LAND OF BIG CITIES

BEFORE YOU READ

Reach Into Your Background

Draw a quick sketch of your neighborhood. Do the houses have big yards, or are they close together? Do you live in an apartment with other families next door, or is your nearest neighbor some distance away? How do you think closeness to other people affects the ways people live?

Questions to Explore

1. How do the large cities of the Northeast contribute to the economy of the United States?
2. Why is the Northeast a region of many cultures?

Key Terms
commute
megalopolis
population density

Key Places
New York City
Philadelphia
Boston

For at least a century, life in New York City has been described in one way: crowded. One hundred years ago, horse-drawn carriages caused traffic jams. Now, 5 million riders squeeze into New York's subway cars every day. Others travel the 1,745 miles (2,807 km) of bus lines or catch one of the city's 12,000 taxis. And many people drive their own cars through the city's busy streets. The ferryboat is another way to travel in New York.

New York is not unique. Washington, D.C., Philadelphia, and Boston are also crowded. In these big cities, millions of people **commute**, or travel to work, each day. Many drive to work from suburbs that are far from the city's center. Even people who live in the city must travel from one area to another to work.

▼ During rush hour, New York City's streets fill with cars. If you are in a hurry, try walking or grabbing a subway train instead of driving.

A Region of Cities

Did you ever hear of Bowash? That is what some people call the chain of cities from Boston to New York to Washington, D.C. This coastal region of the Northeast is a **megalopolis** (meg uh LAHP uh lis). In this type of region, cities and suburbs have

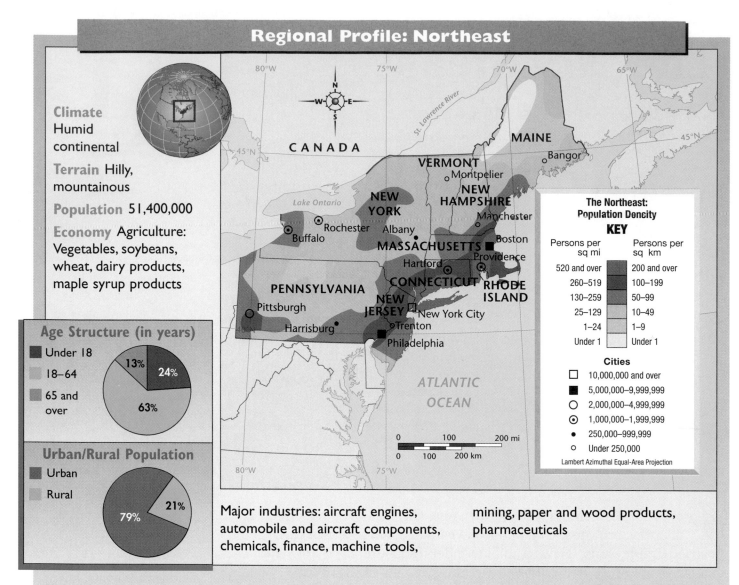

Climate Humid continental

Terrain Hilly, mountainous

Population 51,400,000

Economy Agriculture: Vegetables, soybeans, wheat, dairy products, maple syrup products

Age Structure (in years)
- Under 18
- 18–64
- 65 and over

13%
24%
63%

Urban/Rural Population
- Urban
- Rural

79%
21%

The Northeast: Population Dencity

KEY

Persons per sq mi	Persons per sq km
520 and over	200 and over
260–519	100–199
130–259	50–99
25–129	10–49
1–24	1–9
Under 1	Under 1

Cities
- ☐ 10,000,000 and over
- ■ 5,000,000–9,999,999
- ○ 2,000,000–4,999,999
- ◉ 1,000,000–1,999,999
- • 250,000–999,999
- ○ Under 250,000

Lambert Azimuthal Equal-Area Projection

Major industries: aircraft engines, automobile and aircraft components, chemicals, finance, machine tools, mining, paper and wood products, pharmaceuticals

Map and Chart Study This map shows the population density of the Northeast. Note that city population figures in the key are for the metropolitan area, or the city and its surrounding suburbs. **Regions** Where are the most densely populated parts of the Northeast? Where are the least densely populated areas? **Critical Thinking** Compare the urban/rural population chart with the map. In which part of the region do you think most northeasterners live?

grown so close together that they form one big urban area. Look at the map on the next page to see how large this area is.

The Northeast is the most densely populated region of the United States. A region's **population density** is the average number of people per square mile (or square kilometer). The population is denser in parts of New Jersey than in crowded countries like India or Japan!

The Northeast's economy is based on cities. Many were founded in colonial times, along rivers or near the Atlantic Ocean. These cities began as transportation and trade centers. Today, manufacturing, finance, communications, and government employ millions of urban Northeasterners.

Philadelphia and Boston Philadelphia and Boston were important in our nation's early history. In Philadelphia, America's founders adopted the Declaration of Independence and the Constitution. Some early struggles against the British took place in Boston. In Philadelphia and Boston, you can visit buildings that date from before the American Revolution. Yet you will find that they are very modern cities, too.

Today, Philadelphia is an industrial powerhouse. It is located near the mouth of the Delaware River. Important land and water transportation routes pass through here. Ships, trucks, and trains bring in raw materials from other parts of Pennsylvania and from all over the world. Thousands of factories process food, refine petroleum, and manufacture chemicals. Hundreds of products are then shipped out for sale.

The Boston area is famous for its more than 20 colleges and universities. Cambridge (KAYM brij) is the home of Harvard, which is America's oldest university. The city is also famous for its science and technology centers. Boston's universities and scientific companies often work together to design new products and to carry out medical research.

LINKS TO LANGUAGE ARTS

Good-bye City Life In 1845, Henry Thoreau moved to Walden Pond in Massachusetts. His life there was an experiment in living alone and with only the essentials. He cut down trees and built a one-room house. He planted a vegetable garden and gathered wild fruit. And he wrote *Walden,* a classic of American literature.

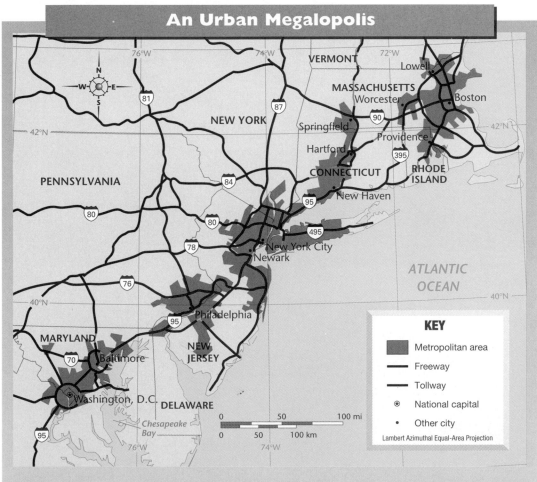

An Urban Megalopolis

KEY

■ Metropolitan area
— Freeway
— Tollway
⊛ National capital
• Other city

Lambert Azimuthal Equal-Area Projection

0   50   100 mi
0   50   100 km

Map Study You can drive from Washington, D.C., to Boston, Massachusetts, without leaving the urban areas. **Place** Compare this map with the one in the Regional Profile. What similarities are there between the two maps?

EXPLORING TECHNOLOGY

The Brooklyn Bridge

The Brooklyn Bridge is a suspension bridge in New York City. A suspension bridge hangs from cables that are anchored at either end and supported by several towers along the bridge's length. Completed in 1883, the bridge crosses the East River, connecting two boroughs, or sections, of the city—Manhattan and Brooklyn. At the time of its completion, the Brooklyn Bridge was the longest suspension bridge in the world. There are six lanes for traffic. A wide walkway for pedestrians runs along the center of the bridge.

The suspender cables connect the cables and the roadbed.

Each tower is 275 feet (84 m) tall. The two towers are seated firmly in underwater piers buried deep in the riverbed.

The anchorages at either end of the bridge are huge blocks of concrete, set deep in the ground.

The roadbed, or deck, has special braces, called *trusses*, that prevent the bridge from swinging during high winds.

The main cable runs from one anchorage, across two towers, to a second anchorage. This cable is nearly 16 inches (41 cm) thick and is made of steel.

New York City   One word describes New York City—huge. In terms of population, it is the largest city in the United States and one of the 10 largest in the world. More than 7 million people live in New York City. Most states do not have populations that large. The city covers an area of about 320 square miles (830 sq km) on islands and the mainland around the mouth of the Hudson River. The various parts of the city are connected by tunnels and bridges. One of the oldest and most interesting bridges is the Brooklyn Bridge. The diagram on the opposite page shows how the Brooklyn Bridge was built.

New York City is our nation's "money capital." The word *millionaire* was invented here. About 500,000 New Yorkers work for banks and other financial institutions. The headquarters of many of the country's wealthiest corporations are in New York. The famous New York Stock Exchange is on Wall Street.

New York is also a center of fashion, publishing, advertising, television, radio, and the arts. New York's Broadway is famous for its plays. About eight million people see plays in New York every year.

◀ New York City's financial district is a maze of skyscrapers. One of the streets hidden among these towers is Wall Street, the heart of New York's banking and financial industries.

Ask Questions What questions would you like to ask a recent immigrant to the United States?

A Gateway for Immigrants

On January 1, 1892, 15-year-old Annie Moore made her way down the gangplank of a steamship onto American soil. Annie and her two younger brothers had sailed from Ireland. Annie stepped into the registry room of the Ellis Island Immigrant Station. Here she received a $10 gold piece for being the first immigrant to arrive at the new station.

From 1892 to 1943, the first stop for millions of immigrants to the United States was Ellis Island. From here, immigrants could see the Statue of Liberty, half a mile away in New York Harbor. Today, Ellis Island and the Statue of Liberty are national monuments.

New York and other port cities of the Northeast have been important gateways for immigrants. In the 1800s, many Irish and Germans immigrated to New York. Later, immigrants poured in from southern and Eastern Europe. During the 1900s, people also have come from the Caribbean, Asia, and Africa. In one recent year, New York City welcomed immigrants from more than 100 different countries.

After entering through the port cities, many immigrants stayed in those cities and built a new life. Today, New York is rich in ethnic diversity. You can visit Little Italy, Little India, and Chinatown. To get a real sense of the ethnic diversity of the United States, just look at a list of restaurants in a big city like New York.

▶ The Statue of Liberty symbolizes the United States' tradition of providing a home to immigrants. The statue stands on Liberty Island in New York Harbor.

SECTION 1 REVIEW

1. **Define** (a) commute, (b) megalopolis, (c) population density.

2. **Identify** (a) New York City, (b) Philadelphia, (c) Boston.

3. (a) How does the population density in the Northeast compare with densities in other regions of the country? (b) How does population density affect the ways people live and work?

4. If you were looking for work in the Northeast, what kinds of jobs might you find?

5. How have immigrants affected the culture of the Northeast?

Critical Thinking

6. **Making Comparisons** Think about the histories of, and major industries in, Philadelphia and Boston. How are the two cities similar? How have they developed differently?

Activity

7. **Writing to Learn** Which city described in this section are you most interested in learning more about? Make a list of things you would like to learn about this city. Then write a brief paragraph explaining why you want to learn these things.

The South

A CHANGING LANDSCAPE

Reach Into Your Background

Think about a time in your life when you experienced a big change. Perhaps you moved to another community or started at a new school. How did you adapt to the change? Did you find yourself thinking and behaving in new ways?

Questions to Explore

1. How is the South's land and water important to its economy?
2. How has the growth of industry changed the South?

Key Terms

petrochemical
industrialization
Sun Belt

Key Places

Atlanta
Washington, D.C.

From July 19 to August 4, 1996, the city of Atlanta, Georgia, was the center of the world. More than two million people from 172 countries visited the city during that time. They came to see a very special event. It was the 1996 Summer Olympic Games.

The people who watched the 1996 Olympics saw more than great athletes. They also saw a world-class city. Atlanta today is a center of trade, transportation, and communication. Atlanta is also in one of the fastest-growing regions of the United States: the South. With strong urban areas like Atlanta, plus rich agriculture, the South is helping to lead the United States into the future.

▼ Famous boxer Muhammad Ali lights the Olympic torch at the 1996 Summer Olympic Games in Atlanta, Georgia.

The Varied Land of the South

People in the South today can make a living in many different ways. The South's geography makes many of these jobs possible. The South is warmer than regions of the United States that are farther north. Most parts of the region also receive plenty of rain. The wide coastal plains along the Atlantic

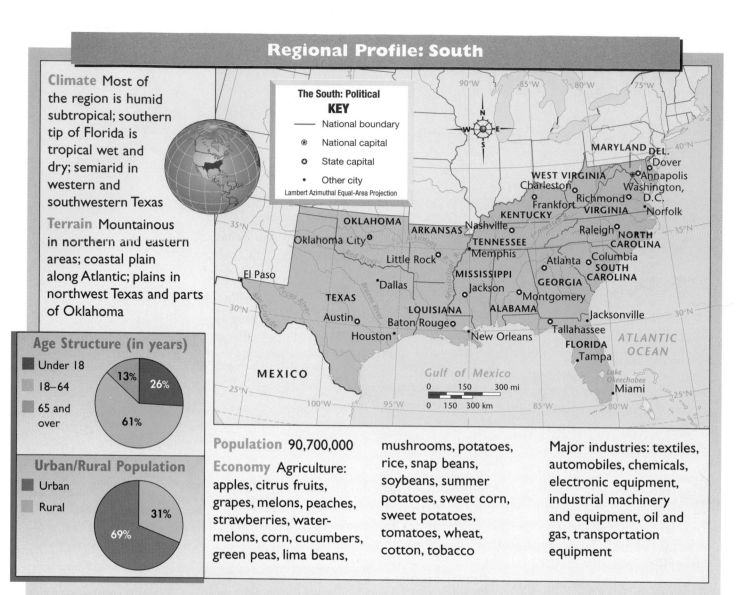

Regional Profile: South

Climate Most of the region is humid subtropical; southern tip of Florida is tropical wet and dry; semiarid in western and southwestern Texas

Terrain Mountainous in northern and eastern areas; coastal plain along Atlantic; plains in northwest Texas and parts of Oklahoma

The South: Political
KEY
— National boundary
⊛ National capital
◎ State capital
• Other city
Lambert Azimuthal Equal-Area Projection

Age Structure (in years)
- Under 18
- 18–64
- 65 and over

13% 26% 61%

Urban/Rural Population
- Urban
- Rural

31% 69%

Population 90,700,000

Economy Agriculture: apples, citrus fruits, grapes, melons, peaches, strawberries, watermelons, corn, cucumbers, green peas, lima beans, mushrooms, potatoes, rice, snap beans, soybeans, summer potatoes, sweet corn, sweet potatoes, tomatoes, wheat, cotton, tobacco

Major industries: textiles, automobiles, chemicals, electronic equipment, industrial machinery and equipment, oil and gas, transportation equipment

Map and Chart Study This map shows the borders and major cities of the southern states of the United States. **Interaction** Notice that most southern cities are located near waterways, such as rivers and the ocean. How do you think southern cities benefit from this location? **Critical Thinking** Look at the urban/rural population chart. Earlier in the 1900s, the South was a mostly rural region. Today, however, more southerners live in urban areas than live in rural areas. Based on your reading of this section, what change in the South's economy might have contributed to this population change?

Ocean and the Gulf of Mexico have rich soil. Together, these features make much of the South a great place for growing crops. Some places in the region are also good for raising animals for food. People in the South can take advantage of many different natural resources.

Farming in the South Farming has always been one of the most important parts of the South's economy. For years, the South's most important crop was cotton. Southern farmers once depended on cotton as their only source of income. Today, cotton still brings a lot of money to the South, especially to Alabama, Mississippi, and Texas. But

"King Cotton" no longer rules this region. In the 1890s, the boll weevil (bowl WEE vuhl)—a kind of beetle—began to attack cotton plants in the South. Over the next 30 years, it destroyed fields across the area. Without money from cotton, many farmers went bankrupt. Most southern farmers now try to raise more than one crop. Together they produce a wide variety of crops and farm animals.

Some of these crops need very special growing conditions. Citrus fruits require year-round warmth and sunshine. Florida has plenty of both. More oranges, tangerines, grapefruits, and limes are grown here than in any other state. Rice needs warm, moist growing conditions. Farmers in Arkansas, Louisiana, and Mississippi can supply this. They grow rice along the coast of the Gulf of Mexico and in the Mississippi River valley.

Some areas of the South have become famous for their agricultural products. Georgia has taken one of its products as its nickname. It is the Peach State. Georgia is also known for its peanuts and pecans. Texas raises more cattle than any other state. Arkansas raises the most chickens and turkeys. All of these items are just a sample of what southern agriculture produces. You can read about more of the South's farm products in the Regional Profile.

Drilling and Mining in the South In some parts of the South, what is under the soil is as important as what grows in it. In Louisiana, Oklahoma, and Texas, companies drill for oil and natural gas. These can be used as fuel. They are also made into **petrochemicals.** These are substances, like plastics, paint, and asphalt, that come from petroleum. In Alabama, Kentucky, West Virginia, and Tennessee, miners dig for coal. Southern states are also leading producers of salt, sulfur, lead, zinc, and bauxite—a mineral used to make aluminum.

READ ACTIVELY

Predict Think about what happened when oil and natural gas were discovered In Louisiana, Oklahoma, and Texas. How do you think that discovery affected the economies of those states?

◀ Cotton is no longer the South's major crop, but it still plays an important part in the region's economy.

Southern Fish and Forests People in the South can also make a living in fishing and forestry. The Chesapeake Bay area near Maryland and Virginia is famous for its shellfish. However, the South's fishing industry is strongest in Louisiana and Texas. The timber industry works in every southern state except for Delaware. Softwood trees like southern pine are used for building or for paper. People use hardwood trees to make furniture. North Carolina has the nation's largest hardwood furniture industry.

Southern Cities and Industries

Until recently, people often thought of the South as a slow-moving, mostly rural region. But over the past 50 years, this region has gone through lots of changes. Though the South's rural areas are still important, most people in the South today live in cities. Some work in factories or in high-technology firms. Others work in tourism or in one of the other industries in this region's growing economy. This change from an agriculture-based economy to an industry-based economy is called **industrialization.**

Textiles and Technology One of the most important industries in the South is the textile industry. Textile mills make cloth. They were first built in this region to use the South's cotton. Today, many mills still make cotton cloth. Many others now make cloth from synthetic, or human-made, materials. The textile industry is strongest in Georgia, the Carolinas, and Virginia.

Visualize Visualize how a rural area might change to an urban area. What do you think might be built? What features might disappear?

▼ One of the largest cities in the United States, Dallas, Texas, is a center of banking, industry, and trade.

The tourists on this steamboat are getting a taste of what it was like to travel on the Mississippi River more than 100 years ago. They are taking a trip on the *Natchez,* which sails out of New Orleans, Louisiana. In the 1800s and early 1900s, steamboats were an important form of transportation on rivers in the United States. **Critical Thinking** What part of a steamboat is used to push the ship through the water?

The textile industry was an early arrival in the South. The first mills in the region were built in the 1800s. Now, more than 100 years later, new industries are growing all across the South. One is the high-technology industry. Workers in this industry try to improve computers and figure out better ways to use them. Some centers of high technology are Raleigh, North Carolina, and Austin, Texas. Another forward-looking industry is the aerospace business. In Cape Canaveral, Florida; Houston, Texas; and Huntsville, Alabama, people work for the National Aeronautics and Space Administration (NASA). Some train as astronauts and run the space shuttle program. Atlanta, Georgia, is now a center for the cable television industry. If you watch the news on cable television, you are probably watching a program from Atlanta.

Transportation and Tourism A big part of the South's economy depends on moving goods and people into and out of the region. Most of the South's largest cities play big roles in this transportation industry. Miami, Florida, and New Orleans, Louisiana, are major ports. Miami is a center for goods and people going to and from Central and South America. New Orleans is a gateway between the Gulf of Mexico and the Mississippi River system. It is also an important port for oil tankers.

Some of the people the transportation industry brings to the South come to stay. Thousands come to work in the South's new industries. Thousands more choose to move to the South because of its climate. The South is part of the **Sun Belt.** This broad area of the United States

Jazz Jazz music is arguably the South's greatest contribution to the arts in America. Most people consider New Orleans to be the birthplace of jazz. Mainly African in origin, jazz grew out of many different kinds of music. African American work songs, hymns, and spirituals are all part of its roots. Today, musicians in New Orleans play many forms of jazz. One of the most popular is called Dixieland or New Orleans jazz.

stretches from the southern Atlantic Coast to the coast of California. It is known for its warm weather. The population of the Sun Belt has been rising for the past few decades. Some arrivals are older adults who want to retire to places without cold winters. Others come to take advantage of both the weather and the work that the Sun Belt offers.

Warm weather also brings people to the South who only plan to visit. These people fuel the region's tourist industry. In winter, tourists come to enjoy the sunny beaches of Florida and the Gulf Coast. In the summer, they can hike in the mountains of the Appalachians and Ozarks. They can visit historic cities like Charleston, South Carolina, or New Orleans, Louisiana, at any time of the year. In states throughout the South, there are always fun and exciting things to see and to do.

Our Nation's Capital The city of Washington is not in any state. Instead, it is in the District of Columbia, which lies between the states of Maryland and Virginia. This area of land was chosen as the site for the nation's capital in 1790. Located on the shore of the Potomac River, Washington, D.C., was the first planned city in the nation. It has wide avenues, public buildings, and dramatic monuments. Many people consider Washington to be one of the most beautiful cities in the world. As the nation's capital, it is home to the nation's leaders and to hundreds of foreign diplomats.

U.S. Space Camp

Every year, people from ages 10 to 92 come to Huntsville, Alabama, to go to U.S. Space Camp. Here, a student experiences "weightlessness."

SECTION 2 REVIEW

1. **Define** (a) petrochemical, (b) industrialization, (c) Sun Belt.

2. **Identify** (a) Atlanta, (b) Washington, D.C.

3. How have the geography and climate of the South shaped its economy?

4. How has the South changed in the 1900s?

Critical Thinking

5. **Recognizing Cause and Effect** In this section, you have learned that the population of the South is growing. How have the South's geography and economy affected this growth?

Activity

6. **Writing to Learn** You work in an advertising firm in Atlanta, Georgia; Houston, Texas; or Miami, Florida. Create an advertisement to persuade people to move to your city or state. The advertisement can be designed for a newspaper or a magazine. It can also be for radio, television, or the Internet.

The Midwest

MOVING FROM THE FARM

Reach Into Your Background

Have you ever introduced a new food or activity to your family? Can you think of a time when you pursued a new interest on your own? In the Midwest, many people are building ways of life very different from the ways their parents lived.

Questions to Explore

1. How is technology changing agriculture in the Midwest?
2. How is the change in agriculture affecting the growth of cities?

Key Terms

mixed-crop farm
recession
corporate farm

Key Places

Chicago
Detroit
St. Louis
Minneapolis-St. Paul

Camille LeFevre grew up in Black River Falls, Wisconsin. Her family included many generations of farmers. Camille spent her childhood on her parents' sheep farm.

> "As a skinny, pigtailed youngster, I spent a lot of time naming lambs, . . . falling off horses named Ginger and Lucky, building hay forts, riding tractors, stuffing freshly sheared wool into gunny sacks and perching on fence gates staring dreamily into space."

Camille remembers her childhood with deep affection. Yet, like thousands of farm children who grew up in the 1980s and 1990s, she did not follow in her parents' footsteps. Farming in the Midwest changed, and Camille chose a different path.

Technology Brings Changes to the Midwest

The Midwest is often called "the heartland" because it is the agricultural center of our nation. The soil is rich, and the climate is suitable for producing corn, soybeans, and livestock. Technology helped make farms productive. Inventions like the

▼ On most farms, sheep-shearing takes place once a year. The wool from this breed of sheep—the Suffolk—is used to make industrial and upholstery fabrics.

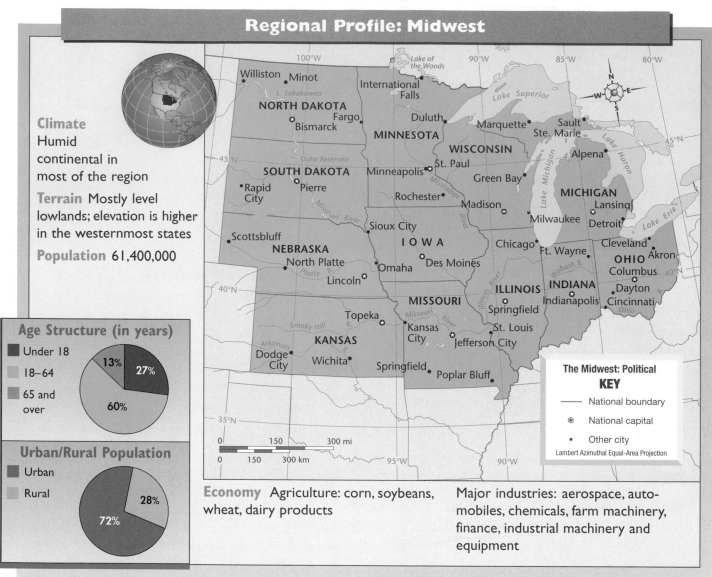

Climate Humid continental in most of the region

Terrain Mostly level lowlands; elevation is higher in the westernmost states

Population 61,400,000

Age Structure (in years)

- Under 18
- 18–64
- 65 and over

13%
27%
60%

Urban/Rural Population

- Urban
- Rural

28%
72%

The Midwest: Political
KEY
— National boundary
⊛ National capital
• Other city
Lambert Azimuthal Equal-Area Projection

Economy Agriculture: corn, soybeans, wheat, dairy products

Major industries: aerospace, automobiles, chemicals, farm machinery, finance, industrial machinery and equipment

Map and Chart Study This map shows the borders and major cities of states in the Midwest United States.
Location The Great Lakes are part of a major shipping route. What Midwest states border the Great Lakes?

Critical Thinking Read the information about the Midwest's economy. Then look at the urban/rural population chart. How do you think most people in the Midwest make a living—in farming or in industry and services? Why?

steel plow, the windmill, and barbed wire helped settlers carve out farms on the plains. Today, technology continues to change the way people farm the land.

Family Farms Dwindle Until the 1980s, small family farms operated in this region. Many of these farms were **mixed-crop farms.** That is, they grew several different kinds of crops. This was a sensible way for farmers to work. If one crop failed, the farm had others. Camille's family, for example, sometimes raised cattle as well as sheep.

In the 1960s and 1970s, family farms prospered. The world population was rising, and demand for American farm products was high. Farmers felt that they could increase their business if they enlarged their farms. To build bigger farms, farmers bought more land and equipment. But all of this cost money. Many farmers borrowed from local banks.

In the early 1980s, there was a country-wide **recession** (rih SESH un), or a downturn in business activity. The demand for farm products dropped. At the same time, interest rates on loans increased. As a result, many farmers were not able to make enough money to pay their loans. Some families sold or left their farms. Over one million American farmers have left their land since 1980.

Corporate Farms Expand   What happened to the farms that were sold? Many of them were bought by agricultural companies. Small farms were combined to form large ones called **corporate farms.** These large farms could be run more efficiently. Large agricultural companies could afford to buy the expensive land and equipment that modern farming requires. And they could still make a profit.

Corporate farmers rely on machines and computers to do much of the work. This means that corporate farms employ fewer workers. Kansas offers a good example of corporate farming—having fewer

Dwindling Farms in Minnesota In Minnesota, the number of farms has fallen quickly. In 1959, Minnesota had 146,000 farms. In 1992, 88,000 farms were left. Further, about 38 percent of Minnesota's population was rural in 1960. In 1990, only 30 percent of the population lived in rural areas.

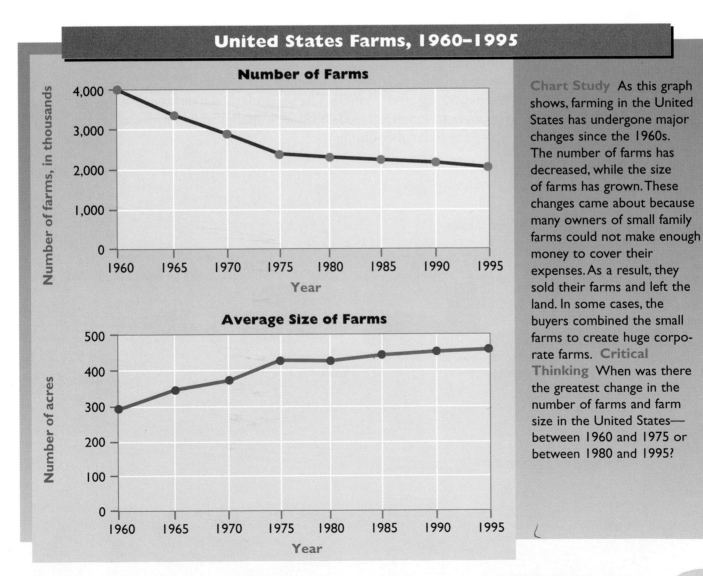

United States Farms, 1960–1995

Number of Farms

Average Size of Farms

Chart Study As this graph shows, farming in the United States has undergone major changes since the 1960s. The number of farms has decreased, while the size of farms has grown. These changes came about because many owners of small family farms could not make enough money to cover their expenses. As a result, they sold their farms and left the land. In some cases, the buyers combined the small farms to create huge corporate farms. **Critical Thinking** When was there the greatest change in the number of farms and farm size in the United States— between 1960 and 1975 or between 1980 and 1995?

workers and larger farms. In Kansas, 90 percent of the land is farmland, but only 10 percent of the people are farmers.

Not every farm in the Midwest is a corporate farm. But most small farms do not earn enough money to support a family. Family farmers usually have another job as well. Camille LeFevre's father, for example, advises other farmers on the best foods for their livestock.

Camille's parents did not lose their farm, but they did sell all their livestock to send Camille to college. When she graduated, she did not go back to the land. Farming these days is a very difficult way to make a living, she explains. She felt that she would have more opportunities in the city.

The Midwest Grows Cities

Camille is not alone. Most people in the Midwest today live in towns and cities. Yet many of these cities got their start as places to process and ship farm products.

Chicago: At the Center of Things   Chicago, Illinois, is a good example. Located on Lake Michigan, it was surrounded by prairies and farms in the mid-1800s. Farmers sent their corn, wheat, cattle, and hogs to Chicago. Mills and meat-packing plants turned these products into foods and shipped them east on the Great Lakes. When railroads were built, Chicago really boomed. By the late 1800s, it had become a steel-making and manufacturing center. What was one of the most important manufactured products made in Chicago? You probably guessed it: farm equipment.

Ask Questions What questions would you like to ask a person who grew up on a farm and later moved to a city?

▼This view from the shores of Lake Michigan shows the many skyscrapers in Chicago's downtown area. The Sears Tower, to the left, is the tallest building in the United States.

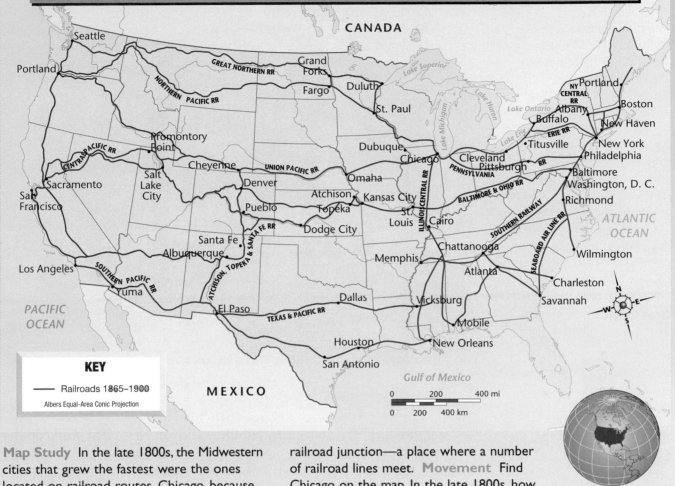

United States: Railroad Routes of the Late 1800s

KEY

—— Railroads 1865–1900

Albers Equal-Area Conic Projection

Map Study In the late 1800s, the Midwestern cities that grew the fastest were the ones located on railroad routes. Chicago, because of its central location in the region, became a railroad junction—a place where a number of railroad lines meet. **Movement** Find Chicago on the map. In the late 1800s, how many railroad routes met in Chicago?

Today, Chicago is the biggest city in the heartland. It is known for its ethnic diversity and lively culture. It is the hub of major transportation routes—highways, railroads, airlines, and shipping routes. Chicago is also the home of the first skyscraper—and many other architectural wonders. For a bird's-eye view of Chicago, go to the top of the Sears Tower, one of the tallest buildings in the world.

Other Cities The Midwest has other large cities. Two of them—Detroit and St. Louis—have played an important role in the country's history. Why do you think Detroit, Michigan, is called "the Motor City"? Here, you will find the headquarters of the American automobile industry. General Motors, Ford, and Chrysler have plants here.

Covered wagons, not cars, used to roll through St. Louis, Missouri. Located on the Mississippi River, this city was the starting point for pioneers heading west. Today, a huge stainless steel arch beside the river marks St. Louis as the "Gateway to the West." St. Louis is also a banking and commercial center.

LINKS ACROSS THE WORLD

Higher and Higher Until 1996, Chicago's Sears Tower, at 1,454 feet (443 m), was the world's tallest building. Now, the Petronas Twin Towers in Malaysia holds that title. It is 1,476 feet (452 m) high. But the world record may change again soon. When completed, the World Financial Center in Shanghai, China, will top out at 1,509 feet (460 m).

The metropolitan area of Minneapolis-St. Paul covers about 4,620 square miles (11,965 sq km) around the point where the Mississippi and Minnesota rivers join. The area's population stands at about 2.7 million people and is growing steadily. The greatest population growth has taken place in Minneapolis-St. Paul's suburban areas, like the one pictured here. **Critical Thinking** Compare this photograph with the photograph of Chicago earlier in this section. How are the two scenes different? What similarities, if any, do you see?

Camille LeFevre moved to another Midwestern city, Minneapolis-St. Paul, Minnesota. These "Twin Cities" face each other on opposite sides of the Mississippi River. Publishing, medical, computer, and arts businesses are flourishing here. The city's suburbs have replaced the fertile land once used for farming. But the city has offered Camille the opportunity to build a career as a journalist. Camille's father still has his farm, and she visits him on the weekends. Perhaps Camille enjoys the best of both worlds.

SECTION 3 REVIEW

1. **Define** (a) mixed-crop farm, (b) recession, (c) corporate farm.

2. **Identify** (a) Chicago, (b) Detroit, (c) St. Louis, (d) Minneapolis-St. Paul.

3. Why did family farmers face hard times in the 1980s?

4. How are mixed-crop farming and corporate farming different?

Critical Thinking

5. **Identifying Central Issues** Think of how farming has changed and the development of corporate farms. List the advantages and disadvantages of corporate farming.

Activity

6. **Writing to Learn** Suppose you are a farmer and you have decided to sell your farm and move to a city. Write a letter to a friend explaining your decision.

The West

USING RESOURCES WISELY

Reach Into Your Background

Do you and your family take part in a recycling program, try to conserve water, or control the amount of electricity you use? In the western United States, people are trying to improve how they use resources.

Questions to Explore

1. What are the resources of the West?

2. How are people working to balance conservation with the need to use natural resources?

Key Terms

forty-niner
mass transit

Key Places

Sierra Nevada
Pacific Northwest
Portland
San Jose

An American President stood before Congress and made the following statement:

"The conservation of our natural resources and their proper use constitute the fundamental problem which underlies almost every other problem of our national life. . . . But there must be . . . a realization . . . that to waste, to destroy our natural resources, to skin and exhaust the land instead of using it so as to increase its usefulness, will result in undermining . . . the very prosperity which we ought by right to hand down to [our children]."

Do you think this sounds like a modern plea for the environment? Actually, President Theodore Roosevelt made this statement nearly one hundred years ago. He understood that the vast resources of the West would not last without proper care.

▼ Congress declared Yosemite a national park in 1890. Yosemite Falls, which drop some 2,425 feet (740 m), are higher than any big-city skyscraper.

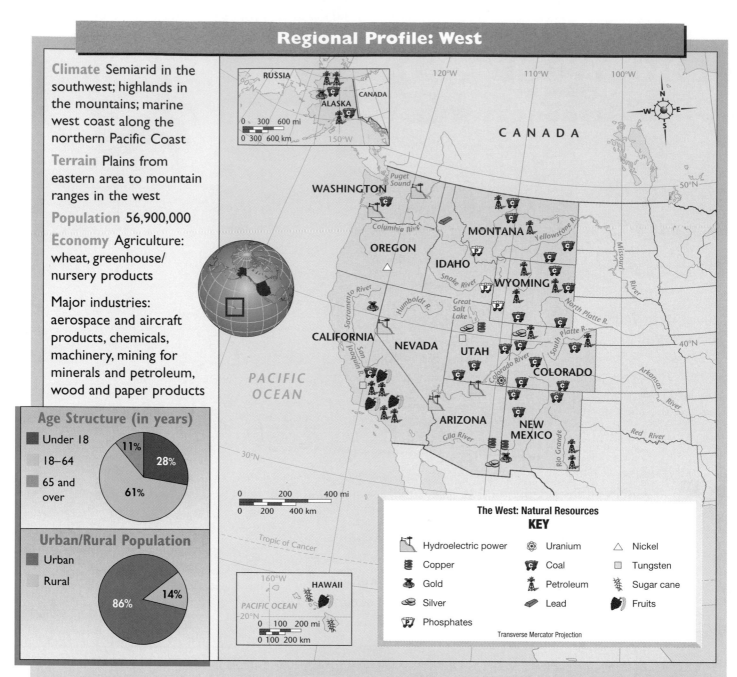

Climate Semiarid in the southwest; highlands in the mountains; marine west coast along the northern Pacific Coast

Terrain Plains from eastern area to mountain ranges in the west

Population 56,900,000

Economy Agriculture: wheat, greenhouse/nursery products

Major industries: aerospace and aircraft products, chemicals, machinery, mining for minerals and petroleum, wood and paper products

Age Structure (in years)
- Under 18 — 28%
- 18–64 — 61%
- 65 and over — 11%

Urban/Rural Population
- Urban — 86%
- Rural — 14%

The West: Natural Resources KEY

Hydroelectric power, Copper, Gold, Silver, Phosphates, Uranium, Coal, Petroleum, Lead, Nickel, Tungsten, Sugar cane, Fruits

Transverse Mercator Projection

Map and Chart Study This map shows the natural resources of the western states of the United States. **Place** What states have deposits of petroleum? What state's resources are mostly agricultural? **Movement** What states do you think are most likely to have been part of the Gold Rush in the late 1800s? **Critical Thinking** In the early 1800s, many people moved to the West to live in the region's wide open spaces. Look at the urban/rural population chart. Do you think that most people move to the West for the same reason today? Why or why not?

A Land of Precious Resources

An incredible wealth of natural resources has drawn people to the West for well over 400 years. The Spanish were well established on the West Coast even before the Pilgrims settled in New England in the 1620s. Then, after Lewis and Clark's exploration of the Louisiana Territory in the early 1800s, more people began to move westward.

Resources and Population   With the California Gold Rush in 1849, the population of the region exploded. The sleepy port of San Francisco boomed into a prosperous city. Hopeful miners arrived there, bought supplies, and headed off to the Sierra Nevada expecting to strike it rich.

A gold strike in Colorado led to the founding of the city of Denver. Further discoveries of valuable minerals drew more and more people to the region. New settlers here needed homes, and the place to find timber to build them was in the Pacific Northwest. After the Civil War, logging camps, sawmills, and paper mills sprang up in Washington, Oregon, and northern California.

At first, the resources of the West seemed unlimited. The use of these resources did create wealth and many jobs. However, it also created new challenges.

Managing Resources in the Sierras   Do you know the story of the goose that laid the golden egg? Its owner cut the goose open to see what was inside. For many years, people treated the Sierra Nevada in a similar way. The **forty-niners,** the first miners of the Gold Rush, washed small bits of gold from the streams. To get at larger deposits, big mining companies brought in water cannons that could blast away entire hillsides. They got their gold but left behind huge, ugly piles of rock.

After the Gold Rush, California's population soared. To meet the demand for new houses, loggers leveled many forests. Engineers built dams to send water through pipes to coastal cities. Next to the dams, they built hydroelectric (hy droh ee LEK trik) plants. Cities like San Francisco got water and power this way, but the dams flooded whole valleys of the Sierras.

READ ACTIVELY

Visualize What would it be like to be a part of the Gold Rush? What would you see?

▼ The magnificent views at Grand Canyon National Park in Arizona attract crowds of tourists from all over the world.

Predict What methods would you suggest to preserve and conserve natural resources in the West?

To save parts of the West as natural wilderness, Congress created several national parks and forests. Yet these, too, have developed problems. Yosemite (yoh SEM ut ee) National Park now gets so many visitors that it has traffic jams and air pollution in the summer.

Westerners are wrestling with new ways to manage the West's resources. For example, Yosemite now limits the number of campers in the park. Dam-building has stopped. Laws protect the habitats of certain animals. In addition, logging companies are limited in the amount of timber they can cut down.

The Urban West

Most Westerners today are not miners, farmers, or loggers. Rather, they work and live in cities. Their challenge is to figure out how to use natural resources wisely.

Portland, Oregon "Your town or mine?" two land developers asked each other in 1845. The two developers were at the same site and predicted the development of a major port city. With such a great location near the junction of the Willamette and Columbia rivers, how could they lose? Francis W. Pettigrove of Portland, Maine, won the coin toss. He named the site after his hometown in the East.

Portland became a trade center for lumber, furs, grain, salmon, and wool. In the 1930s, new dams produced cheap electricity. Portland attracted many manufacturing industries. Over time, the factories polluted the Willamette River. Federal, state, and local governments—and industries—have worked to clean up this valuable resource.

A Black Bear in Its Natural Habitat

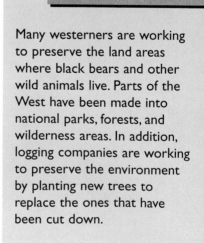

Many westerners are working to preserve the land areas where black bears and other wild animals live. Parts of the West have been made into national parks, forests, and wilderness areas. In addition, logging companies are working to preserve the environment by planting new trees to replace the ones that have been cut down.

Phoenix, Arizona

Half of Arizona's people live in Phoenix, which is Arizona's capital and an important industrial center. As the city has grown, it has sprawled out across the surrounding desert.

San Jose, California   Urban sprawl is a problem in San Jose. The area around San Jose was known as "Valley of the Heart's Delight" for its beautiful orchards and farms. Now it is called "Silicon Valley," because it is the heart of the computer industry.

Instead of good soil and climate, San Jose's most valuable resource is its people. They come from all parts of the world. The greater population density has created crowded freeways and air pollution. To counter these problems, San Jose has built a light-rail **mass transit** system. Mass transit replaces individual cars with energy-saving buses or trains.

CITIZEN HEROES

To Be a Leader Cesar Chavez and his family made a living as migrant farmworkers. Pay was low, and working conditions were hard. Chavez wanted to build a better future for migrant farmworkers. He helped to set up a farmworkers' union. Chavez's union organized national boycotts of farm products. As a result, farm owners agreed to improve pay and working conditions. Chavez had achieved his goal—fair treatment of migrant farmworkers.

SECTION 4 REVIEW

1. **Define**   (a) forty-niner, (b) mass transit.

2. **Identify**   (a) Sierra Nevada, (b) Pacific Northwest, (c) Portland, (d) San Jose.

3. (a) How have people used the resources of the West? (b) How are these resources being protected today?

4. What natural resources made Portland a good location for a city?

Critical Thinking

5. **Recognizing Cause and Effect**   How has rapid urban growth affected the natural resources of the West?

Activity

6. **Writing to Learn**   Do you think that there are better ways to use natural resources in your community? Write a letter to your representative in Congress expressing your ideas. To help you in this task, think about the efforts in the West to preserve and conserve resources.

Understanding Circle Graphs

Chris walked across the playground with his new friend Kyung, who had just moved to Texas from Korea. Kyung looked up at the burning sun.

"Boy, it's really hot here. Does the whole United States get weather like this?"

"It depends," said Chris. "Let me think . . . in the Northwest it rains a lot, and I don't think it gets quite as hot as here. But Arizona and New Mexico do, for sure. In the Midwest, they have some really hot summers, but freezing cold winters. They have tornadoes, too. And then there's Alaska—their summers don't get too hot, even though the sun shines all night long. You know, it's hard to say. This country gets a lot of different weather."

▼ A typical sunny day in Myakka River State Park, Florida

Get Ready

Trying to describe the weather of the United States is no easy task. The United States has a great variety of weather. It can be hard to keep it all straight, but graphs can make it easier.

One common type of graph is a circle graph. Circle graphs show proportion, or the parts of a whole. The entire circle represents all, or 100 percent, of something. Half the circle represents 50 percent. Smaller slices represent smaller amounts, and larger slices represent larger amounts.

Try It Out

The best way to understand how circle graphs work is to try making one yourself. Working with a few other students, make a circle graph showing last week's weather. Follow the steps on the next page.

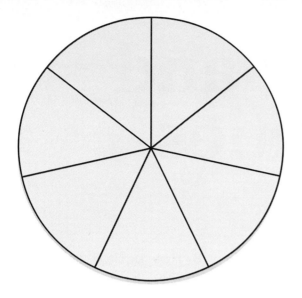

A. Record last week's weather. Write the days of the week in a column down the left-hand side of a sheet of paper. Working with your group, recall last week's weather. Which days had precipitation? Which days did not? Next to each day, note that day's weather activity as either *precipitation* or *no precipitation*. Now count the number of days with precipitation and with no precipitation and make a note of each on your paper.

B. Draw your circle graph. On another sheet of paper, copy the circle above. For your graph, the circle represents one week. Notice how the circle is divided into seven sections, one for each day of the week.

C. Fill in your circle graph. Using one color for each weather category, fill in your circle graph. You should color in one section of the graph for every day. For example, suppose there were three rainy days last week and you chose blue to represent precipitation. Color three sections blue. Be sure to keep the sections with the same color together.

D. Label your circle graph. Finally, label each color on your circle graph or create a key to show what each color stands for. Give your graph a title that tells what the graph is about.

E. Study your circle graph. Your graph lets you quickly see what proportion of last week had precipitation and what proportion did not. How would you describe last week's weather—as mostly wet or mostly dry?

Apply the Skill

A circle graph can show more than two categories of data. It can also be compared with other graphs showing the same kind of data, like the graphs on this page. Use the graphs to answer the questions below.

① **Become familiar with the illustration.** Read the title. What is the subject of these two graphs? Read the graph key. What data do the graphs provide?

② **Study the graphs.** Look at the graph for Los Angeles. How would you describe the weather in Los Angeles? Now study the graph for Boston. What percent of the year had no precipitation in this city?

③ **Use the graphs to make comparisons.** Which city has the most rain? What other comparisons can you make?

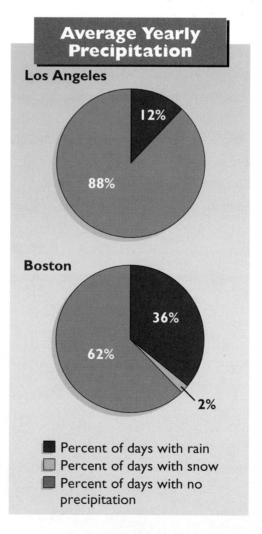

Average Yearly Precipitation

Los Angeles
12%
88%

Boston
36%
62%
2%

■ Percent of days with rain
□ Percent of days with snow
■ Percent of days with no precipitation

Review and Activities

Reviewing Main Ideas

1. What are some of the large cities of the Northeast?
2. How does the Northeast serve as a gateway to the country?
3. How do people in the South make a living?
4. How does warm weather affect the economy of the South?
5. What major changes have occurred in the Midwest since the 1980s?
6. Describe the differences between family farms and corporate farms.
7. What are the main natural resources of the West?
8. How has life in the West changed since the days of the California Gold Rush?
9. How has the way people manage natural resources in the West changed since the 1800s?

Reviewing Key Terms

Use each key term below in a sentence that shows the meaning of the term.

1. commute
2. megalopolis
3. population density
4. petrochemical
5. industrialization
6. Sun Belt
7. mixed-crop farm
8. recession
9. corporate farm
10. forty-niner
11. mass transit

Critical Thinking

1. **Making Comparisons** Identify at least one major trend that two or more regions of the United States have in common.
2. **Drawing Conclusions** If the unwise use of resources continues in the West, what are some likely results?

Graphic Organizer

Copy the chart onto a separate sheet of paper. Then, using information from the chapter, fill in the empty boxes.

	Resources	Cities	Current Industries
Northeast			
South			
Midwest			
West			

Map Activity

United States

For each place listed below, write the letter from the map that shows its location.

1. Boston
2. New York City
3. Washington, D.C.
4. Atlanta
5. Chicago
6. Detroit
7. Portland
8. San Jose

Writing Activity

Writing a Travel Guide

If you had friends who were visiting the United States for the first time, what information would you want to share with them? Which cities would you tell them to visit? Write a brief travel guide for your friends that takes them to all four regions of the United States. Do research to plan the trip. Suggest activities for each region. Provide background information to help your friends understand the history and culture of each region.

Internet Activity

Use a search engine to find **CityNet.** Take a virtual trip to cities in the Northeast, South, Midwest, and West. Make a chart to compare and contrast the cities. Work in small groups to write a television commercial to welcome tourists to one of the cities. Choose a group member to present the commercial to the class.

Skills Review

Turn to the Skills Activity.

Review how special graphs can give information. Then complete the following: (a) Explain what a circle graph shows. (b) Give two examples of kinds of information that could be shown in a circle graph.

How Am I Doing?

Answer these questions to help you check your progress.

1. Do I understand the history and economic development of the four regions of the United States?
2. Can I describe the major cities in the Northeast?
3. Can I identify the major resources and economic challenges in the South, the Midwest, and the West?
4. What information from this chapter can I use in my book project?

FROM

Childtimes

BY ELOISE GREENFIELD AND LESSIE JONES LITTLE,
WITH MATERIAL BY PATTIE RIDLEY JONES

BEFORE YOU READ

Reach Into Your Background

How much do people know about the lives of their grandparents? What about the lives of their parents as children? Suppose someone wanted to write a history of his or her family—how could they find information?

You can learn a lot from seeing how a single family lives through several generations. Every family history reflects the history of the country or region where that family lives. The following excerpts come from a book written by a mother and daughter, with help from the grandmother. They have written a *memoir,* or a true story of personal experience. This memoir tells the story of their family, and it also takes a peek into the history of the growth of their hometown, Parmele, North Carolina.

Questions to Explore

1. How does the town of Parmele change over three generations?
2. What do the memoirs of the three generations have in common?

Pattie Frances Ridley Jones
Born in Bertie County, North Carolina, December 15, 1884

Parmele, North Carolina

Towns build up around work, you know. People go and live where they can find jobs. And that's how Parmele got started.

At first, it was just a junction, a place where two railroads crossed. Two Atlantic Coast Line railroads, one running between Rocky Mount and Plymouth, and one running between Kinston and Weldon. Didn't too many people live around there then, and those that did were pretty much spread out.

Well, around 1888, a Yankee named Mr. Parmele came down from New York and looked the place over, and he saw all those big trees and decided to start a lumber company. Everybody knew what that meant. There were going to be jobs! People came from everywhere to get work. I was right little at that time, too little to know what was going on, but everybody says it was something to see how fast that town grew. All those people moving in and houses going up. They named the town after the man who made the jobs, and they called it *Pomma-lee.*

The lumber company hired a whole lot of people. They hired workers to lay track for those little railroads they call tram roads that they were going to run back and forth between the town and the woods. They hired lumberjacks to chop the trees down and cut them up into logs and load them on the tram cars. They hired men to build the mill and put the machinery in, and millworkers to run the machines that would cut the logs into different sizes and dry them and make them nice and smooth.

Lessie Blanche Jones Little
Born in Parmele, North Carolina,
    October 1, 1906

Parmele

I used to hear Papa and Mama and their friends talking about the lumber mill that had been the center of life in Parmele before I was born, but there wasn't any mill when I was growing up. The only thing left of it was the sawdust from all the wood they had sawed there. The sawdust was about a foot thick on the land where the mill had been. I used to love to walk on it. It was spongy, and it made me feel like I was made of rubber. I'd take my shoes off and kind of bounce along on top of it. But that was all that was left of the mill.

My Parmele was a train town. The life of my town moved around the trains that came in and out all day long. About three hundred people lived in Parmele, most of them black. There were three black churches, a Baptist, a Methodist, and a Holiness, and one white church. Two black schools, one white. There wasn't even one doctor, and not many people would have had the money to pay one, if there had been. If somebody got down real bad sick, a member of the family would go by horse and buggy to a nearby town and bring the doctor back, or sometimes the doctor would ride on his own horse.

Most of the men and women in Parmele earned their living by farming. Some did other things like working at the tobacco factory in Robersonville, but most worked on the farms that were all around in the area, white

▼ These people were picking peppers in 1921 on a farm in Louisiana.

▲ Going to church in the South in the 1930s

Ask Questions What more would you like to know about farm life?

Pamlico Sound (PAM lih koh sound) a long body of water off the coast of North Carolina that separates the Hatteras Islands from the mainland

people's farms usually. When I was a little girl, they earned fifty cents a day, a farm day, sunup to sundown, plus meals. After they got home, they had all their own work to do, cooking and cleaning, laundry, chopping wood for the woodstove, and shopping.

* * *

Parmele had trains coming in and going out all day long. Passenger trains and freight trains. There was always so much going on at the station that I wouldn't know what to watch. People were changing trains and going in and out of the cafe and the restaurant. They came from big cities like New York and Chicago and Boston, and they were all wearing the latest styles. Things were being unloaded, like furniture and trunks and plows and cases of fruit and crates of clucking chickens, or a puppy, or the body of somebody who had died and was being brought back home. And every year around the last two weeks in May, a special

train would come through. It had two white flags flying on the locomotive, and it was carrying one hundred carloads of white potatoes that had been grown down near Pamlico Sound, where everybody said the soil was so rich they didn't even have to fertilize it.

The train station was a gathering place, too. A lot of people went there to relax after they had finished their work for the day. They'd come downtown to pick up their mail, or buy a newspaper, and then they'd just stand around laughing and talking to their friends. And on Sundays fellas and their girls would come all the way from other towns, just to spend the afternoon at the Parmele train station.

* * *

It was hard for Papa to find work. Not long after Sis Clara died, we moved to Mount Herman, a black section of Portsmouth, Virginia. Papa worked on the docks there, and even though he didn't make much money, the work was steady. But when we moved back to Parmele, it was hard for him to find any work at all.

* * *

Eloise Glynn Little Greenfield
Born in Parmele, North Carolina, May 17, 1929

Daddy Makes a Way

When I was three months old, Daddy left home to make a way for us. He went North, as thousands of black people had done, during slavery and since.

They went North looking for safety, for justice, for freedom, for work, looking for a good life. Often one member of a family would go ahead of the others to make a way—to find a job and a place to live. And that's what my father did.

In the spring of 1926, Daddy had graduated from high school, Parmele Training School. He had been offered a scholarship by Knoxville College in Tennessee, but he hadn't taken it. He and Mama had gotten married that fall, and now they had Wilbur and me to take care of. Mama had been teaching school since her graduation from Higgs, but she had decided to stop.

Nineteen twenty-nine was a bad time for Daddy to go away, but a worse time for him not to go. The Great Depression was about to begin, had already begun for many people. All over the United States, thousands of people were already jobless and homeless.

In Parmele, there were few permanent jobs. Some seasons of the year, Daddy could get farm work, harvesting potatoes and working in the tobacco fields. Every year, from August to around Thanksgiving, he worked ten hours a day for twenty-five cents an hour at a tobacco warehouse in a nearby town, packing tobacco in huge barrels and loading them on the train for shipping. And he and his father were house movers. Whenever somebody wanted a house moved from one place to another, Daddy and Pa would jack it up and attach it to a windlass, the machine that the horse would turn to move the house. But it was only once in a while that they were called on to do that.

So, one morning in August 1929, Mama went with Daddy to the train station and tried to hold back her tears as the Atlantic Coast Line train pulled out, taking him toward Washington, D.C. Then she went home, sat in the porch swing, and cried.

In Washington, friends helped Daddy find a room for himself and his family to live in, and took him job hunting. He found a job as a dishwasher in a restaurant, and in a few weeks, he had saved enough money for our train fare.

READ ACTIVELY

Visualize Picture the trains arriving at the station and the people and goods as they come off board.

Great Depression a period of time in the 1930s when businesses did not do well, causing many people to lose their jobs

EXPLORING YOUR READING

Look Back

1. How did the town of Parmele first begin to grow? What did adding a lumber company do that made more people come to the town?

Think It Over

2. Why were trains such an important part of Parmele?

Go Beyond

3. What do these memoirs tell you about the time period they cover?

Ideas for Writing: Memoir

4. Write a memoir of your own childhood from the point of view of yourself as an older person. What forces have most shaped your life?

CHAPTER 5

Exploring Canada

SECTION 1
Quebec
PRESERVING A CULTURE

SECTION 2
Saskatchewan
CANADA'S BREADBASKET

SECTION 3
British Columbia
TIES TO THE PACIFIC RIM

KEY

— National boundary

⊛ National capital

✪ Provincial capital

• Other city

Lambert Azimuthal Equal-Area Projection

MAP ACTIVITIES

Canada is a nation of many cultures. People from all over the world have immigrated to Canada. This has given each region a distinct cultural identity. To get acquainted with some of these regions, do the following activities.

Study the map
Find the provinces of Quebec, Saskatchewan, and British Columbia on the map. Using information on the map, describe the relative location of each province.

Make historical connections
Which of the three provinces do you think was first settled by Europeans? Explain your answer.

Quebec

PRESERVING A CULTURE

BEFORE YOU READ

Reach Into Your Background

In a democracy, citizens choose their leaders by voting. Sometimes they also vote on issues. The person or position on an issue that gets the most votes wins. Suppose that two of your classmates want to be class president. There is a vote—and each person gets half of the votes. What happens next? How can your class decide on the winner?

Questions to Explore

1. Why do French Canadians worry about preserving their culture?

2. What have French Canadians in Quebec done to preserve their culture?

Key Terms

Francophone
separatist
Quiet Revolution
referendum

Key People and Places

Jacques Cartier
Quebec City
Montreal

In 1977, a new law in the province of Quebec said that all street signs must be in French only. That pleased the majority of Quebeckers who speak French, but it upset other Quebeckers. In 1993, a change in the law allowed English on signs as well. But French is still the only language used in Quebec government, commerce, and education.

Canadian law states that the country has two official languages—English and French. French-speaking people live in every province. In Quebec, however, the first language of 83 percent of the people is French. The first language of 12 percent is English. The remaining 5 percent speak 35 different languages! Still, until the 1960s, government and business in Quebec were conducted in English, just as they were in the rest of Canada. It took a long political battle to change things in Quebec.

The French Influence in Quebec

Canada's history explains why Quebec is so French. In the 1530s, Jacques Cartier (zhahk kahr TYAY), a French explorer, sailed along the St. Lawrence River. In 1535, he landed near today's Quebec City. In his journal, Cartier wrote that he and his crew saw a land "as full of beautiful fields and

▼ In Quebec, bright red signs yell "STOP" in Canada's two official languages, French and English.

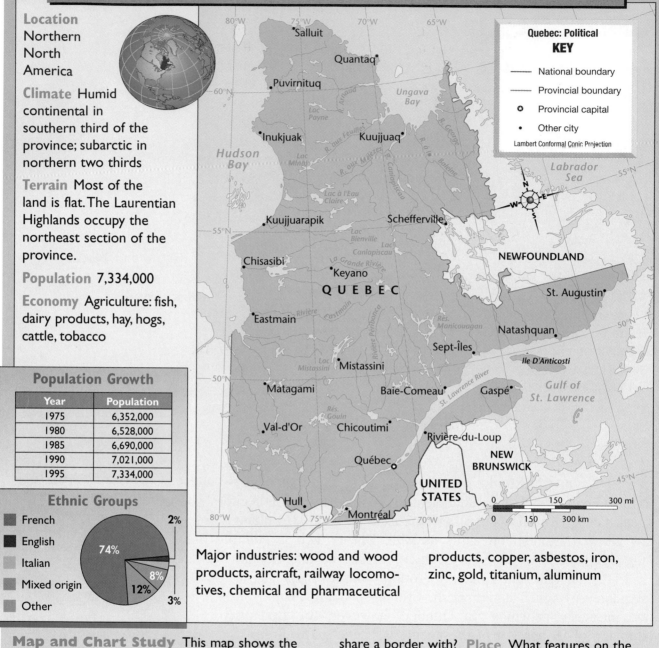

Location Northern North America

Climate Humid continental in southern third of the province; subarctic in northern two thirds

Terrain Most of the land is flat. The Laurentian Highlands occupy the northeast section of the province.

Population 7,334,000

Economy Agriculture: fish, dairy products, hay, hogs, cattle, tobacco

Population Growth

Year	Population
1975	6,352,000
1980	6,528,000
1985	6,690,000
1990	7,021,000
1995	7,334,000

Ethnic Groups

- French
- English
- Italian
- Mixed origin
- Other

74%
2%
3%
12%
8%

Major industries: wood and wood products, aircraft, railway locomotives, chemical and pharmaceutical products, copper, asbestos, iron, zinc, gold, titanium, aluminum

Map and Chart Study This map shows the borders and major cities of Quebec, Canada's largest province. **Location** Quebec shares a border with several Canadian provinces, including Newfoundland and New Brunswick. What country does Quebec share a border with? **Place** What features on the map show Quebec's French heritage? **Critical Thinking** Look at the charts on this page. What percentage of Quebeckers are French? About how much has Quebec's population grown since 1975?

meadows as any we have ever seen." The men became friends with the Stadacona (stad uh KOH nuh), the indigenous people of the area. Soon both groups were living in the area. Some places in Quebec and elsewhere in Canada have Stadacona names. Cartier and later explorers gave other places French names. *Montreal,* for instance, is French for "Mount Royal."

Cartier claimed the region we now know as Quebec for his nation and named it New France. But England also claimed the region. The two countries eventually fought over it. France lost, and in 1763 the territory went to the British. However, tens of thousands of French colonists lived in the region. Today, their descendants make up the majority of Quebec's population. They are **Francophones** (FRANG koh fohnz), or people who speak French as their first language.

Quebec—A Distinct Society Within Canada   In the 1960s, many Francophones began to express concern about life in Quebec. They did not like using English at school and at work. They did not like the fact that new immigrants to Quebec learned English, not French. They felt that if this situation did not change, their language and culture might die. They also believed that they were contributing much to Canada but getting little back. Quebec is rich in natural resources, which are important to Canada's economy. For the most part, however, Francophones got only lower-paying jobs. They faced prejudice because they were French speakers.

Soon some Francophone Quebeckers began to demand independence. They were called **separatists.** They wanted Quebec to separate, or break away, from Canada. To do this, they formed a political party called the *Parti Québécois* (PAHR tee keh beh KWAH). In a 1976 election, the party won control of the Quebec provincial legislature. This peaceful change in Quebec's government is called the **Quiet Revolution.**

Predict What problems developed when Britain took over French colonies in Canada?

◀ Quebec City's French heritage is shown in the French style of architecture. The Château Frontenac (sha TOH FRAHNT uh nak) Hotel, built in 1893, looks very much like the great country houses built by French nobles.

121

Just before the 1995 referendum, a Quebecker displays her opposition to separation. She has a "no" sign on her forehead and the maple leaf—the symbol of Canada—on her cheeks (left). Other Quebeckers, carrying signs calling for "independence" and "sovereignty," rallied to support the split from Canada (above). By the narrowest of margins, Quebeckers voted to remain part of Canada. **Critical Thinking** Why do you think that so many Quebeckers want their province to be an independent country?

Connect Suppose that California or New York state wanted to leave the United States and become a separate nation. What would be your response?

French became the official language, to be used in education, government, and commerce. Immigrants were required to learn French. Still, Quebec remained a province of Canada.

Not everyone in Quebec supported the idea of separation from Canada. In 1980, the provincial government held a referendum. In a **referendum,** voters cast ballots for or against an issue. This referendum asked voters whether Quebec should become a separate nation. A majority voted no.

The Canadian government knew that the separatists could force the nation to separate. For this reason, the government tried to meet their demands. Quebeckers wanted their province to be a "distinct society" within Canada. It would have its own special way of life. If this was guaranteed, they would stay part of Canada. There was only one way to do this—change Canada's constitution. In 1990 and 1992, the government held referendums about the issue. Quebeckers voted to change the constitution. Both times, Canadians in other provinces voted not to. The referendums failed.

In 1995, Quebec held another referendum. Again, Quebeckers voted to remain part of Canada. But the margin was very slim. The "no" vote was 50.6 percent; the "yes" vote was 49.4 percent. Canada's Prime Minister promised to try to change the constitution again, "so that Canada will move into the twenty-first century united." But Quebec's separatist leader warned, "The battle for a country is not over. And it will not be until we have one." The close vote on election day guaranteed that the issue will continue to be discussed.

Preserving Quebec's Culture

One of the ways in which Quebeckers celebrate their culture is through festivals. The *Fête des Neiges* (fet day NEZH), or winter festival, lasts 17 days. It even includes canoe races among the ice floes along the St. Lawrence River. A Quebec author notes that the city of Quebec

> "is liveliest in winter during the carnival . . . when the city is ruled by the carnival snowman and the newly elected carnival queen. Then a fairy ice palace is built on the hill facing the Quebec Parliament; people dance in the streets . . . visitors come from all over to admire the ice sculpture along the sidewalks of Sainte-Therese Street: a marvelous exhibition of dinosaur monsters . . . boats from the ice race, famous people, and all kinds of animals. . . . This fantasy world becomes really weird at night when all the sculptures are brilliantly lit by thousands of lamps."

A Copy of St. Peter's Basilica One sign of Quebec's religious heritage is Montreal's Cathedral-Basilica of Mary, Queen of the World. Built in 1870, this church was designed to look like Saint Peter's Basilica in Vatican City, in Rome, Italy. Montreal's church is one third as large as St. Peter's.

▼ During Quebec's Winter Carnival, artists compete to make the best sculptures of ice or packed snow.

A Summer Night in Quebec City

Quebeckers jam the sidewalk cafés in Upper Town, the old section of Quebec City. The capital of Quebec province, Quebec City is located on the site where the first permanent French settlement in Canada was set up. **Critical Thinking** Many French Canadians consider Quebec City to be an almost sacred place. Why do you think this is so?

This is only one festival in French-Canadian culture. Another honors Jean Baptiste (zhahn bah TEEST), the patron saint, or special guardian, of French Canadians. The festival is held June 24. All over the province, people celebrate with bonfires, firecrackers, and street dances.

French style and cooking are alive in Quebec—with Quebec variations. Sugar pie, for example, uses maple sugar from the province's forests. Quebec has French architecture—with Quebec variations. All in all, Quebeckers have a lively culture to preserve and protect.

SECTION 1 REVIEW

1. **Define** a) Francophone, (b) separatist, (c) Quiet Revolution, (d) referendum.

2. **Identify** (a) Jacques Cartier, (b) Quebec City, (c) Montreal.

3. What are some features of Quebec culture?

4. List several reasons for the Quiet Revolution.

5. What steps have Quebeckers and other Canadians taken to preserve French culture?

Critical Thinking

6. **Expressing Problems Clearly** Explain why many people in Quebec want to separate from Canada.

Activity

7. **Writing to Learn** List some features of Quebec culture that you would like to learn more about.

Saskatchewan
CANADA'S BREADBASKET

BEFORE YOU READ

Reach Into Your Background

Think about something you heard that led you to believe that some experience was going to be wonderful. Were you ever disappointed when the real experience turned out to be less than what you had hoped for? What did you do? Did you try to maintain a good attitude?

Questions to Explore

1. Why did many immigrants from central and Eastern Europe come to Saskatchewan in the mid-1800s?

2. How do ethnic communities maintain their traditions in Saskatchewan?

Key Term
immunity

Key Places
Regina
Saskatoon

One August day in 1821, after a long, difficult journey, about 195 Swiss immigrants reached their new land. It was summertime. But it was chilly on the Hudson Bay in northern Canada. The Swiss watchmakers, mechanics, pastry cooks, and musicians wanted to become Canadian farmers in this region called "Rupert's Land." Later, the region became the Northwest Territory. The settlers had heard that these vast plains had good land and an excellent climate. Then they looked around. No shelter, food, or supplies were waiting for them. The settlers survived only because the native people of the region, the Saulteaux (sawl TOH), helped them.

The Rindisbacher (RIN dis baw kur) family was part of the group. All of them—father, mother, and seven children—later moved to the Red River region. Today it is part of Manitoba. One of the children, 15-year-old Peter, loved to draw. He sketched and painted pictures of life on the Canadian plains. He also drew the indigenous peoples, carefully adding details about their tools, clothing, and canoes.

Rindisbacher's pictures also tell us about the hard life of the settlers. During harsh winters they fought snow and ice. During summers they fought drought, floods, and swarms of grasshoppers.

▼ This photograph, taken in 1928, shows a group of young men on board the ship *Montcalm*. They are on their way to Canada to start a new life in the Prairie Provinces.

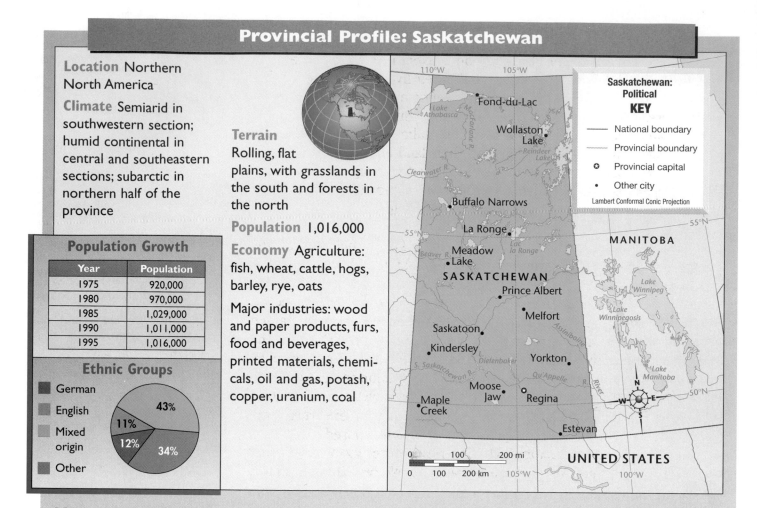

Provincial Profile: Saskatchewan

Location Northern North America

Climate Semiarid in southwestern section; humid continental in central and southeastern sections; subarctic in northern half of the province

Terrain Rolling, flat plains, with grasslands in the south and forests in the north

Population 1,016,000

Economy Agriculture: fish, wheat, cattle, hogs, barley, rye, oats

Major industries: wood and paper products, furs, food and beverages, printed materials, chemicals, oil and gas, potash, copper, uranium, coal

Population Growth

Year	Population
1975	920,000
1980	970,000
1985	1,029,000
1990	1,011,000
1995	1,016,000

Ethnic Groups

- German
- English
- Mixed origin
- Other

43%
11%
12%
34%

Saskatchewan: Political KEY
- National boundary
- Provincial boundary
- ⊕ Provincial capital
- • Other city

Lambert Conformal Conic Projection

Map and Chart Study This map shows the borders and major cities of Saskatchewan. **Location** Where are most of Saskatchewan's major cities located? Why do you think these cities are located in this area?

Critical Thinking Look at the chart of Saskatchewan's ethnic groups. Is any one ethnic group much larger than the others? What conclusions can you draw about Saskatchewan's culture based on this chart?

There were few trees on the plains, so many people built their homes out of sod. They cut prairie sod into blocks and piled them up to make walls. "Soddies" were cheap, but if it rained, the roofs leaked! Most settlers had little experience in farming and had not expected such hardships.

Changing Ways of Life

Throughout the 1800s, European settlers continued to trickle into the Plains region. As they did, they changed the cultures of the indigenous peoples. In part, changes came from European trade goods, such as pots, needles, and guns. European diseases, such as measles, caused other changes. In Europe, people had suffered from measles for centuries. As a result, Europeans had **immunity,** or natural resistance. But measles had not existed in North America. Indigenous peoples had no immunity. In some groups, as many as 75 percent of the people died. European diseases killed millions of indigenous peoples in South America, too.

READ ACTIVELY

Ask Questions What do you want to know about the effects that European settlers had on indigenous peoples of the prairies?

A Way of Life Lost   In the late 1870s, the ways of life of many indigenous peoples in the Plains region of North America came to an end. For centuries, these people had built their lives around the buffalo. Then people of European descent began killing off the buffalo herds. In a few years, nearly all were gone. At the same time, the governments of Canada and the United States began to take over the indigenous peoples' land. Most agreed to give up their land and live on reserves. These were small areas of land set aside for the indigenous peoples. With a few exceptions, indigenous peoples in Canada did not go to war to protect their land as they did in the United States.

Free Land Draws Newcomers   The population of the indigenous peoples was shrinking. The European population, however, was increasing. Many early settlers, like the Rindisbacher family, moved away after a while. Other immigrants replaced them. The new people, too, were ready to farm the prairie. The Canadian government wanted even more people. Newcomers would help the economy grow. In the late 1800s and early 1900s, Canada advertised free land in European newspapers. The advertisements worked. Immigration increased.

Until then, most Canadians were indigenous peoples or settlers from France or Britain. That quickly changed. The newcomers were from many ethnic groups. The people in each group shared a history, religion, language, and customs. The Prairie Provinces saw an amazing variety of newcomers. Some were Ukrainians, Norwegians, or Finns.

Sanctuary Visitors to Saskatchewan's Grasslands National Park see some of North America's last untouched prairies. Ancient grasses called wheat grass, snowberry, and silver sage blow in the wind. The park is also home to 12 endangered and threatened species. They include certain kinds of hawks, burrowing owls, and short-horned lizards.

◄Settlers in the southwest of Saskatchewan made a living by ranching. Rodeos have become a popular form of entertainment in this area.

Connect If you wanted to move to a new location, what kinds of things would attract you?

Others were Russians or Poles. The names of new settlements illustrated the changes. Swedes settled in New Stockholm. Icelanders founded Thingvalla. Danes founded New Denmark. Hungarians founded Esterhazy. And Germans founded Ebenezer. By the turn of the century, the Canadian prairies were a checkerboard of ethnic settlements. Each had its own language and customs.

All came looking for a better life. Life in Saskatchewan was not always as easy as the advertisements had claimed, however. One newspaper writer summed up the situation bluntly. He described the capital city of Regina as a village "in the midst of a vast plain of inferior soil . . . with about enough water in the miserable little creek . . . to wash a sheep." Nevertheless, the settlers stayed. Hope became an important part of Saskatchewan culture. When crops failed one year, people did not moan and complain. They just looked forward to the next year. This is how Saskatchewan earned the nickname "Next Year Country." The hard work of the people of Saskatchewan paid off. In 1923, the Saskatchewan Wheat Pool was started. Today, it is one of the world's largest grain cooperatives and is the leading company in the province.

Maintaining Tradition on the Prairies

About one quarter of Canada's farmland is in Saskatchewan. Most European immigrants became wheat farmers. Two thirds of Saskatchewan's farmland is still devoted to wheat. For this reason, the province is sometimes called "Canada's Breadbasket."

Wheat Fields Near Saskatoon

This farmer is harvesting wheat near Saskatoon, Saskatchewan's largest city. Saskatchewan has more farmland than any other province in Canada. Saskatchewan is Canada's largest wheat producer. In fact, it is one of the largest wheat producers in the world. **Critical Thinking** What part of the United States is similar to this part of Canada?

Religious Diversity in Saskatchewan

The onion-shaped domes of St. Julien's Greek Orthodox Church pierce the blue sky of Alvena. This small town is located in central Saskatchewan about 150 miles (240 km) northwest of Regina. Saskatchewan's other Christian churches include Roman Catholic, Ukrainian Orthodox, and various Protestant denominations. **Critical Thinking** Why do you think that immigrant groups maintain the traditions and ways of life of the countries they came from?

Today, immigrants still come to the Canadian prairies. Most move to cities like Regina and Saskatoon. Each year, these cities celebrate ethnic festivals. Ukrainian, Icelandic, and German festivals include traditional dancing, art, and music. Every summer, indigenous peoples also host powwows. In some small towns, people still maintain the European languages and customs of their ancestors.

SECTION 2 REVIEW

1. **Define** immunity.

2. **Identify** (a) Regina, (b) Saskatoon.

3. What attracted thousands of European immigrants to the Canadian prairies?

4. How did the lives of indigenous peoples in Canada change after Europeans arrived?

5. How have European immigrants influenced the culture of Saskatchewan?

Critical Thinking

6. **Drawing Conclusions** Many immigrants came to the Canadian prairies in the 1800s. What advantages and disadvantages do you think this move had for them?

Activity

7. **Writing to Learn** Suppose that it is the year 1900. You want to encourage people to come and start farms in Saskatchewan. The government will give 160 acres of land to anyone willing to try. Make a poster advertising free land. You may show weather, soil, scenery, or settler communities. Describe conditions so many will want to come.

British Columbia
TIES TO THE PACIFIC RIM

BEFORE YOU READ

Reach Into Your Background

Think about the ways in which people use natural resources. How do we benefit from natural resources? What are some of the problems that using natural resources can cause?

Questions to Explore

1. Before the 1880s, what major events influenced British Columbia's culture?
2. Why does British Columbia have such a diverse population?
3. How does geography tie British Columbia to the Pacific Rim?

Key Terms

totem pole
boomtown

Key Places

Vancouver
Fraser River
Victoria
Cariboo Mountains
Pacific Rim

▼ Brightly painted totem poles are sometimes used to tell the history of a family or tribe.

A visitor starts her day at a tiny coffee shop. All around her, people are speaking Dutch, Japanese, Spanish, German, and English. After having breakfast, the visitor gets into her car. On the radio, she hears country music—sung in French. Driving downtown, she passes street signs in Chinese, Indian men wearing turbans, a Korean travel agency, and a Thai restaurant. Where in the world is she? It may seem like the United Nations. But it is Vancouver (van KOO vur), British Columbia—a truly international city.

Fishers, Hunters, Traders, Miners

The first people came to what is now British Columbia about 10,000 to 12,000 years ago. They belonged to several ethnic groups and spoke many different languages. Each group had its own customs and a complex society. The people along the coast caught fish, whales, and clams. They also carved giant **totem poles,** which were symbols for a group, a clan, or a family. Other groups lived and hunted game

Provincial Profile: British Columbia

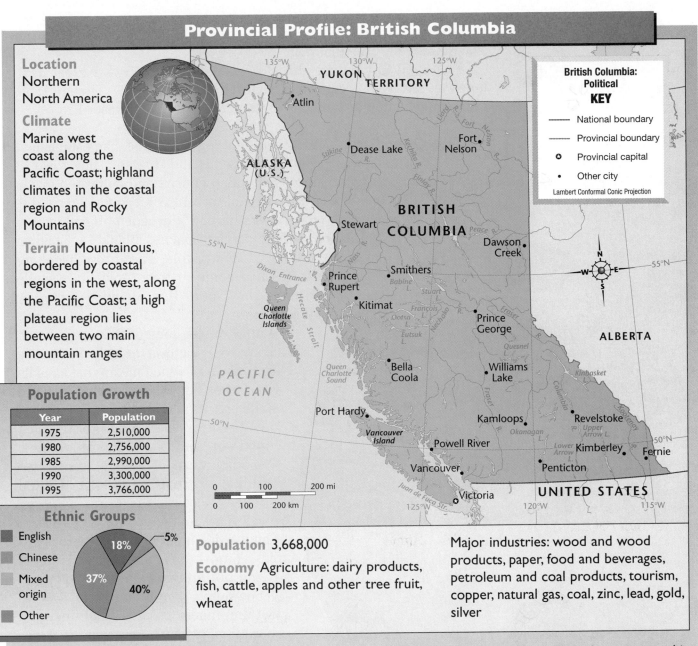

Location
Northern North America

Climate
Marine west coast along the Pacific Coast; highland climates in the coastal region and Rocky Mountains

Terrain Mountainous, bordered by coastal regions in the west, along the Pacific Coast; a high plateau region lies between two main mountain ranges

Population Growth

Year	Population
1975	2,510,000
1980	2,756,000
1985	2,990,000
1990	3,300,000
1995	3,766,000

Ethnic Groups

- English
- Chinese
- Mixed origin
- Other

18% 5% 37% 40%

Population 3,668,000

Economy Agriculture: dairy products, fish, cattle, apples and other tree fruit, wheat

Major industries: wood and wood products, paper, food and beverages, petroleum and coal products, tourism, copper, natural gas, coal, zinc, lead, gold, silver

British Columbia: Political
KEY
— National boundary
— Provincial boundary
⊕ Provincial capital
• Other city
Lambert Conformal Conic Projection

Map and Chart Study This map shows the borders and major cities of British Columbia. **Location** What U.S. state is separated from the rest of the United States by British Columbia? What other parts of Canada does British Columbia border? **Critical Thinking**

Look at the charts and the economic information on this page. Is any one ethnic group much larger than the others? About how much has the population grown since 1975? How does British Columbia's growing population make a living?

in the dense inland forests. Some groups traded with each other and got along well. Others fought.

New Arrivals   In the late 1500s, Spanish, British, and Russian explorers began to arrive in the area to trade. In 1778, James Cook, a British explorer, sailed to Vancouver Island, off the coast of British Columbia. A group of Nootka (NOOT kuh) people met the British and agreed to trade. These coastal people wanted iron tools, while the

THE UNITED STATES AND CANADA   **131**

British wanted furs. When the British built a fur-trading post on the island, trade began to flourish.

Trade did not change the indigenous peoples' lives a great deal, however. Fur traders came and went. They did not settle. Then in 1858, everything changed. Someone discovered gold along Fraser River.

The Gold Rush   A few years earlier, the British had established Victoria, a trading village on Vancouver Island. It was a tidy town of traders and farmers. Its citizens attended church and cultivated lovely gardens. Then, one Sunday morning in April 1858, an American paddle-wheeler entered Victoria's harbor. It dropped off 450 men in red shirts. They carried packs, blankets, spades, pickaxes, knives, and pistols. These rough-looking characters had come to mine gold. In a single morning, they more than doubled Victoria's population.

Within weeks, tens of thousands more had arrived. Victoria quickly became a "stumptown"—which meant that all of its great trees had been chopped down to build shacks and boats.

Two years later, miners also struck gold in the Cariboo Mountains. Another wave of miners came from China, Europe, and the United States. Because the Cariboo region was hard to reach, the government built a 400-mile (666-km) highway to it. Almost overnight, settlements called **boomtowns** sprang up along it. A boomtown's only purpose was to meet the miners' needs. When the gold rush was over, many boomtowns died out.

Changes for Indigenous Peoples

The indigenous peoples, said the governor of Victoria, were "naturally annoyed" that thousands were coming and taking gold from their land—even taking over the land itself. In 1888, the British government wanted to confine some indigenous peoples to a small reserve. The indigenous peoples protested. They had always lived on the land where the reserve was located. How, they asked, could the government now "give" it to them?

The indigenous peoples had little choice. In a few short years, they had gone from being the great majority to being the smallest minority of the population. They were pushed onto small reserves. Laws banned many of their customs, religions, and languages. Children were taken from their parents to be raised in European-run schools.

▲ This photograph, taken in 1900, shows a group of people looking for gold at Pine Creek, British Columbia. During the gold rush, most people mined gold from creeks and streams, not by digging deep into the ground.

Recently, the indigenous peoples of British Columbia have found new pride in their history and culture. They are demanding land and political rights, and their art is thriving.

The Canadian Pacific Railway In the spring of 1881, Canadians began work on an enormous project—building a railroad all the way from Montreal to Vancouver. The goal of the project was to unite Canada. Look at the map of British Columbia in the Provincial Profile and you may see what a major task this was. There were countless obstacles—soaring mountains, steep valleys, freezing weather, and glaciers. Workers built 600 bridges and blasted 27 tunnels through the mountains.

The railroad project brought more change. Immigrants from all over the world came to work on the railroad. Towns grew up along the railroad, and more newcomers moved in. All this activity attracted criminals, too. They caused so much trouble that the Mounted Police were brought in. In a few short years, British Columbia went from being a sparsely inhabited region to a settled one, complete with cities.

LINKS TO SCIENCE

Trapping Shells Many native peoples of the Northwest used a shell called *dentalia* as money. The shells were difficult to gather. They live on the ocean bottom, in beds 50 to 60 feet (15 to 18 m) deep. Native peoples would lower a broom-like device from a canoe. Stabbing the broom into the sand, they would trap a few shells at a time.

Hauling Freight

A huge freight train heads for Vancouver along the banks of the Thompson River, high in the mountains of British Columbia. **Critical Thinking** What difficulties do you think faced the workers who laid the railroad along the Thompson River?

Predict How has physical geography affected the culture of British Columbia?

British Columbia Today

The Canadian Pacific Railroad did unite all of Canada. However, the mountains have always been a big barrier between British Columbia and the rest of the country. Today, about two thirds of British Columbians live along the coast, west of the mountains. Many feel that their future lies with Pacific Rim countries—nations that border the Pacific Ocean—not with the rest of Canada.

Trade Routes Across the Pacific Ocean

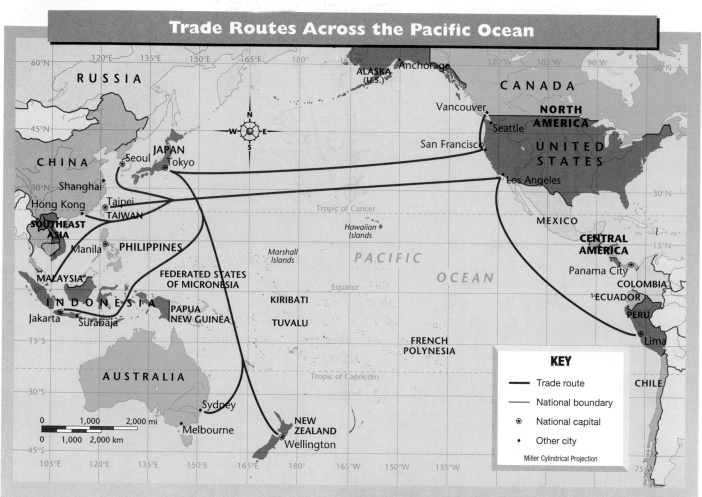

Map Study Traditionally, the United States and Europe have been Canada's most important trade partners. However, Canada is developing a thriving relationship with the countries that border the Pacific Ocean. In the mid-1970s, Japan replaced the United Kingdom as the second largest market for Canadian exports. Most of Canada's Pacific Rim trade passes through British Columbia's major port, Vancouver (right). **Movement** Name three Pacific countries, other than Japan, with which Canada might trade.

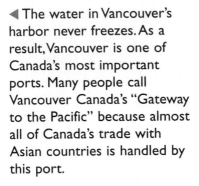
◄ The water in Vancouver's harbor never freezes. As a result, Vancouver is one of Canada's most important ports. Many people call Vancouver Canada's "Gateway to the Pacific" because almost all of Canada's trade with Asian countries is handled by this port.

Another link between British Columbia and the Pacific Rim is British Columbia's diverse people. About 11 percent have Asian ancestors. Trade is still another link between British Columbia and the Pacific Rim. Forty percent of the province's trade is with Asian countries. British Columbia wants good relationships with them. As a result, in British Columbian schools, students learn Asian languages. They learn Japanese, Cantonese Chinese, or Mandarin Chinese. Some even learn Punjabi (pun JAH bee), a language of India and Pakistan!

SECTION 3 REVIEW

1. **Define** (a) totem pole, (b) boomtown.

2. **Identify** (a) Vancouver, (b) Fraser River, (c) Victoria, (d) Cariboo Mountains, (d) Pacific Rim.

3. What brought Europeans to British Columbia between the late 1500s and the late 1800s?

4. Explain the effects of the gold rush on British Columbia.

5. What ties are there between the people of British Columbia and the Pacific Rim?

Critical Thinking

6. **Identifying Central Issues** What was the importance of the completion of the Canadian Pacific Railroad?

Activity

7. **Writing to Learn** What do you think it would be like to be a gold prospector in one of the gold rushes in Canada? Write a journal entry describing a gold prospector's typical workday.

SKILLS ACTIVITY

Writing for a Purpose

Think about the last three or four conversations you have had.

You might have been talking with friends at school, a teacher, family members, a clerk in a store, or a friend. Chances are, the conversations were all very different. However, they probably also had something in common.

No matter what you talked about, or with whom you spoke, one of you probably *informed* the other. To inform someone simply means to give someone information. You might have informed a friend about how you were feeling, informed a store clerk about what you wanted to buy, or informed your mother that you had basketball practice after school.

People often write to inform, too. This entire book, for example, was written to inform you about the United States and Canada.

Get Ready

As a student and as an adult, you will often write to inform your readers. You may write reports to inform your teacher about a subject you have researched. You may write letters to inform friends about your life. You may fill in a job application to inform an employer about your work experience.

Try It Out

Writing to inform means writing to provide information. It involves five basic steps. As you read through the following steps, think about a one-page paper you could write to inform someone about something. Complete the activity at the end of each step.

A. Choose your topic. What will you write about? What do you want to tell your readers? Of course, there are millions of subjects. You can write about anything you want—a hobby, your last weekend, or a football game. Write down a few possibilities, then circle the one you like best.

Writing to Inform

about a process

Organize your writing around the steps in the process.

B. Choose your audience. You need to know to whom you are writing. You would write differently for a group of second-graders than you would for your parents. For this paper, your audience will be your teacher and your classmates.

C. Research your topic. In order to inform your audience, you have to first inform yourself. Read and take notes from books, magazines, newspapers, and other sources of information. Gather your information and know what you want to write before you begin the next step.

D. Plan your paper. This is how you will inform your audience. When you write to inform, you should organize your paper in the way that will make your topic easiest for your audience to understand. The box to the right tells you how to choose the best way.

Will you write about a process, an event, or a thing? How will you organize your paper? Write it down.

E. Write. Now you can start writing a one-page paper to inform. Make an outline before you start. Make sure it is organized in the same way that you will organize your final paper. Try to start your paper with an interesting opening and write clearly.

Apply the Skill

Now write a one-page paper to inform your teacher and classmates about a subject in this chapter of your textbook. Choose one of the following ideas, or choose your own subject.

- The immigration of Chinese Americans and other Americans to Canada from California (a process)
- The election to decide on Quebec's independence (an event)
- A wheat farm in Saskatchewan (a thing)

about a thing

Write about the object's purpose and its parts.

about an event

Organize your writing in chronological order, or order based on time.

Review and Activities

Reviewing Main Ideas

1. What is the largest cultural group in Quebec?

2. What is the main political aim of many French Canadians?

3. How has immigration shaped Saskatchewan's culture?

4. What is Saskatchewan's main contribution to Canada's economy?

5. Identify different groups of people who have shaped British Columbia's culture.

6. What part of the world has the strongest cultural ties with British Columbia today? Why?

Reviewing Key Terms

Use each key term below in a sentence that shows the meaning of the term.

1. Francophone

2. separatist

3. Quiet Revolution

4. referendum

5. immunity

6. totem pole

7. boomtown

Critical Thinking

1. **Recognizing Bias** The slogans "Masters in Our Own House" and "United From Sea to Sea" are from the dispute over Quebec. Determine which side of the issue each slogan supports.

2. **Recognizing Cause and Effect** Identify several different events in western Canada that led to the decline of the native peoples' cultures.

Graphic Organizer

Each of the provinces mentioned in this chapter has natural resources that attracted settlers. Copy this chart. Then fill in the blanks with resources found in each province.

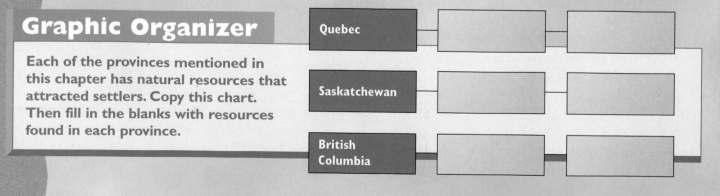

Quebec

Saskatchewan

British Columbia

Map Activity

Canada

For each place listed below, write the letter from the map that shows its location.

1. Quebec

2. Montreal

3. Saskatchewan

4. Regina

5. British Columbia

6. Rocky Mountains

7. Vancouver

Writing Activity

Writing a Paragraph
Make a list of the distinguishing characteristics of Quebec, Saskatchewan, and British Columbia. Then pick one province. Write a letter to a friend, trying to convince your friend to move to the province.

Internet Activity

Use a search engine to find **QuebecWeb.** Click **Regions,** then choose Quebec. Explore the various links to learn about the Quebecois heritage. What evidences of French culture did you find in Quebec? Use the information to make a time line of Quebecois heritage and history.

Skills Review

Turn to the Skills Activity.

Review the basic steps of writing to inform. Then complete the following: (a) Name some types of writing that inform. (b) Tell how you could organize informative writing about a process, an event, or an object.

How Am I Doing?

Answer these questions to help you check your progress.

1. Can I explain why French Canadians are worried about preserving their culture?

2. Can I visualize what life was like in Saskatchewan in the past?

3. Can I explain how the gold rush affected growth in British Columbia?

4. What information from this chapter can I use in my book project?

THE
UNITED STATES AND CANADA
PROJECT POSSIBILITIES

As you study the United States and Canada, you will be reading and thinking about these important questions.

☞ **How has physical geography affected the cultures of the United States and Canada?**

☞ **How have historical events affected the cultures of the United States and Canada?**

☞ **How has the variety of peoples in the United States and Canada benefited and challenged the two nations?**

☞ **How has modern technology benefited and challenged the United States and Canada?**

☞ **How did the United States and Canada become two of the wealthiest nations in the world?**

What do you know about the United States and Canada? It's time to show it.

GEO CLEO

Project Menu

The chapters in this book have some answers to these questions. Now you can find your own answers by doing projects on your own or with a group. Here are some ways to make your own discoveries about the United States and Canada.

Write a Children's Book Choose a topic from this book that interests you. Then write a short book about it for younger students. Take careful notes before you write, to be sure you get all the facts right. Write with simple language that younger children can understand. Include the main points of this topic in your book, along with a few interesting details. Illustrate your book with drawings and magazine photographs. Draw at least one map of the area you are writing about. Be sure to use the kind of map—physical, political, or other—that shows the right information for your topic. Finally, design a book cover, and bind your book. Share the book with younger students in your school.

From Questions to Careers

PARK RANGER

The national parks of the United States and Canada preserve and protect many of the great treasures of these two countries. Some parks preserve natural wonders, like deep forests and unusual geological formations. Other parks preserve important historic sites. Some simply give people a place to picnic, play, and camp outside.

Many people work for the park services in all kinds of jobs. Tour guides show visitors around historic sites, telling the story of each place. Scientists and park rangers often work together to keep wildernesses healthy and to protect the original land, water, plants, and animals. Writers create brochures for park visitors. On top of all that, the parks always hire people to work in gift shops, visitor offices, and snack bars, to help the thousands of people who visit the parks every year.

▼ This United States park ranger shows the famous cracked Liberty Bell to visitors in Philadelphia, Pennsylvania.

Set Up a Weather Station Set up a weather station to measure and record your local weather as you read this book. Measure the temperature each day at the same time. Also record the amount of precipitation and wind direction. Record all of your findings in a weather log.

Each day, compare your local weather with the weather in other parts of the country. You can get this information from television, radio, the newspaper, or the Internet. When you have finished your measurements and recordings, create graphs to display your local readings. In the end, compare your findings with the climate map in the Activity Atlas.

Make a Time Line of Local History Create a time line of the history of your community. What do you know about it? When was it founded? What famous people have lived there? What important events have shaped its history?

Find the answers to these and other questions about the history of your town, village, city, or county. Read about its history at the local public library. Write down the dates and descriptions of the most important events. Try to find between 10 and 20 events. On a sheet of paper, list the events in the order in which they happened. Then, make a time line large enough to hang on the wall of your classroom. Draw a picture of each event and place it next to its description on the time line. Add several major events of United States history.

Create a Diorama Make a diorama that represents a physical map of the United States and Canada, or of a smaller geographic region within the two countries. Use clay or dough to sculpt the major geographic forms, such as mountain ranges, valleys, rivers, and large bodies of water. Make your diorama with as much detail as possible, showing forests, farms, towns, and other landscapes. You can use materials such as rocks, twigs, and miniature buildings. Make a key that explains what each material represents. Display your finished diorama for the class.

Reference

TABLE OF CONTENTS

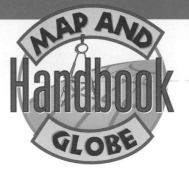

Table of Contents

This Map and Globe Handbook is designed to help you develop some of the skills you need to be a world explorer. These can help you whether you explore from the top of an elephant in India or from a computer at school.

You can use the information in this handbook to improve your map and globe skills. But the best way to sharpen your skills is to practice. The more you practice the better you'll get.

GEO CLEO and GEO LEO

Five Themes of Geography

Studying the geography of the entire world can be a huge task. You can make that task easier by using the five themes of geography: location, place, human-environment interaction, movement, and regions. The themes are tools you can use to organize information and to answer the where, why, and how of geography.

1 **Location** answers the question, "Where is it?" You can think of the location of a continent or a country as its address. You might give an absolute location such as "22 South Lake Street" or "40°N and 80°W." You might also use a relative address, telling where one place is by referring to another place. "Between school and the mall" and "eight miles east of Pleasant City" are examples of relative locations.

2 **Place** identifies the natural and human features that make one place different from every other place. You can identify a specific place by its landforms, climate, plants, animals, people, or cultures. You might even think of place as a geographic signature. Use the signature to help you understand the natural and human features that make one place different from every other place.

1. Location
Chicago, Illinois, occupies one location on the Earth. No other place has exactly the same absolute location.

2. Place
Ancient cultures in Egypt built distinctive pyramids. Use the theme of place to help you remember features that exist only in Egypt.

3 **Human-Environment Interaction** focuses on the relationship between people and the environment. As people live in an area, they often begin to make changes to it, usually to make their lives easier. For example, they might build a dam to control flooding during rainy seasons. Also, the environment can affect how people live, work, dress, travel, and communicate.

4 **Movement** answers the question "How do people, goods, and ideas move from place to place?" Remember that, often, what happens in one place can affect what happens in another. Use the theme of movement to help you trace the spread of goods, people, and ideas from one location to the next.

5 **Regions** is the last geographic theme. A region is a group of places that share common features. Geographers divide the world into many types of regions. For example, countries, states, and cities are political regions. The people in these places live under the same type of government. Other features can be used to define regions. Places that have the same climate belong to a particular climate region. Places that share the same culture belong to a cultural region. The same place can be found in more than one region. The state of Hawaii is in the political region of the United States. Because it has a tropical climate, Hawaii is also part of a tropical climate region.

PRACTICE YOUR WORLD EXPLORER SKILLS

❶ What is the absolute location of your school? What is one way to describe its relative location?

❷ What might be a "geographic signature" of the town or city you live in?

❸ Give an example of human-environment interaction where you live.

❹ Name at least one thing that comes into your town or city and one that goes out. How is each moved? Where does it come from? Where does it go?

❺ What are several regions you think your town or city belongs in?

3. Human-Environment Interaction
Peruvians have changed steep mountain slopes into terraces suitable for farming. Think how this environment looked before people made changes.

4. Movement
Arab traders brought not only goods to Kuala Lumpur, Malaysia, but also Arab building styles and the Islamic religion.

5. Regions
Wheat farming is an important activity in Kansas. This means that Kansas is part of a farming region.

Understanding Movements of the Earth

lanet Earth is part of our solar system. The Earth revolves around the sun in a nearly circular path called an orbit. A revolution, or one complete orbit around the sun, takes 365 1/4 days, or a year. As the Earth revolves around the sun, it is also spinning around in space. This movement is called a rotation. The Earth rotates on its axis—an invisible line through the center of the Earth from the North Pole to the South Pole. The Earth makes one full rotation about every 24 hours. As the Earth rotates, it is daytime on the side facing the sun. It is night on the side away from the sun.

The Earth's axis is tilted at an angle. Because of this tilt, sunlight strikes different parts of the Earth at certain points in the year, creating different seasons.

Earth's Revolution and the Seasons

Summer On June 21 or 22, the sun's direct rays are over the Tropic of Cancer. The Northern Hemisphere receives the greatest number of sunlight hours. It is the beginning of summer there.

Spring On March 20 or 21, the sun's rays shine strongest near the Equator. The Northern and Southern Hemispheres each receive almost equal hours of sunlight and darkness. It is the beginning of spring in the Northern Hemisphere.

Sun

Autumn On September 22 or 23, the sun's rays shine strongest near the Equator. Again, the Northern and Southern Hemispheres each receive almost equal hours of sunlight and darkness. It is the beginning of fall in the Northern Hemisphere.

Winter Around December 21, the sun is over the Tropic of Capricorn in the Southern Hemisphere. The Northern Hemisphere is tilted away from the sun and it is the beginning of winter there.

▲ **Location** This diagram shows how the Earth's tilt and orbit around the sun combine to create the seasons. Remember, in the Southern Hemisphere the seasons are reversed.

1 What causes the seasons in the Northern Hemisphere to be the opposite of those in the Southern Hemisphere?

2 During which two months of the year do the Northern and Southern Hemispheres have about equal hours of daylight and darkness?

Maps and Globes Represent the Earth

Globes

A globe is a scale model of the Earth. It shows the actual shapes, sizes, and locations of all the Earth's landmasses and bodies of water. Features on the surface of the Earth are drawn to scale on a globe. This means a smaller unit of measure on the globe stands for a larger unit of measure on the Earth.

Because a globe is made in the true shape of the Earth, it offers these advantages for studying the Earth.

- The shape of all land and water bodies are accurate.
- Compass directions from one point to any other point are correct.
- The distance from one location to another is always accurately represented.

However, a globe presents some disadvantages for studying the Earth. Because a globe shows the entire Earth, it cannot show small areas in great detail. Also, a globe is not easily folded and carried from one place to another. For these reasons, geographers often use maps to learn about the Earth.

Maps

A map is a drawing or representation, on a flat surface, of a region. A map can show details too small to be seen on a globe. Floor plans, mall directories, and road maps are among the maps we use most often.

While maps solve some of the problems posed by globes, they have some disadvantages of their own. Maps flatten the real round world. Mapmakers cut, stretch, push, and pull some parts of the Earth to get it all flat on paper. As a result, some locations may be distorted. That is, their size, shape, and relative location may not be accurate. For example, on most maps of the entire world, the size and shape of the Antarctic and Arctic regions are not accurate.

PRACTICE YOUR WORLD EXPLORER SKILLS

1. What is the main difference between a globe and a map?

2. What is one advantage of using a globe instead of a map?

Global Gores

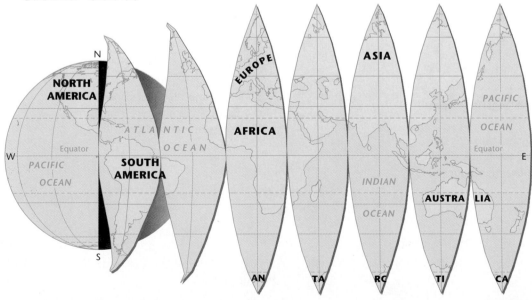

◀ Location
When mapmakers flatten the surface of the Earth, curves become straight lines. As a result, size, shape, and distance are distorted.

Locating Places on a Map or a Globe

The Hemispheres

Another name for a round ball like a globe is a sphere. The Equator, an imaginary line halfway between the North and South Poles, divides the globe into two hemispheres. (The prefix *hemi* means "half.") Land and water south of the Equator are in the Southern Hemisphere. Land and water north of the Equator are in the Northern Hemisphere.

Mapmakers sometimes divide the globe along an imaginary line that runs from North Pole to South Pole. This line, called the Prime Meridian, divides the globe into the Eastern and Western Hemispheres.

Northern Hemisphere

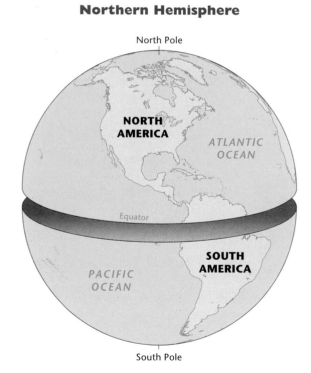

Southern Hemisphere

▲ The Equator divides the Northern Hemisphere from the Southern Hemisphere.

Western Hemisphere   **Eastern Hemisphere**

▲ The Prime Meridian divides the Eastern Hemisphere from the Western Hemisphere.

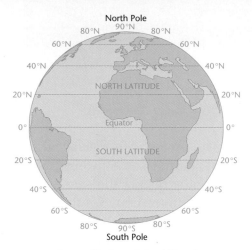

Parallels of Latitude

The Equator, at 0° latitude, is the starting place for measuring latitude or distances north and south. Most globes do not show every parallel of latitude. They may show every 10, 20, or even 30 degrees.

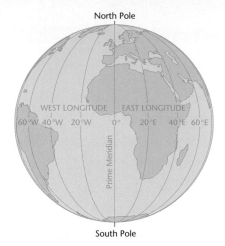

Meridians of Longitude

The Prime Meridian, at 0° longitude, runs from pole to pole through Greenwich, England. It is the starting place for measuring longitude or distances east and west. Each meridian of longitude meets its opposite longitude at the North and South Poles.

The Global Grid

Two sets of lines cover most globes. One set of lines runs parallel to the Equator. These lines, including the Equator, are called *parallels of latitude*. They are measured in degrees (°). One degree of latitude represents a distance of about 70 miles (112 km). The Equator has a location of 0°. The other parallels of latitude tell the direction and distance from the Equator to another location.

The second set of lines runs north and south. These lines are called *meridians of longitude*. Meridians show the degrees of longitude east or west of the Prime Meridian, which is located at 0°. A meridian of longitude tells the direction and distance from the Prime Meridian to another location. Unlike parallels, meridians are not the same distance apart everywhere on the globe.

Together the pattern of parallels of latitude and meridians of longitude is called the global grid. Using the lines of latitude and longitude, you can locate any place on Earth. For example, the location of 30° north latitude and 90° west longitude is usually written as 30°N, 90°W. Only one place on Earth has these coordinates—the city of New Orleans, in the state of Louisiana.

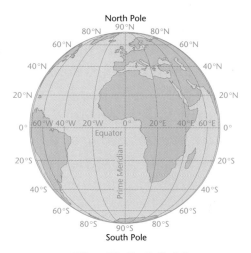

The Global Grid

By using lines of latitude and longitude, you can give the absolute location of any place on the Earth.

1. Which continents lie completely in the Northern Hemisphere? The Western Hemisphere?

2. Is there land or water at 20°S latitude and the Prime Meridian? At the Equator and 60°W longitude?

Map Projections

magine trying to flatten out a complete orange peel. The peel would split. The shape would change. You would have to cut the peel to get it to lie flat. In much the same way, maps cannot show the correct size and shape of every landmass or body of water on the Earth's curved surface. Maps shrink some places and stretch others. This shrinking and stretching is called distortion—*a change made to a shape.*

To make up for this disadvantage, mapmakers use different map projections. Each map projection is a way of showing the round Earth on flat paper. Each type of projection has some distortion. No one projection can accurately show the correct area, shape, distance, and direction for the Earth's surface. Mapmakers use the projection that has the least distortion for the information they are studying.

Same-Shape Maps

Some map projections can accurately show the shapes of landmasses. However, these projections often greatly distort the size of landmasses as well as the distance between them.

One of the most common same-shape maps is a Mercator projection, named for the mapmaker who invented it. The Mercator projection accurately shows shape and direction, but it distorts distance and size. In this projection, the northern and southern areas of the globe appear stretched more than areas near the Equator. Because the projection shows true directions, ships' navigators use it to chart a straight line course between two ports.

Mercator Projection

Equal-Area Maps

Some map projections can show the correct size of landmasses. Maps that use these projections are called equal-area maps. In order to show the correct size of landmasses, these maps usually distort shapes. The distortion is usually greater at the edges of the map and less at the center.

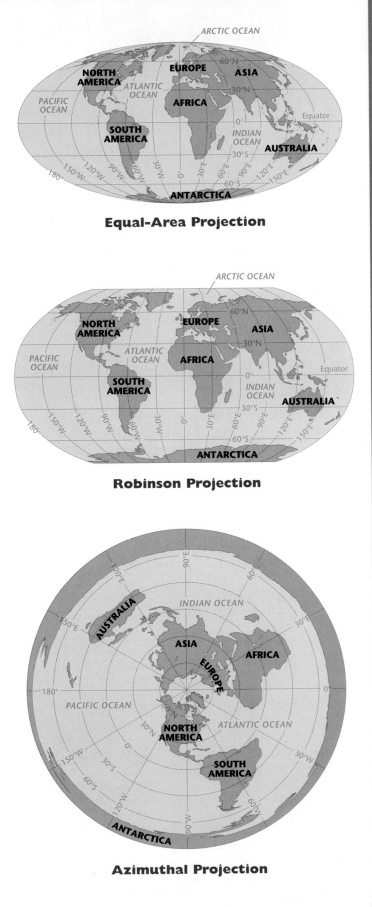

Equal-Area Projection

Robinson Maps

Many of the maps in this book use the Robinson projection. This is a compromise between the Mercator and equal-area projections. It gives a useful overall picture of the world. The Robinson projection keeps the size and shape relationships of most continents and oceans but does distort size of the polar regions.

Robinson Projection

Azimuthal Maps

Another kind of projection shows true compass direction. Maps that use this projection are called azimuthal maps. Such maps are easy to recognize—they are usually circular. Azimuthal maps are often used to show the areas of the North and South Poles. However, azimuthal maps distort scale, area, and shape.

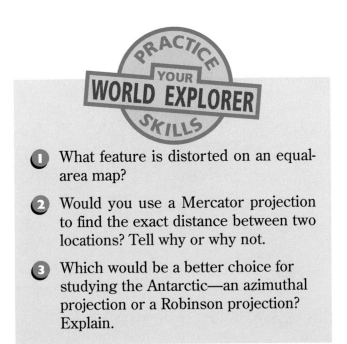

PRACTICE YOUR WORLD EXPLORER SKILLS

1. What feature is distorted on an equal-area map?

2. Would you use a Mercator projection to find the exact distance between two locations? Tell why or why not.

3. Which would be a better choice for studying the Antarctic—an azimuthal projection or a Robinson projection? Explain.

Azimuthal Projection

Parts of a Map

Mapmakers provide several clues to help you understand the information on a map. As an explorer, it is your job to read and interpret these clues.

Compass

Many maps show north at the top of the map. One way to show direction on a map is to use an arrow that points north. There may be an N shown with the arrow. Many maps give more information about direction by displaying a compass showing the directions, north, east, south, and west. The letters N, E, S, and W are placed to indicate these directions.

Title

The title of a map is the most basic clue. It signals what kinds of information you are likely to find on the map. A map titled *West Africa: Population Density* will be most useful for locating information about where people live in West Africa.

West Africa: Population Density

20°W 10°W 0° 10°E 20°E 30°E 40°E 50°E

Algiers Tunis
Rabat
Casablanca TUNISIA *Mediterranean Sea*
MOROCCO Tripoli
30°N
WESTERN SAHARA (MOROCCO) ALGERIA LIBYA

S A H A R A
CAPE VERDE MAURITANIA
Dakar MALI NIGER CHAD
SENEGAL
GAMBIA
GUINEA-BISSAU BURKINA FASO
10°N GUINEA NIGERIA
SIERRA LEONE CÔTE D'IVOIRE Abuja
Abidjan GHANA Ibadan
LIBERIA Accra Lagos CENTRAL AFRICAN REPUBLIC
TOGO BENIN CAMEROON
Equator EQUATORIAL GUINEA
SÃO TOMÉ AND PRÍNCIPE
GABON CONGO

ATLANTIC OCEAN

0   500   1,000 mi
0   500   1,000 km

20°W 10°W 0° 10°E 20°E

KEY

Persons per sq mi		Persons per sq km
520 and over		200 and over
260–519		100–199
130–259		50–99
25–129		10–49
1–24		1–9
Under 1		Under 1

Cities

◯	2,000,000–4,999,999
◉	1,000,000–1,999,999
●	250,000–999,999
○	Under 250,000

Lambert Azimuthal Equal-Area Projection

Scale

A map scale helps you find the actual distances between points shown on the map. You can measure the distance between any two points on the map, compare them to the scale, and find out the actual distance between the points. Most map scales show distances in both miles and kilometers.

Key

Often a map has a key, or legend, that shows the symbols used on the map and what each one means. On some maps, color is used as a symbol. On those maps, the key also tells the meaning of each color.

PRACTICE YOUR WORLD EXPLORER SKILLS

1 What part of a map tells you what the map is about?

2 Where on the map should you look to find out the meaning of this symbol? ●

3 What part of the map can you use to find the distance between two cities?

Comparing Maps of Different Scale

Here are three maps drawn to three different scales. The first map shows Moscow's location in the northeastern portion of Russia. This map shows the greatest area—a large section of northern Europe. It has the smallest scale (1 inch = about 900 miles) and shows the fewest details. This map can tell you what direction to travel to reach Moscow from Finland.

Find the red box on Map 1. It shows the whole area covered by Map 2. Study Map 2. It gives a closer look at the city of Moscow. It shows the features around the city, the city's boundary, and the general shape of the city. This map can help you find your way from the airport to the center of town.

Now find the red box on Map 2. This box shows the area shown on Map 3. This map moves you closer into the city. Like the zoom on a computer or camera, Map 3 shows the smallest area but has the greatest detail. This map has the largest scale (1 inch = about 0.8 miles). This is the map to use to explore downtown Moscow.

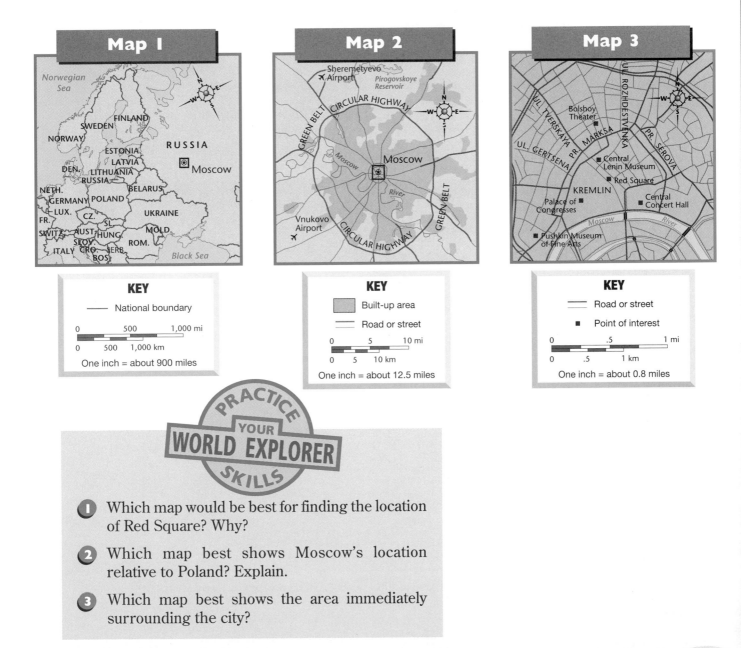

Map 1

Map 2

Map 3

KEY

National boundary

0   500   1,000 mi
0   500   1,000 km

One inch = about 900 miles

KEY

Built-up area

Road or street

0   5   10 mi
0   5   10 km

One inch = about 12.5 miles

KEY

Road or street

■ Point of interest

0   .5   1 mi
0   .5   1 km

One inch = about 0.8 miles

PRACTICE YOUR WORLD EXPLORER SKILLS

1. Which map would be best for finding the location of Red Square? Why?

2. Which map best shows Moscow's location relative to Poland? Explain.

3. Which map best shows the area immediately surrounding the city?

Political Maps

Mapmakers create maps to show all kinds of information. The kind of information presented affects the way a map looks. One type of map is called a political map. Its main purpose is to show continents, countries, and divisions within countries such as states or provinces. Usually different colors are used to show different countries or divisions within a country. The colors do not have any special meaning. They are used only to make the map easier to read.

Political maps also show where people have built towns and cities. Symbols can help you tell capital cities from other cities and towns. Even though political maps do not give information that shows what the land looks like, they often include some physical features such as oceans, lakes, and rivers.

Political maps usually have many labels. They give country names, and the names of capital and major cities. Bodies of water such as lakes, rivers, oceans, seas, gulfs, and bays are also labeled.

PRACTICE YOUR WORLD EXPLORER SKILLS

1 What symbol shows the continental boundary?

2 What symbol is used to indicate a capital city? A major city?

3 What kinds of landforms are shown on this map?

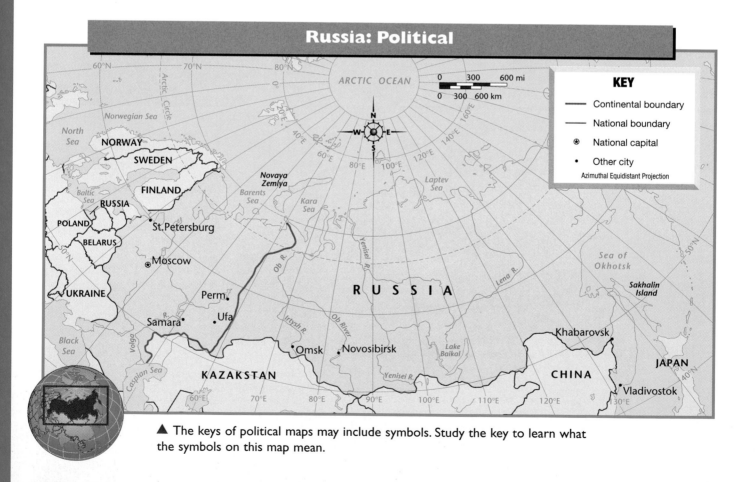

Russia: Political

KEY

— Continental boundary

— National boundary

⊛ National capital

• Other city

Azimuthal Equidistant Projection

▲ The keys of political maps may include symbols. Study the key to learn what the symbols on this map mean.

Physical Maps

Like political maps, physical maps show country labels and labels for capital cities. However, physical maps also show what the land of a region looks like by showing the major physical features such as plains, hills, plateaus, or mountains. Labels give the names of features such as mountain peaks, mountains, plateaus, and river basins.

In order to tell one landform from another, physical maps often show elevation and relief.

Elevation is the height of the land above sea level. Physical maps in this book use color to show elevation. Browns and oranges show higher lands while blues and greens show lands that are at or below sea level.

Relief shows how quickly the land rises or falls. Hills, mountains, and plateaus are shown on relief maps using shades of gray. Level or nearly level land is shown without shading. Darkly shaded areas indicate steeper lands.

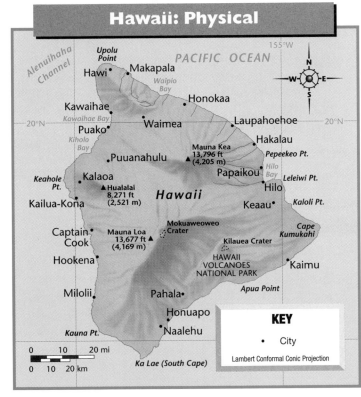

Hawaii: Physical

▲ On a physical map, shading is sometimes used to show relief. Use the shading to locate the moutains in Hawaii.

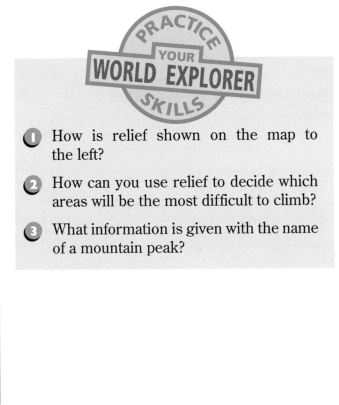

1. How is relief shown on the map to the left?

2. How can you use relief to decide which areas will be the most difficult to climb?

3. What information is given with the name of a mountain peak?

▼ Mauna Kea, an extinct volcano, is the highest peak in the state of Hawaii. Find Mauna Kea on the map.

Special Purpose Maps

As you explore the world, you will encounter many different kinds of special purpose maps. For example, a road map is a special purpose map. The title of each special purpose map tells the purpose and content of the map. Usually a special purpose map highlights only one kind of information. Examples of special purpose maps include land use, population distribution, recreation, transportation, natural resources, or weather.

The key on a special purpose map is very important. Even though a special purpose map shows only one kind of information, it may present many different pieces of data. This data can be shown in symbols, colors, or arrows. In this way, the key acts like a dictionary for the map.

Reading a special purpose map is a skill in itself. Look at the map below. First, try to get an overall sense of what it shows. Then, study the map to identify its main ideas. For example, one main idea of this map is that much of the petroleum production in the region takes place around the Persian Gulf.

1. What part of a special purpose map tells what information is contained on the map?

2. What part of a special purpose map acts like a dictionary for the map?

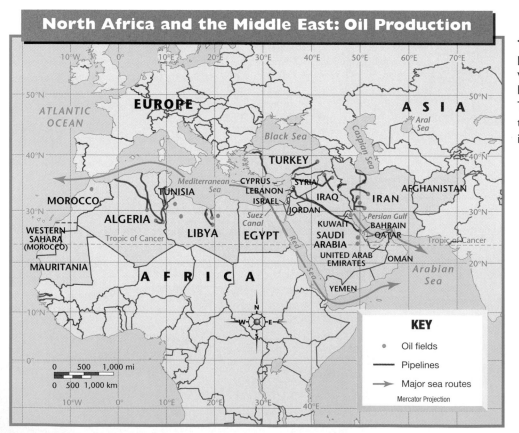

North Africa and the Middle East: Oil Production

KEY
- Oil fields
- Pipelines
- Major sea routes

Mercator Projection

◀ The title on a special purpose map indicates what information can be found on the map. The symbols used on the map are explained in the map's key.

Landforms, Climate Regions, and Natural Vegetation Regions

Maps that show landforms, climate, and vegetation regions are special purpose maps. Unlike the boundary lines on a political map, the boundary lines on these maps do not separate the land into exact divisions. A tropical wet climate gradually changes to a tropical wet and dry climate. A tundra gradually changes to an ice cap. Even though the boundaries between regions may not be exact, the information on these maps can help you understand the region and the lives of people in it.

Landforms

Understanding how people use the land requires an understanding of the shape of the land itself. The four most important landforms are mountains, hills, plateaus, and plains. Human activity in every region in the world is influenced by these landforms.

- **Mountains** are high and steep. Most are wide at the bottom and rise to a narrow peak or ridge. Most geographers classify a mountain as land that rises at least 2,000 feet (610 m) above sea level. A series of mountains is called a mountain range.

- **Hills** rise above surrounding land and have rounded tops. Hills are lower and usually less steep than mountains. The elevation of surrounding land determines whether a landform is called a mountain or a hill.

- A **plateau** is a large, mostly flat area of land that rises above the surrounding land. At least one side of a plateau has a steep slope.

- **Plains** are large areas of flat or gently rolling land. Plains have few changes in elevation. Many plains areas are located along coasts. Others are located in the interior regions of some continents.

▶ A satellite view of the Earth showing North and South America. What landforms are visible in the photograph?

Climate Regions

   Another important influence in the ways people live their lives is the climate of their region. Climate is the weather of a given location over a long period of time. Use the descriptions in the table below to help you visualize the climate regions shown on maps.

Climate	Temperatures	Precipitation
Tropical		
Tropical wet	Hot all year round	Heavy all year round
Tropical wet and dry	Hot all year round	Heavy when sun is overhead, dry other times
Dry		
Semiarid	Hot summers, mild to cold winters	Light
Arid	Hot days, cold nights	Very light
Mild		
Mediterranean	Hot summers, cool winters	Dry summers, wet winters
Humid subtropical	Hot summers, cool winters	Year round, heavier in summer than in winter
Marine west coast	Warm summers, cool winters	Year round, heavier in winter than in summer
Continental		
Humid continental	Hot summers, cold winters	Year round, heavier in summer than in winter
Subarctic	Cool summers, cold winters	Light
Polar		
Tundra	Cool summers, very cold winters	Light
Ice Cap	Cold all year round	Light
Highlands	Varies, depending on altitude and direction of prevailing winds	Varies, depending on altitude and direction of prevailing winds

Natural Vegetation Regions

Natural vegetation is the plant life that grows wild without the help of humans. A world vegetation map tells what the vegetation in a place would be if people had not cut down forests or cleared grasslands. The table below provides descriptions of natural vegetation regions shown on maps. Comparing climate and vegetation regions can help you see the close relationship between climate and vegetation.

Vegetation	Description
Tropical rain forest	Tall, close-growing trees forming a canopy over smaller trees, dense growth in general
Deciduous forest	Trees and plants that regularly lose their leaves after each growing season
Mixed forest	Both leaf-losing and cone-bearing trees, no type of tree dominant
Coniferous forest	Cone-bearing trees, evergreen trees and plants
Mediterranean vegetation	Evergreen shrubs and small plants
Tropical savanna	Tall grasses with occasional trees and shrubs
Temperate grassland	Tall grasses with occasional stands of trees
Desert scrub	Low shrubs and bushes, hardy plants
Desert	Little or no vegetation
Tundra	Low shrubs, mosses, lichens; no trees
Ice Cap	No vegetation
Highlands	Varies, depending on altitude and direction of prevailing winds

PRACTICE YOUR WORLD EXPLORER SKILLS

 1 How are mountains and hills similar? How are they different?

2 What is the difference between a plateau and a plain?

Atlas

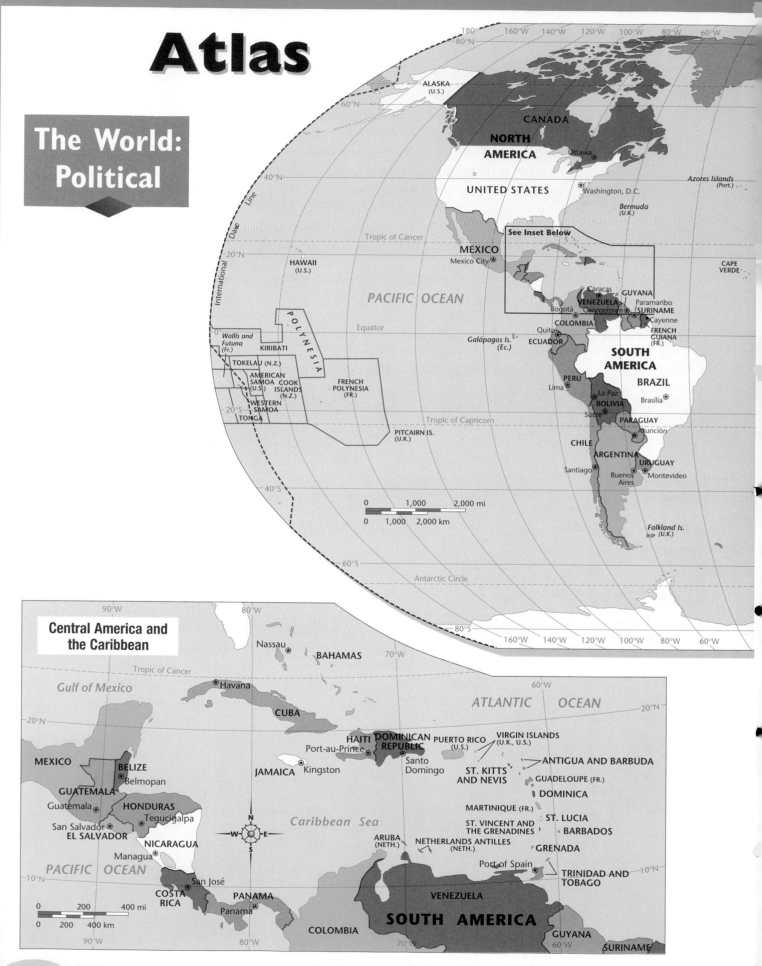

The World: Political

ALASKA (U.S.)

CANADA

NORTH AMERICA

Ottawa

UNITED STATES

Washington, D.C.

Azores Islands (Port.)

Bermuda (U.K.)

Tropic of Cancer

See Inset Below

MEXICO

Mexico City

CAPE VERDE

Caracas GUYANA

VENEZUELA Paramaribo

Bogotá Georgetown SURINAME

COLOMBIA Cayenne

FRENCH GUIANA (FR.)

Quito

Galápagos Is. (Ec.) ECUADOR

SOUTH AMERICA

PERU

Lima

BRAZIL

La Paz

BOLIVIA Brasília

Sucre

PARAGUAY

CHILE Asunción

ARGENTINA URUGUAY

Santiago Buenos Aires Montevideo

Falkland Is. (U.K.)

PACIFIC OCEAN

Equator

HAWAII (U.S.)

International Date Line

POLYNESIA

Wallis and Futuna (Fr.)

KIRIBATI

TOKELAU (N.Z.)

AMERICAN SAMOA (U.S.) COOK ISLANDS (N.Z.)

FRENCH POLYNESIA (FR.)

WESTERN SAMOA

TONGA

Tropic of Capricorn

PITCAIRN IS. (U.K.)

| 0 | 1,000 | 2,000 mi |
| 0 | 1,000 | 2,000 km |

Antarctic Circle

Central America and the Caribbean

Tropic of Cancer

Nassau

BAHAMAS

Gulf of Mexico

Havana

CUBA

ATLANTIC OCEAN

HAITI DOMINICAN REPUBLIC PUERTO RICO (U.S.) VIRGIN ISLANDS (U.K., U.S.)

Port-au-Prince

MEXICO

BELIZE

Belmopan

JAMAICA Kingston

Santo Domingo

ANTIGUA AND BARBUDA

ST. KITTS AND NEVIS GUADELOUPE (FR.)

GUATEMALA

Guatemala

DOMINICA

HONDURAS

Tegucigalpa

MARTINIQUE (FR.) ST. LUCIA

San Salvador

EL SALVADOR

Caribbean Sea

ST. VINCENT AND THE GRENADINES BARBADOS

NICARAGUA

Managua

ARUBA (NETH.)

NETHERLANDS ANTILLES (NETH.) GRENADA

PACIFIC OCEAN

Port of Spain TRINIDAD AND TOBAGO

COSTA RICA

San José

PANAMA

Panama

VENEZUELA

SOUTH AMERICA

COLOMBIA GUYANA

SURINAME

| 0 | 200 | 400 mi |
| 0 | 200 | 400 km |

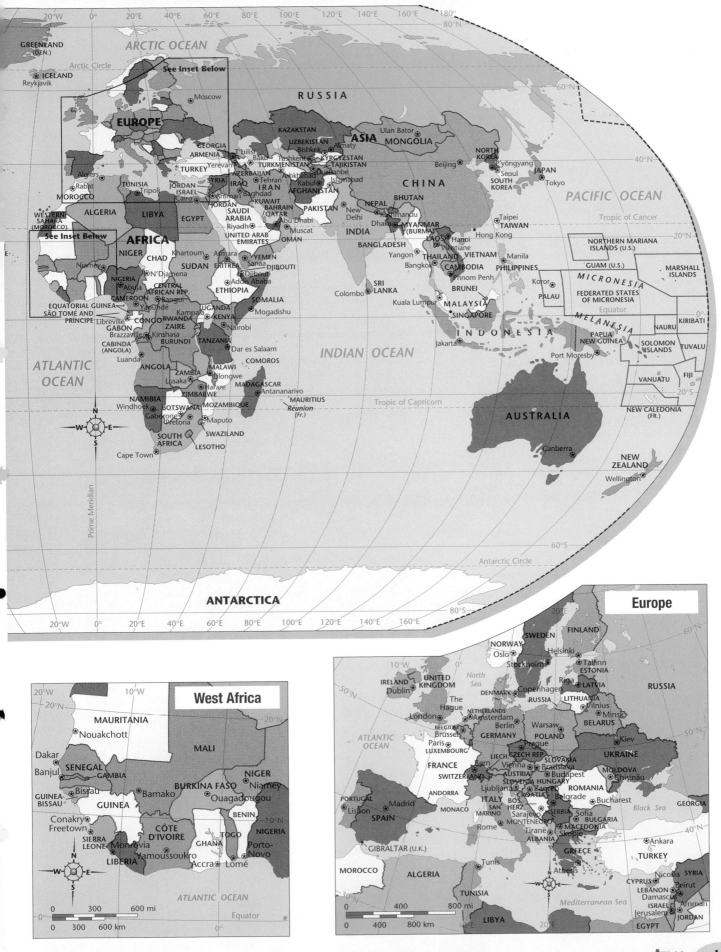

ARCTIC OCEAN

GREENLAND
(DEN.)

ICELAND
Reykjavik

Arctic Circle

Moscow

RUSSIA

EUROPE

ASIA

KAZAKSTAN

GEORGIA
ARMENIA
T'bilisi
Baku
Tashkent
KYRGYZSTAN
Almaty

MONGOLIA
Ulan Bator

TURKEY
Yerevan
AZERBAIJAN
SYRIA
TURKMENISTAN
TAJIKISTAN

Algiers
Rabat
TUNISIA
Tripoli
JORDAN
ISRAEL
Cairo
IRAQ
Baghdad
Amman
Tehran
Kabul
Ashkhabad
Dushanbe
Islamabad

NORTH
KOREA
Beijing
P'yǒngyang
SOUTH
KOREA
Seoul
JAPAN
Tokyo

MOROCCO

WESTERN
SAHARA
(MOROCCO)

ALGERIA
LIBYA
EGYPT

SAUDI
ARABIA
Riyadh
KUWAIT
BAHRAIN
QATAR
Abu Dhabi
UNITED ARAB
EMIRATES
OMAN
Muscat

AFGHANISTAN
IRAN

PAKISTAN
New
Delhi
NEPAL
Kathmandu
BHUTAN
Dhaka

CHINA

Taipei
TAIWAN

PACIFIC OCEAN

Tropic of Cancer

See Inset Below

AFRICA
NIGER
CHAD
Khartoum
SUDAN
Asmara
ERITREA
YEMEN
Sanaa
DJIBOUTI
Djibouti

INDIA
BANGLADESH
MYANMAR
(BURMA)
Yangon
LAOS
Hanoi
Vientiane
Hong Kong
Manila

NORTHERN MARIANA
ISLANDS (U.S.)

GUAM (U.S.)

MARSHALL
ISLANDS

Niamey
NIGERIA
Abuja
N'Djamena
CENTRAL
AFRICAN REP.
Bangui
CAMEROON
Yaoundé
ETHIOPIA
Addis Ababa
SOMALIA
Mogadishu

THAILAND
VIETNAM
Bangkok
CAMBODIA
Phnom Penh
PHILIPPINES
BRUNEI
Kuala Lumpur
MALAYSIA
SINGAPORE

MICRONESIA

Koror
PALAU
FEDERATED STATES
OF MICRONESIA

Equator

KIRIBATI

See Inset Below

EQUATORIAL GUINEA
SÃO TOMÉ AND
PRÍNCIPE
Libreville
GABON
CONGO
Brazzaville
Kinshasa
ZAIRE
BURUNDI
RWANDA
UGANDA
Kampala
KENYA
Nairobi
TANZANIA
Dar es Salaam
Colombo
SRI
LANKA

INDONESIA

Jakarta

MELANESIA

PAPUA
NEW GUINEA
Port Moresby

SOLOMON
ISLANDS

NAURU

TUVALU

ATLANTIC
OCEAN

Luanda
CABINDA
(ANGOLA)
ANGOLA
ZAMBIA
Lusaka
MALAWI
Lilongwe
COMOROS

INDIAN OCEAN

VANUATU

FIJI

NEW CALEDONIA
(FR.)

NAMIBIA
Windhoek
BOTSWANA
Gaborone
ZIMBABWE
Harare
MOZAMBIQUE
MADAGASCAR
Antananarivo
MAURITIUS
Réunion
(Fr.)

Tropic of Capricorn

AUSTRALIA

Pretoria
Maputo
SWAZILAND
SOUTH
AFRICA
LESOTHO

Cape Town

Canberra

NEW
ZEALAND

Wellington

Prime Meridian

ANTARCTICA

Antarctic Circle

Europe

NORWAY
Oslo
SWEDEN
FINLAND
Helsinki
Stockholm

IRELAND
Dublin
UNITED
KINGDOM
North
Sea
ESTONIA
Tallinn
Riga
LATVIA
RUSSIA

DENMARK
Copenhagen
LITHUANIA
Vilnius
Minsk
BELARUS

The Hague
London
NETHERLANDS
Amsterdam
Berlin
Warsaw
POLAND
Kiev
UKRAINE

ATLANTIC
OCEAN

BELGIUM
Brussels
GERMANY
Prague
LUXEMBOURG
Paris
LIECH.
CZECH REP.
SLOVAKIA
MOLDOVA
Chișinău

FRANCE
Bern
Vienna
Bratislava
Budapest
SWITZERLAND
AUSTRIA
HUNGARY
SLOVENIA
ROMANIA
Bucharest

PORTUGAL
Lisbon
ANDORRA
Madrid
Ljubljana
Zagreb
CROATIA
BOS.
HERZ.
Belgrade
SERBIA
Sofia
BULGARIA
GEORGIA

SPAIN
MONACO
ITALY
SAN
MARINO
Rome
Sarajevo
MONTENEGRO
Tirane
ALBANIA
MACEDONIA
Skopje
Ankara
Black Sea

GIBRALTAR (U.K.)
Tunis
GREECE
Athens
TURKEY
Nicosia
CYPRUS
SYRIA
Beirut
LEBANON

MOROCCO
ALGERIA
Mediterranean Sea
ISRAEL
Jerusalem
Amman
JORDAN

TUNISIA
LIBYA
EGYPT

West Africa

MAURITANIA
Nouakchott

MALI

Dakar
SENEGAL
GAMBIA
Banjul
Bissau
GUINEA-
BISSAU
GUINEA
NIGER
Niamey
BURKINA FASO
Bamako
Ouagadougou
BENIN
Conakry
Freetown
SIERRA
LEONE
CÔTE
D'IVOIRE
GHANA
TOGO
NIGERIA
Porto-
Novo
Monrovia
Yamoussoukro
Accra
Lomé
LIBERIA

ATLANTIC OCEAN

Equator

0   300   600 mi

0   300   600 km

0   400   800 mi

0   400   800 km

The World: Physical

ARCTIC OCEAN
80°N
GREENLAND (DEN.)
Beaufort Sea
Yukon R.
Mackenzie R.
60°N
Bering Sea
Hudson Bay
CANADIAN SHIELD
ROCKY MOUNTAINS
GREAT PLAINS
NORTH AMERICA
Aleutian Islands
40°N
Missouri R.
Great Lakes
St. Lawrence R.
APPALACHIAN MTS.
Colorado R.
Mississippi R.
ATLANTIC OCEAN
Hawaiian Islands
Tropic of Cancer
SIERRA MADRE OCCIDENTAL
Rio Grande
SIERRA MADRE ORIENTAL
Gulf of Mexico
20°N
West Indies
Caribbean Sea
PACIFIC OCEAN
Orinoco R.
GUIANA HIGHLANDS
P O L Y N E S I A
Equator
0°
AMAZON BASIN
Amazon R.
SOUTH AMERICA
ANDES MOUNTAINS
BRAZILIAN HIGHLANDS
20°S
Tropic of Capricorn
PAMPAS
Rio de la Plata
40°S
PATAGONIA
Cape Horn
Drake Passage
60°S
Antarctic Circle
ANTARCTIC PENINSULA
80°S
180° 160°W 140°W 120°W 100°W 80°W 60°W
160°W 140°W 120°W 100°W 80°W 60°W

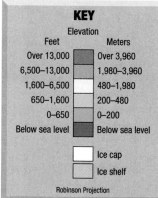

KEY

Elevation

Feet	Meters
Over 13,000	Over 3,960
6,500–13,000	1,980–3,960
1,600–6,500	480–1,980
650–1,600	200–480
0–650	0–200
Below sea level	Below sea level
	Ice cap
	Ice shelf

Robinson Projection

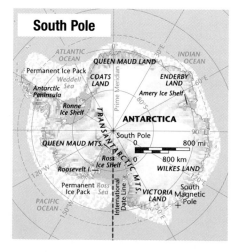

South Pole

ATLANTIC OCEAN
0°
QUEEN MAUD LAND
INDIAN OCEAN
Permanent Ice Pack
COATS LAND
ENDERBY LAND
Weddell Sea
Antarctic Peninsula
Amery Ice Shelf
Prime Meridian
Ronne Ice Shelf
TRANSANTARCTIC MTS.
ANTARCTICA
South Pole
90°E
QUEEN MAUD MTS.
0   800 mi
0   800 km
WILKES LAND
Roosevelt I.
Ross Ice Shelf
VICTORIA LAND
South Magnetic Pole
Permanent Ice Pack
Ross Sea
International Date Line
PACIFIC OCEAN

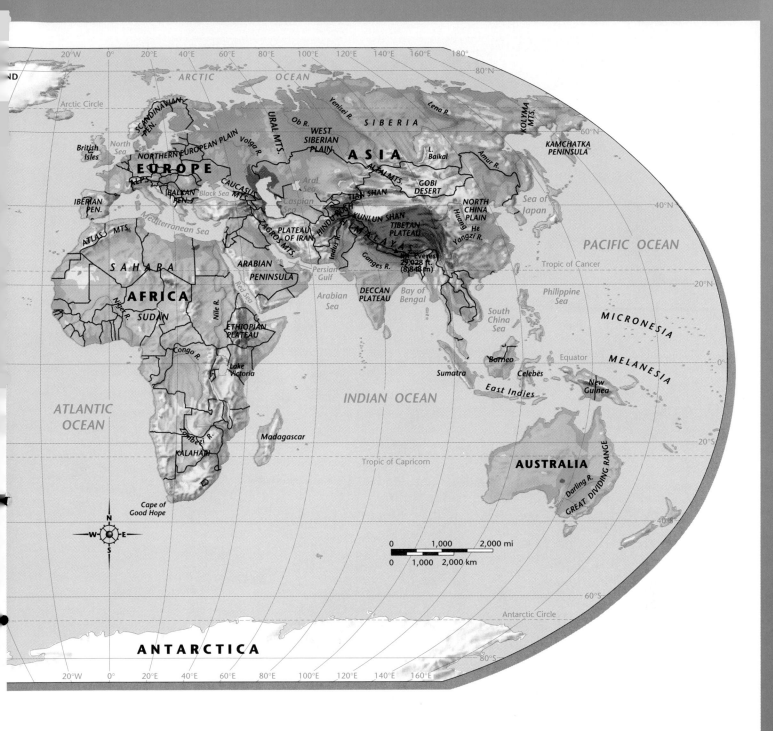

ARCTIC OCEAN

20°W 0° 20°E 40°E 60°E 80°E 100°E 120°E 140°E 160°E 180°

80°N

Arctic Circle

SCANDINAVIAN PEN.

British Isles

North Sea

SIBERIA

Yenisei R. Lena R.

Ob R.

WEST SIBERIAN PLAIN

URAL MTS.

KOLYMA MTS.

60°N

NORTHERN EUROPEAN PLAIN

Volga R.

KAMCHATKA PENINSULA

ASIA

EUROPE

L. Baikal

Amur R.

ALPS

CAUCASUS MTS.

Aral Sea

ALTAI MTS.

GOBI DESERT

40°N

BALKAN PEN.

Black Sea

Caspian Sea

TIAN SHAN

Sea of Japan

IBERIAN PEN.

NORTH CHINA PLAIN

ZAGROS MTS.

HINDU KUSH

KUNLUN SHAN

ATLAS MTS.

Mediterranean Sea

PLATEAU OF IRAN

TIBETAN PLATEAU

Huang He

PACIFIC OCEAN

HIMALAYAS

Indus R.

Yangzi R.

SAHARA

ARABIAN PENINSULA

Ganges R.

Tropic of Cancer

Mt. Everest 29,028 ft. (8,848 m)

20°N

AFRICA

Red Sea

Persian Gulf

DECCAN PLATEAU

Bay of Bengal

Philippine Sea

Nile R.

Niger R.

SUDAN

Arabian Sea

MICRONESIA

ETHIOPIAN PLATEAU

South China Sea

Congo R.

Borneo

Celebes

Equator

MELANESIA

Lake Victoria

Sumatra

New Guinea

0°

INDIAN OCEAN

East Indies

ATLANTIC OCEAN

Zambezi R.

Madagascar

20°S

KALAHARI

Tropic of Capricorn

AUSTRALIA

GREAT DIVIDING RANGE

Darling R.

Cape of Good Hope

N
W   E
S

40°S

0 1,000 2,000 mi

0 1,000 2,000 km

60°S

Antarctic Circle

ANTARCTICA

80°S

20°W 0° 20°E 40°E 60°E 80°E 100°E 120°E 140°E 160°E

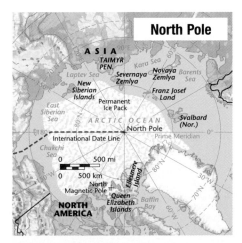

North Pole

ASIA

TAIMYR PEN.

Laptev Sea

Kara Sea

Severnaya Zemlya

Novaya Zemlya

Barents Sea

New Siberian Islands

Franz Josef Land

East Siberian Sea

Permanent Ice Pack

Svalbard (Nor.)

ARCTIC OCEAN

North Pole

International Date Line

Prime Meridian

Chukchi Sea

0 500 mi

0 500 km

North Magnetic Pole

Ellesmere Island

Queen Elizabeth Islands

Baffin Bay

NORTH AMERICA

United States: Political

RUSSIA

ARCTIC OCEAN

Arctic Circle

70°N

70°N

ALASKA

Yukon River

CANADA

60°N

N
W-E
S

Anchorage

Bering Sea

Gulf of Alaska

Juneau

0   250   500 mi
0   250   500 km

160°W

140°W

PACIFIC OCEAN

50°N

120°W

110°W

WASHINGTON

Seattle

Olympia

Spokane

River

Columbia

Missouri River

Minot

Bismarck

Portland

Salem

Helena

MONTANA

OREGON

IDAHO

Billings

Klamath Falls

Boise

Sheridan

Pierre

Eureka

40°N

Snake River

Jackson

Rapid City

Twin Falls

WYOMING

Winnemucca

Great Salt Lake

Cheyenne

NEBRASKA

Carson City

Salt Lake City

Sacramento

NEVADA

UTAH

Denver

San Francisco

Grand Junction

COLORADO

Pueblo

Cedar City

Colorado River

Arkans

CALIFORNIA

Las Vegas

PACIFIC OCEAN

Los Angeles

Albuquerque

Santa Fe

ARIZONA

NEW MEXICO

San Diego

Phoenix

Rio Grande

Roswell

Tucson

El Paso

160°W

155°W

Honolulu

N
W-E
S

PACIFIC OCEAN

HAWAII

20°N

20°N

Hilo

MEXICO

0   50   100 mi
0   50   100 km

155°W

120°W

Tropic of Cancer

110°W

CANADA

90°W   80°W   70°W

MAINE
Presque Isle
Augusta
Portland

NORTH DAKOTA

Duluth

Sault Ste. Marie

MINNESOTA

MICHIGAN

Lake Superior

Lake Huron

Montpelier
VERMONT
NEW HAMPSHIRE
Concord
Boston

NEW YORK
Albany
MASSACHUSETTS
Providence
RHODE ISLAND
Hartford
CONNECTICUT
New Haven

SOUTH DAKOTA

Minneapolis   St. Paul
WISCONSIN

Milwaukee   Lansing
Madison   Detroit

Chicago

Lake Michigan

Lake Ontario

Lake Erie
Cleveland

Buffalo

PENNSYLVANIA
Harrisburg
Pittsburgh

New York City
Trenton
NEW JERSEY
Philadelphia

Dover
Baltimore   Annapolis   **DELAWARE**

40°N

IOWA
Cedar Rapids
Des Moines

Omaha
Lincoln

INDIANA
Indianapolis

OHIO
Columbus

Washington, D.C.

MARYLAND

ILLINOIS
Springfield

Cincinnati
WEST VIRGINIA
Charleston
Richmond
VIRGINIA
Norfolk

Topeka   Kansas City
KANSAS
Jefferson City
Wichita   **MISSOURI**

St. Louis
Louisville   Frankfort

KENTUCKY

Ohio River

Tennessee River

Raleigh

NORTH CAROLINA
Charlotte

Nashville
TENNESSEE
Memphis

Columbia

Tulsa
OKLAHOMA
ARKANSAS
Oklahoma City   Little Rock
Pine Bluff

Mississippi River

SOUTH CAROLINA
Charleston

Atlanta

Red River

Birmingham
MISSISSIPPI   **ALABAMA**
Jackson
Montgomery

GEORGIA
Columbus
Savannah

Dallas

TEXAS

Shreveport

Hattiesburg

Jacksonville

30°N

Austin

Baton Rouge   Tallahassee
LOUISIANA
New Orleans

FLORIDA

San Antonio   Houston

Gulf   of   Mexico

Tampa
Lake Okeechobee

ATLANTIC OCEAN

N
W · E
S

Miami

KEY

—— National boundary
—— State boundary
✪ National capital
✪ State capital
• Other city

Transverse Mercator Projection

Rio Grande

North and South America: Political

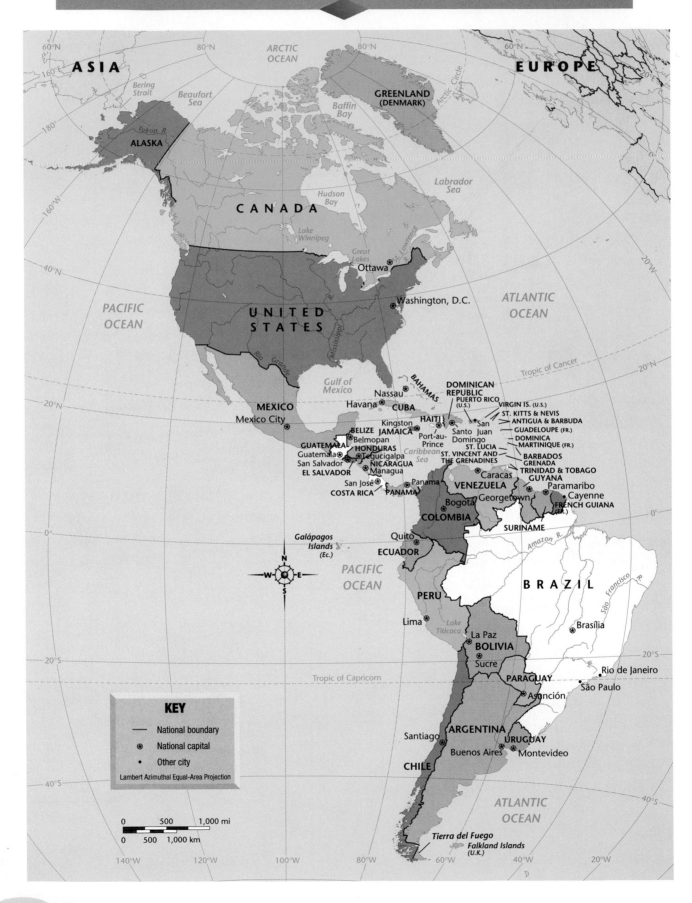

ASIA

Bering Strait

Beaufort Sea

ARCTIC OCEAN

GREENLAND (DENMARK)

EUROPE

ALASKA

Yukon R.

Baffin Bay

Labrador Sea

C A N A D A

Hudson Bay

Lake Winnipeg

Great Lakes

St. Lawrence

⊛ Ottawa

PACIFIC OCEAN

U N I T E D S T A T E S

Mississippi

• Washington, D.C.

ATLANTIC OCEAN

Rio Grande

Gulf of Mexico

BAHAMAS

Nassau

Tropic of Cancer

DOMINICAN REPUBLIC

PUERTO RICO (U.S.)

VIRGIN IS. (U.S.)

MEXICO

Havana

CUBA

ST. KITTS & NEVIS

ANTIGUA & BARBUDA

⊛ Mexico City

Kingston

HAITI

San Juan

GUADELOUPE (FR.)

BELIZE

JAMAICA

Port-au-Prince

Santo Domingo

DOMINICA

MARTINIQUE (FR.)

GUATEMALA

Belmopan

Caribbean Sea

ST. LUCIA

HONDURAS

Tegucigalpa

ST. VINCENT AND THE GRENADINES

BARBADOS

GRENADA

Guatemala ⊛

NICARAGUA

San Salvador

Managua

TRINIDAD & TOBAGO

EL SALVADOR

Caracas

GUYANA

San José ⊛

Panama

VENEZUELA

Paramaribo

Cayenne

COSTA RICA

PANAMA

Georgetown

FRENCH GUIANA (FR.)

Bogotá

COLOMBIA

SURINAME

Galápagos Islands (Ec.)

Quito

0°

ECUADOR

Amazon R.

PACIFIC OCEAN

B R A Z I L

São Francisco R.

PERU

Lima

Lake Titicaca

La Paz

BOLIVIA

Brasília •

Sucre

Tropic of Capricorn

PARAGUAY

Rio de Janeiro •

Asunción ⊛

São Paulo •

KEY

— National boundary

⊛ National capital

• Other city

Lambert Azimuthal Equal-Area Projection

ARGENTINA

Santiago

URUGUAY

Buenos Aires

Montevideo

CHILE

ATLANTIC OCEAN

0 500 1,000 mi

0 500 1,000 km

Tierra del Fuego

Falkland Islands (U.K.)

North and South America: Physical

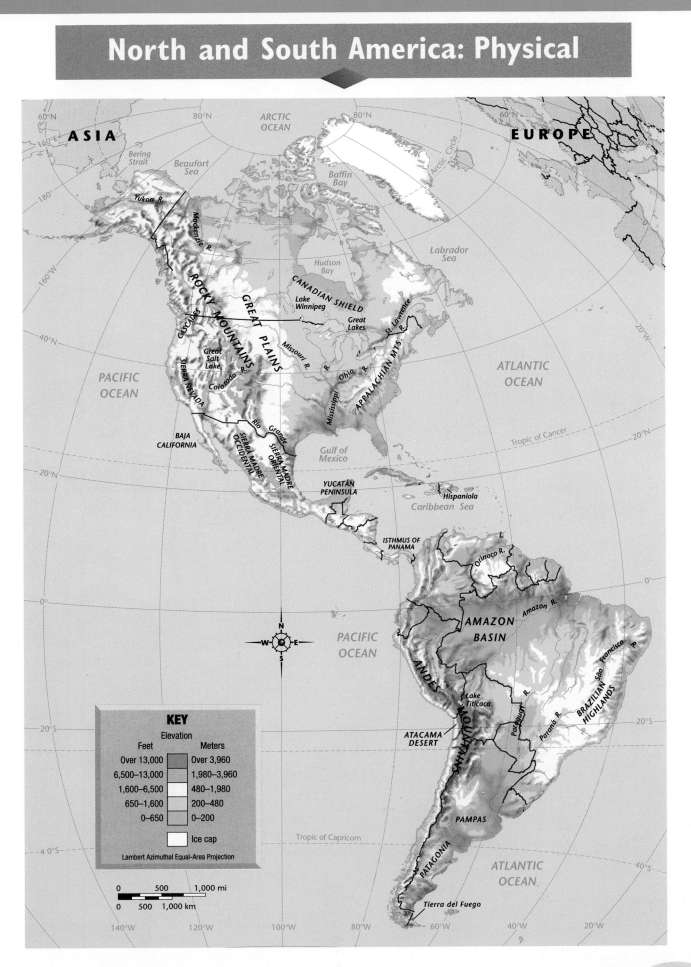

ASIA

EUROPE

ARCTIC OCEAN

60°N · 80°N · 80°N · 60°N

160°E

180°

Bering Strait

Beaufort Sea

Baffin Bay

Arctic Circle

20°W

Yukon R.

Mackenzie R.

ROCKY MOUNTAINS

CASCADES

GREAT PLAINS

CANADIAN SHIELD

Hudson Bay

Lake Winnipeg

Great Lakes

Labrador Sea

St. Lawrence R.

APPALACHIAN MTS.

40°N

160°W

PACIFIC OCEAN

SIERRA NEVADA

Great Salt Lake

Colorado R.

Missouri R.

Mississippi R.

Ohio R.

ATLANTIC OCEAN

20°W

BAJA CALIFORNIA

SIERRA MADRE OCCIDENTAL

Rio Grande

SIERRA MADRE ORIENTAL

Gulf of Mexico

Tropic of Cancer

20°N

YUCATÁN PENINSULA

Hispaniola

Caribbean Sea

ISTHMUS OF PANAMA

Orinoco R.

0°

AMAZON BASIN

Amazon R.

PACIFIC OCEAN

ANDES

São Francisco R.

Lake Titicaca

Paraguay R.

Paraná R.

BRAZILIAN HIGHLANDS

20°S

20°S

KEY

Elevation

Feet	Meters
Over 13,000	Over 3,960
6,500–13,000	1,980–3,960
1,600–6,500	480–1,980
650–1,600	200–480
0–650	0–200
Ice cap	

Lambert Azimuthal Equal-Area Projection

ATACAMA DESERT

ANDES MOUNTAINS

PAMPAS

Tropic of Capricorn

PATAGONIA

ATLANTIC OCEAN

40°S

0   500   1,000 mi

0   500   1,000 km

Tierra del Fuego

140°W   120°W   100°W   80°W   60°W   40°W   20°W

Europe: Political

KEY

— National boundary
⊗ National capital
• Other city

Lambert Azimuthal Equal-Area Projection

ARCTIC OCEAN

Arctic Circle

ICELAND
Reykjavik

Faeroe Is. (Den.)

Shetland Is. (U.K.)

ATLANTIC OCEAN

Prime Meridian

FINLAND

Gulf of Bothnia

SWEDEN

NORWAY
Lillehammer
Oslo
Göteborg

Turku   Helsinki   St. Petersburg

Stockholm   Tallinn   ESTONIA   RUSSIA
                                   Moscow

North Sea

DENMARK
Copenhagen

Baltic Sea

Riga   LATVIA

LITHUANIA
Vilnius

RUSSIA   BELARUS
          Minsk

IRELAND
Dublin

UNITED KINGDOM
Manchester

London

Amsterdam
The Hague
NETHERLANDS

Brussels
BELGIUM

English Channel

LUXEMBOURG
Luxembourg

Paris

FRANCE

Bay of Biscay

Berlin   Gdańsk

GERMANY

Cologne
Bonn
Frankfurt

Munich

LIECHTENSTEIN
Bern
SWITZERLAND

POLAND
Warsaw
Łódź

Katowice   Kraków

CZECH REPUBLIC
Prague
Brno

SLOVAKIA
Bratislava

Vienna
AUSTRIA

Budapest
HUNGARY

Kiev

UKRAINE

MOLDOVA
Chişinău

Cluj
ROMANIA

Milan

Ljubljana
SLOVENIA   Zagreb

CROATIA

BOSNIA & HERZEGOVINA
Sarajevo

Belgrade
SERBIA

Bucharest

Black Sea

PORTUGAL

SPAIN
Madrid
Lisbon

ANDORRA

Marseille

MONACO

SAN MARINO
ITALY

Corsica

VATICAN CITY   Rome

Barcelona

Sardinia

Balearic Is.

Naples

Podgorica
MONTENEGRO

Adriatic Sea

Tyrrhenian Sea

BULGARIA
Sophia

Skopje
ALBANIA   MACEDONIA
Tiranë

GREECE

Aegean Sea

Athens

Ionian Sea

Strait of Gibraltar

GIBRALTAR (U.K.)

Mediterranean Sea

AFRICA

Sicily

MALTA

Crete

Danube R.

0   250   500 mi
0   250   500 km

N   W E   S

Europe: Physical

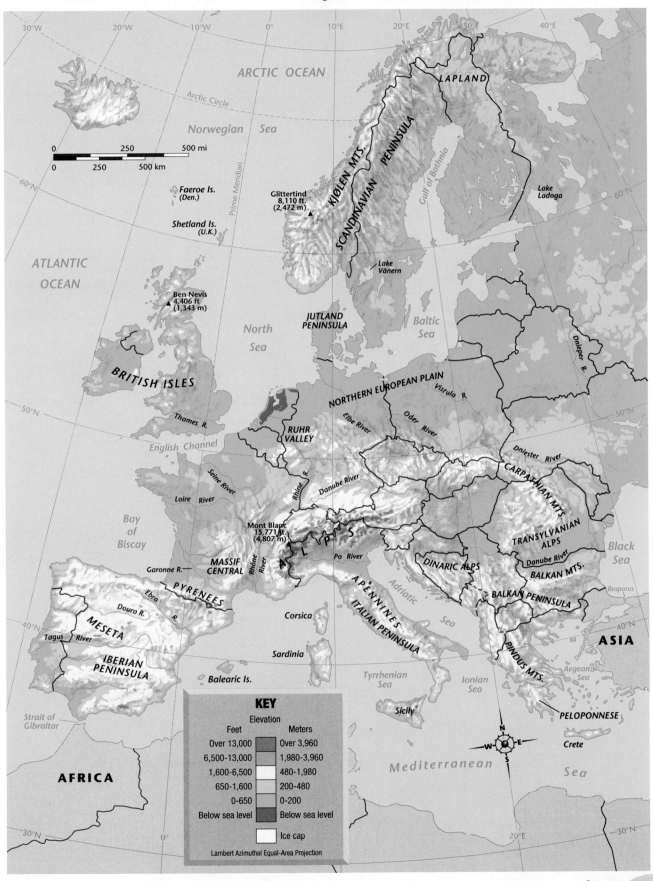

ARCTIC OCEAN

Arctic Circle

Norwegian Sea

LAPLAND

KJØLEN MTS.

SCANDINAVIAN PENINSULA

Gulf of Bothnia

Lake Ladoga

Faeroe Is. (Den.)

Glittertind 8,110 ft. (2,472 m)

Shetland Is. (U.K.)

ATLANTIC OCEAN

Lake Vänern

Ben Nevis 4,406 ft (1,343 m)

JUTLAND PENINSULA

Baltic Sea

North Sea

BRITISH ISLES

Dnieper R.

NORTHERN EUROPEAN PLAIN

Vistula R.

Thames R.

RUHR VALLEY

Elbe River

Oder River

English Channel

Dniester River

Seine R.

Danube River

CARPATHIAN MTS.

Loire River

Rhine R.

Bay of Biscay

Mont Blanc 15,771 ft. (4,807 m)

Rhône River

Po River

TRANSYLVANIAN ALPS

Danube River

A L P S

Garonne R.

MASSIF CENTRAL

DINARIC ALPS

BALKAN MTS.

Black Sea

PYRENEES

Bosporus

Douro R.

Ebro R.

A P E N N I N E S

Adriatic Sea

BALKAN PENINSULA

MESETA

Corsica

ITALIAN PENINSULA

ASIA

Tagus River

IBERIAN PENINSULA

Sardinia

Dardanelles

Balearic Is.

Tyrrhenian Sea

Ionian Sea

PINDUS MTS.

Aegean Sea

Strait of Gibraltar

Sicily

PELOPONNESE

Crete

AFRICA

Mediterranean Sea

KEY

Elevation

Feet	Meters
Over 13,000	Over 3,960
6,500-13,000	1,980-3,960
1,600-6,500	480-1,980
650-1,600	200-480
0-650	0-200
Below sea level	Below sea level
Ice cap	

Lambert Azimuthal Equal-Area Projection

Africa: Political

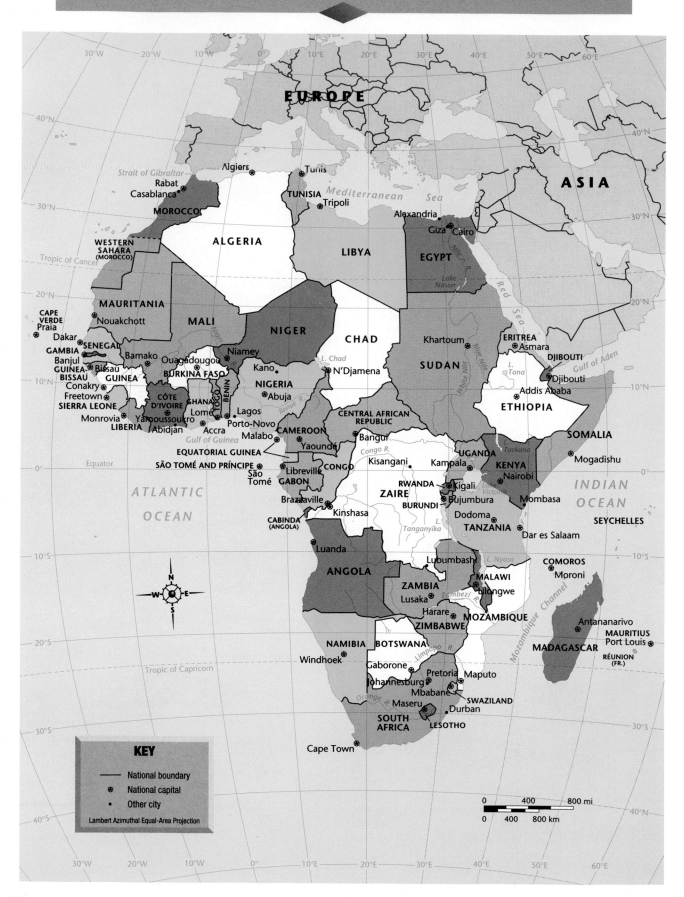

EUROPE

ASIA

Mediterranean Sea

Strait of Gibraltar
Algiers ⊛
Tunis ⊛
Rabat
Casablanca •
TUNISIA
Tripoli •

MOROCCO

Alexandria •
Giza • Cairo ⊛

WESTERN SAHARA (MOROCCO)

Tropic of Cancer

ALGERIA

LIBYA

EGYPT

Lake Nasser

MAURITANIA

MALI

NIGER

CHAD

Khartoum ⊛

ERITREA
Asmara ⊛

DJIBOUTI

Gulf of Aden

CAPE VERDE
Praia ⊛
Nouakchott ⊛
Dakar ⊛

Niamey ⊛

SUDAN

L. Tana

Djibouti ⊛

SENEGAL
Bamako ⊛
GAMBIA
Banjul ⊛
Ouagadougou ⊛
Kano •
N'Djamena •
GUINEA BISSAU
Bissau ⊛
GUINEA
BURKINA FASO
NIGERIA
Abuja ⊛

Addis Ababa •

ETHIOPIA

Conakry ⊛
Freetown ⊛
CÔTE D'IVOIRE
GHANA
Lomé
SIERRA LEONE
Monrovia ⊛ Yamoussoukro
BENIN
TOGO
Lagos •
Porto-Novo ⊛
CENTRAL AFRICAN REPUBLIC

SOMALIA

LIBERIA
Abidjan
Accra ⊛
Malabo ⊛
CAMEROON
Bangui ⊛
UGANDA
KENYA
Mogadishu •

EQUATORIAL GUINEA
Yaoundé ⊛
Kisangani •
Kampala ⊛
Nairobi ⊛

SÃO TOMÉ AND PRÍNCIPE ⊛
São Tomé
Libreville ⊛
CONGO
L. Turkana

Equator

GABON
ZAIRE
RWANDA
Kigali ⊛
Mombasa •

ATLANTIC OCEAN

Brazzaville ⊛
Kinshasa •
Congo R.
BURUNDI
Bujumbura ⊛
Lake Victoria

CABINDA (ANGOLA)
Dodoma ⊛
INDIAN OCEAN

L. Tanganyika
TANZANIA
Dar es Salaam •
SEYCHELLES

Luanda ⊛

Lubumbashi •
L. Nyasa
COMOROS
Moroni •

ANGOLA
ZAMBIA
MALAWI
Lilongwe ⊛

Lusaka ⊛
Zambezi R.

Harare ⊛
MOZAMBIQUE
Antananarivo ⊛
MAURITIUS
Port Louis ⊛

ZIMBABWE

NAMIBIA
BOTSWANA
Limpopo R.
MADAGASCAR
RÉUNION (FR.)

Windhoek ⊛
Gaborone ⊛
Pretoria ⊛ Maputo ⊛

Johannesburg •
Mbabane ⊛
Maseru ⊛
SWAZILAND
Orange R.
Durban •

SOUTH AFRICA
LESOTHO

Tropic of Capricorn

Cape Town ⊛

KEY
— National boundary
⊛ National capital
• Other city

Lambert Azimuthal Equal-Area Projection

0   400   800 mi
0   400   800 km

Africa: Physical

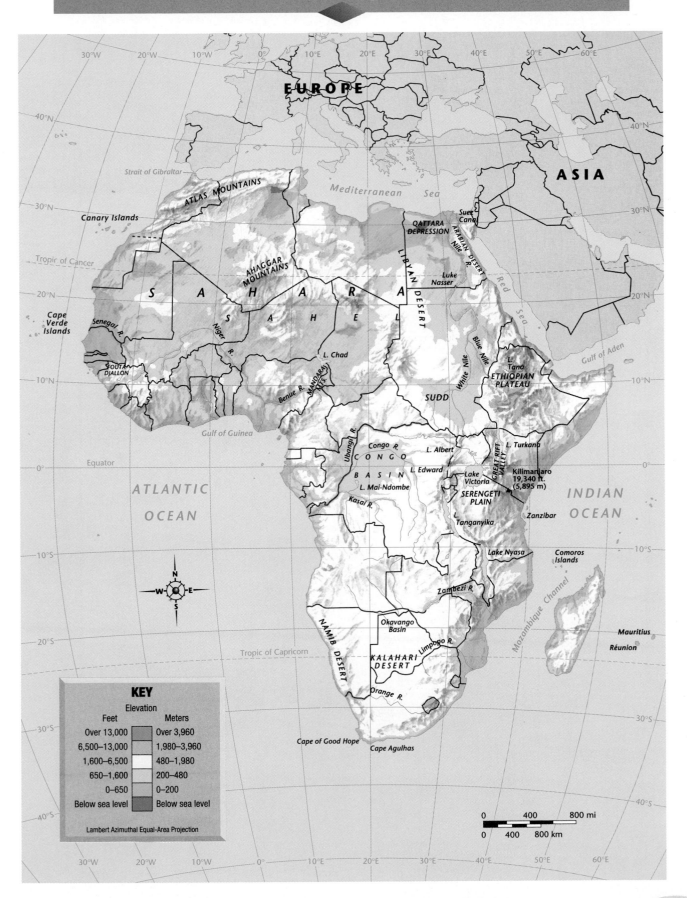

30°W 20°W 10°W 0° 10°E 20°E 30°E 40°E 50°E 60°E

EUROPE

ASIA

40°N

Strait of Gibraltar

Mediterranean Sea

Suez Canal

30°N

ATLAS MOUNTAINS

Canary Islands

QATTARA DEPRESSION

Tropic of Cancer

AHAGGAR MOUNTAINS

LIBYAN DESERT

ARABIAN DESERT

Nile R.

20°N

S   A   H   A   R   A

Luke Nasser

Red Sea

Cape Verde Islands

Senegal R.

S   A   H   E   L

Niger R.

L. Chad

White Nile

Blue Nile

L. Tana

Gulf of Aden

10°N

FOUTA DJALLON

MANDARA MTS.

Benue R.

ETHIOPIAN PLATEAU

Gulf of Guinea

SUDD

Ubangi R.

Congo R.

L. Albert

L. Turkana

Equator 0°

CONGO BASIN

L. Edward

Lake Victoria

GREAT RIFT VALLEY

Kilimanjaro 19,340 ft. (5,895 m)

ATLANTIC OCEAN

L. Mai-Ndombe

SERENGETI PLAIN

INDIAN OCEAN

Kasai R.

Zanzibar

L. Tanganyika

10°S

Lake Nyasa

Comoros Islands

Mozambique Channel

Zambezi R.

Mauritius

NAMIB DESERT

Okavango Basin

Réunion

20°S

Tropic of Capricorn

Limpopo R.

KALAHARI DESERT

Orange R.

30°S

Cape of Good Hope

Cape Agulhas

KEY
Elevation

Feet		Meters
Over 13,000		Over 3,960
6,500–13,000		1,980–3,960
1,600–6,500		480–1,980
650–1,600		200–480
0–650		0–200
Below sea level		Below sea level

Lambert Azimuthal Equal-Area Projection

N W E S

0   400   800 mi

0   400   800 km

KEY

— National boundary
⊛ National capital
• Other city

Two-Point Equidistant Projection

EUROPE

AFRICA

ARCTIC OCEAN

PACIFIC OCEAN

INDIAN OCEAN

North Pole

Arctic Circle

Tropic of Cancer

Equator

Tropic of Cancer

Bering Sea

East Siberian Sea

Barents Sea

Sea of Okhotsk

Sakhalin Island

Kuril Islands (Russia)

Sea of Japan

Yellow Sea

East China Sea

Ryukyu Islands

Philippine Sea

South China Sea

Java Sea

Celebes Sea

Bay of Bengal

Arabian Sea

Gulf of Aden

Red Sea

Persian Gulf

Gulf of Oman

Caspian Sea

Aral Sea

Black Sea

Mediterranean Sea

Lake Baikal

Lake Balkhash

Lena R.

Ob R.

Irtysh R.

Yenisei R.

Volga R.

Huang He

Yangzi R.

Ganges R.

RUSSIA

Verkhoyansk
Vladivostok
Bratsk
Irkutsk
Omsk
Yekaterinburg
Samara
St. Petersburg
Moscow
Kharkov

Tokyo
N. KOREA — Seoul
S. KOREA — Pyŏngyang
JAPAN
Harbin
Beijing
Xi'an
Fuzhou
Hong Kong
Macau (Port.)

CHINA

MONGOLIA — Ulan Bator

ESTONIA — Tallinn
LATVIA — Riga
LITHUANIA — Vilnius
BELARUS — Minsk
UKRAINE — Kiev
MOLDOVA — Chişinău

KAZAKSTAN
Qaraghandy
Almaty
UZBEKISTAN — Tashkent
Bishkek
KYRGYZSTAN
TAJIKISTAN — Dushanbe
Ashkhabad
TURKMENISTAN

GEORGIA — T'bilisi
ARMENIA — Yerevan
AZERBAIJAN — Baku
TURKEY — Ankara
CYPRUS — Nicosia
LEBANON — Beirut
SYRIA — Damascus
ISRAEL — Jerusalem
JORDAN — Amman
IRAQ — Baghdad
Tehran
IRAN — Shiraz
KUWAIT — Kuwait
BAHRAIN
QATAR
UNITED ARAB EMIRATES — Abu Dhabi
SAUDI ARABIA — Riyadh
Mecca
YEMEN — Sanaa
OMAN — Muscat
Socotra (Yemen)

AFGHANISTAN — Kabul
PAKISTAN — Islamabad
New Delhi
INDIA
Mumbai (Bombay)
Madras
NEPAL — Kathmandu
BHUTAN — Thimphu
BANGLADESH — Dhaka
Yangon
MYANMAR (BURMA)
SRI LANKA — Colombo
MALDIVES — Male

LAOS — Vientiane
THAILAND — Bangkok
VIETNAM — Hanoi
CAMBODIA — Phnom Penh
MALAYSIA — Kuala Lumpur
SINGAPORE — Singapore
INDONESIA
Sumatra
Borneo
Java
Jakarta
Celebes
Timor
Tanimbar

BRUNEI — Bandar Seri Begawan
PHILIPPINES — Manila
TAIWAN — Taipei
PALAU — Koror

PAPUA NEW GUINEA — Port Moresby
New Guinea

1,000 mi
1,000 km
500
0

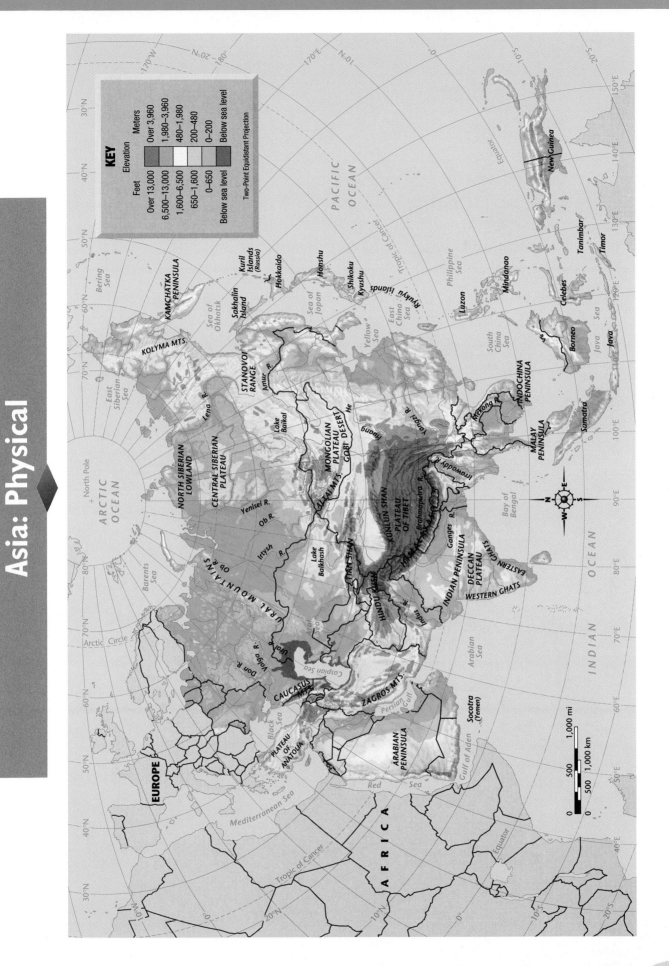

Asia: Physical

KEY

Elevation

Feet	Meters
Over 13,000	Over 3,960
6,500–13,000	1,980–3,960
1,600–6,500	480–1,980
650–1,600	200–480
0–650	0–200
Below sea level	Below sea level

Two-Point Equidistant Projection

ARCTIC OCEAN

North Pole

PACIFIC OCEAN

Bering Sea

KAMCHATKA PENINSULA

KOLYMA MTS.

Sea of Okhotsk

STANOVOI RANGE

Sakhalin Island

Kuril Islands (Russia)

Hokkaido

Honshu

Sea of Japan

Shikoku

Kyushu

Ryukyu Islands

East China Sea

Yellow Sea

Amur R.

Lake Baikal

MONGOLIAN PLATEAU

GOBI DESERT

ALTAI MTS.

Lena R.

NORTH SIBERIAN LOWLAND

CENTRAL SIBERIAN PLATEAU

Yenisei R.

Ob R.

Irtysh R.

Lake Balkhash

URAL MOUNTAINS

Ob R.

He

Huang

Yangzi R.

KUNLUN SHAN

PLATEAU OF TIBET

TIAN SHAN

HINDU KUSH

Brahmaputra R.

Indus R.

Ganges R.

INDIAN PENINSULA

DECCAN PLATEAU

EASTERN GHATS

WESTERN GHATS

Bay of Bengal

Irrawaddy R.

Mekong R.

INDOCHINA PENINSULA

MALAY PENINSULA

South China Sea

Luzon

Mindanao

Celebes

Borneo

Sumatra

Java

Java Sea

Philippine Sea

New Guinea

Tanimbar

Timor

Equator

INDIAN OCEAN

Arabian Sea

Persian Gulf

ZAGROS MTS.

ARABIAN PENINSULA

Socotra (Yemen)

Gulf of Aden

Red Sea

CAUCASUS MTS.

Caspian Sea

Aral Sea

Ural R.

Volga R.

Don R.

Black Sea

PLATEAU OF ANATOLIA

Mediterranean Sea

EUROPE

AFRICA

Tropic of Cancer

Arctic Circle

Barents Sea

East Siberian Sea

0 500 1,000 mi

0 500 1,000 km

Australia, New Zealand, and the Pacific Islands: Physical–Political

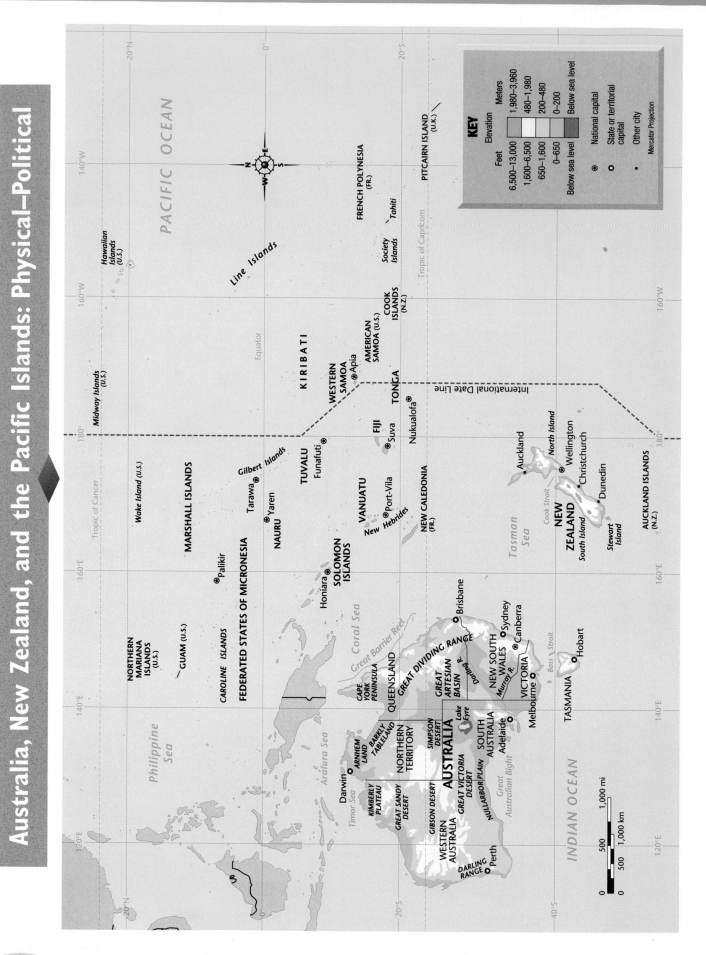

PACIFIC OCEAN

20°N

140°W

160°W

180°

160°E

140°E

120°E

Tropic of Cancer

Equator

Tropic of Capricorn

International Date Line

20°S

40°S

Hawaiian Islands (U.S.)

Midway Islands (U.S.)

Line Islands

FRENCH POLYNESIA (FR.)

Tahiti

Society Islands

PITCAIRN ISLAND (U.K.)

COOK ISLANDS (N.Z.)

AMERICAN SAMOA (U.S.)

KIRIBATI

WESTERN SAMOA

Apia

TONGA

Nukualofa

FIJI

Suva

TUVALU

Funafuti

Gilbert Islands

Tarawa

MARSHALL ISLANDS

Wake Island (U.S.)

NAURU

Yaren

VANUATU

Port-Vila

New Hebrides

NEW CALEDONIA (FR.)

SOLOMON ISLANDS

Honiara

FEDERATED STATES OF MICRONESIA

Palikir

CAROLINE ISLANDS

NORTHERN MARIANA ISLANDS (U.S.)

GUAM (U.S.)

Philippine Sea

Coral Sea

Great Barrier Reef

Arafura Sea

Timor Sea

Darwin

ARNHEM LAND

KIMBERLEY PLATEAU

GREAT SANDY DESERT

GIBSON DESERT

WESTERN AUSTRALIA

GREAT VICTORIA DESERT

Perth

DARLING RANGE

NULLARBOR PLAIN

Great Australian Bight

NORTHERN TERRITORY

BARKLY TABLELAND

SIMPSON DESERT

Lake Eyre

SOUTH AUSTRALIA

Adelaide

AUSTRALIA

CAPE YORK PENINSULA

QUEENSLAND

GREAT DIVIDING RANGE

Brisbane

GREAT ARTESIAN BASIN

NEW SOUTH WALES

Sydney

Canberra

Murray R.

Darling R.

VICTORIA

Melbourne

TASMANIA

Bass Strait

Hobart

Tasman Sea

Cook Strait

North Island

Auckland

Wellington

Christchurch

Dunedin

NEW ZEALAND

South Island

Stewart Island

AUCKLAND ISLANDS (N.Z.)

INDIAN OCEAN

KEY

Elevation

Feet	Meters
6,500–13,000	1,980–3,960
1,600–6,500	480–1,980
650–1,600	200–480
0–650	0–200
Below sea level	Below sea level

⊛ National capital

✪ State or territorial capital

• Other city

Mercator Projection

Scale:
1,000 mi
500 1,000 km

The Arctic

Sea of Okhotsk
VERKHOYANSKI KHREBET
CHERSKOGO RANGE
Lena R.
ASIA
EUROPE
KOLYMA MTS.
TAIMYR PEN.
Kara Sea
KOLA PEN.
Laptev Sea
Severnaya Zemlya
Novaya Zemlya
Baltic Sea
SCANDINAVIAN PENINSULA
New Siberian Islands
Franz Josef Land
Barents Sea
ANADYR RANGE
East Siberian Sea
Arctic Circle
North Cape
International Date Line
Wrangel Island
ARCTIC OCEAN
Svalbard (Nor.)
Norwegian Sea
North Sea
180°
Bering Sea
CHUKOTSKI PEN.
North Pole
Prime Meridian
St. Lawrence Island
Bering Strait
Permanent Ice Pack
Greenland Sea
Chukchi Sea
80°N
Denmark Strait
ATLANTIC OCEAN
Nunivak Island
BROOKS RANGE
Pt. Barrow
70°N
Kodiak I.
ALASKA RANGE
Yukon R.
Beaufort Sea
North Magnetic Pole
Queen Elizabeth Islands
Ellesmere Island
Baffin Bay
Arctic Circle
60°N
Gulf of Alaska
Amundsen Gulf
Banks Island
Davis Strait
0   250   500 mi
Victoria Island
Baffin I.
30°W
0   250   500 km
Mackenzie R.
NORTH AMERICA
Cape Farewell

Antarctica

ATLANTIC OCEAN
Antarctic Circle
South Shetland Is.
QUEEN MAUD LAND
SOUTH AMERICA
Permanent Ice Pack
COATS LAND
ENDERBY LAND
Antarctic Peninsula
Weddell Sea
Filchner Ice Shelf
Prime Meridian
Alexander I.
Berkner I.
Amery Ice Shelf
Ronne Ice Shelf
TRANSANTARCTIC MTS.
Bellingshausen Sea
ANTARCTICA
Vinson Massif 16,066 ft. (4,897 m)
South Pole
90° E
90°W
QUEEN MAUD MTS.
Amundsen Sea
WILKES LAND
INDIAN OCEAN
Ross Ice Shelf
Roosevelt I.
Permanent Ice Pack
PACIFIC OCEAN
Ross Sea
VICTORIA LAND
International Date Line
South Magnetic Pole
0   400   800 mi
0   400   800 km

KEY

Elevation

Feet		Meters
Over 13,000		Over 3,960
6,500–13,000		1,980–3,960
1,600–6,500		480–1,980
650–1,600		200–480
0–650		0–200

	Ice cap
	Ice shelf

Orthographic Projection

175

World View

Afghanistan

CAPITAL: Kabul
POPULATION: 21,251,821
MAJOR LANGUAGES: Pashtu, Afghan Persian, Turkic, and 30 various languages
AREA: 250,010 sq mi; 647,500 sq km
LEADING EXPORTS: fruits and nuts, handwoven carpets, and wool
CONTINENT: Asia

Albania
CAPITAL: Tiranë
POPULATION: 3,413,904
MAJOR LANGUAGES: Albanian, Tosk dialect, and Greek
AREA: 11,101 sq mi; 28,750 sq km
LEADING EXPORTS: asphalt, metals and metallic ores, and electricity
CONTINENT: Europe

Algeria

CAPITAL: Algiers
POPULATION: 28,539,321
MAJOR LANGUAGES: Arabic (official), French, and Berber dialects
AREA: 919,626 sq mi; 2,381,740 sq km
LEADING EXPORTS: petroleum and natural gas
CONTINENT: Africa

Andorra
CAPITAL: Andorra La Vella
POPULATION: 65,780
MAJOR LANGUAGES: Catalan (official), French, and Castilian
AREA: 174 sq mi; 450 sq km
LEADING EXPORTS: electricity, tobacco products, and furniture
CONTINENT: Europe

Angola
CAPITAL: Luanda
POPULATION: 10,069,501
MAJOR LANGUAGES: Portuguese (official), Bantu, and various languages
AREA: 481,370 sq mi; 1,246,700 sq km
LEADING EXPORTS: oil, diamonds, and refined petroleum products
CONTINENT: Africa

Anguilla

CAPITAL: The Valley
POPULATION: 7,099
MAJOR LANGUAGE: English (official)
AREA: 35 sq mi; 91 sq km
LEADING EXPORTS: lobster and salt
LOCATION: Caribbean Sea

Antigua and Barbuda

CAPITAL: Saint John's
POPULATION: 65,176
MAJOR LANGUAGES: English (official) and various dialects
AREA: 170 sq mi; 440 sq km
LEADING EXPORTS: petroleum products and manufactures
LOCATION: Caribbean Sea

Argentina
CAPITAL: Buenos Aires
POPULATION: 34,292,742
MAJOR LANGUAGES: Spanish (official), English, Italian, German, and French
AREA: 1,068,339 sq mi; 2,766,890 sq km
LEADING EXPORTS: meat, wheat, corn, oilseed, and manufactures
CONTINENT: South America

Armenia
CAPITAL: Yerevan
POPULATION: 3,557,284
MAJOR LANGUAGES: Armenian and Russian
AREA: 11,506 sq mi; 29,800 sq km
LEADING EXPORTS: gold and jewelry, and aluminum
CONTINENT: Asia

Australia
CAPITAL: Canberra
POPULATION: 18,322,231
MAJOR LANGUAGES: English and various languages
AREA: 2,968,010 sq mi; 7,686,850 sq km
LEADING EXPORTS: coal, gold, meat, wool, and alumina
CONTINENT: Australia

Austria
CAPITAL: Vienna
POPULATION: 7,986,664
MAJOR LANGUAGE: German
AREA: 32,376 sq mi; 83,850 sq km
LEADING EXPORTS: machinery and equipment, and iron and steel
CONTINENT: Europe

Azerbaijan

CAPITAL: Baku
POPULATION: 7,789,886
MAJOR LANGUAGES: Azeri, Russian, Armenian, and various languages
AREA: 33,438 sq mi; 86,600 sq km
LEADING EXPORTS: oil and gas, chemicals, and oil field equipment
CONTINENT: Europe and Asia

Bahamas
CAPITAL: Nassau
POPULATION: 256,616
MAJOR LANGUAGES: English and Creole
AREA: 5,382 sq mi; 13,940 sq km
LEADING EXPORTS: pharmaceuticals, cement, rum, and crawfish
LOCATION: Caribbean Sea

Bahrain

CAPITAL: Manama
POPULATION: 575,925
MAJOR LANGUAGES: Arabic, English, Farsi, and Urdu
AREA: 239 sq mi; 620 sq km
LEADING EXPORTS: petroleum and petroleum products
CONTINENT: Asia

Bangladesh
CAPITAL: Dhaka
POPULATION: 128,094,948
MAJOR LANGUAGES: Bangla and English
AREA: 55,600 sq mi; 144,000 sq km
LEADING EXPORTS: garments, jute and jute goods, and leather
CONTINENT: Asia

Barbados
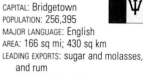
CAPITAL: Bridgetown
POPULATION: 256,395
MAJOR LANGUAGE: English
AREA: 166 sq mi; 430 sq km
LEADING EXPORTS: sugar and molasses, and rum
LOCATION: Caribbean Sea

Belarus

CAPITAL: Minsk
POPULATION: 10,437,418
MAJOR LANGUAGES: Byelorussian and Russian
AREA: 79,926 sq mi; 207,600 sq km
LEADING EXPORTS: machinery and transportation equipment
CONTINENT: Europe

Belgium
CAPITAL: Brussels
POPULATION: 10,081,880
MAJOR LANGUAGES: Dutch, French, and German
AREA: 11,780 sq mi; 30,510 sq km
LEADING EXPORTS: iron and steel, and transportation equipment
CONTINENT: Europe

Belize
CAPITAL: Belmopan
POPULATION: 214,061
MAJOR LANGUAGES: English (official), Spanish, Maya, and Garifuna
AREA: 8,865 sq mi; 22,960 sq km
LEADING EXPORTS: sugar, citrus fruits, bananas, and clothing
LOCATION: Caribbean Sea

Benin

CAPITAL: Porto-Novo
POPULATION: 5,522,677
MAJOR LANGUAGES: Fon, Yoruba, and at least 6 various languages
AREA: 43,484 sq mi; 112,620 sq km
LEADING EXPORTS: cotton, crude oil, palm products, and cocoa
CONTINENT: Africa

Bermuda

CAPITAL: Hamilton
POPULATION: 61,629
MAJOR LANGUAGE: English
AREA: 19.3 sq mi; 50 sq km
LEADING EXPORTS: semitropical produce and light manufactures
CONTINENT: North America

Bhutan
CAPITAL: Thimphu
POPULATION: 1,780,638
MAJOR LANGUAGES: Dzongkha (official), Tibetan dialects, and Nepalese dialects
AREA: 18,147 sq mi; 47,000 sq km
LEADING EXPORTS: cardamon, gypsum, timber, and handicrafts
CONTINENT: Asia

Bolivia
CAPITAL: La Paz
POPULATION: 7,896,254
MAJOR LANGUAGES: Spanish, Quechua, and Aymara
AREA: 424,179 sq mi; 1,098,580 sq km
LEADING EXPORTS: metals, natural gas, soybeans, jewelry, and wood
CONTINENT: South America

Bosnia and Herzegovina

CAPITAL: Sarajevo
POPULATION: 3,201,823
MAJOR LANGUAGE: Serbo-Croatian
AREA: 19,782 sq mi; 51,233 sq km
LEADING EXPORTS: none
CONTINENT: Europe

Botswana

CAPITAL: Gaborone
POPULATION: 1,392,414
MAJOR LANGUAGES: English and Setswana
AREA: 231,812 sq mi; 600,370 sq km
LEADING EXPORTS: diamonds, copper and nickel, and meat
CONTINENT: Africa

Brazil

CAPITAL: Brasília
POPULATION: 160,737,489
MAJOR LANGUAGES: Portuguese, Spanish, English, and French
AREA: 3,286,600 sq mi; 8,511,965 sq km
LEADING EXPORTS: iron ore, soybean, bran, and orange juice
CONTINENT: South America

British Virgin Islands

CAPITAL: Road Town
POPULATION: 13,027
MAJOR LANGUAGE: English
AREA: 58 sq mi; 150 sq km
LEADING EXPORTS: rum, fresh fish, gravel, sand, and fruits
LOCATION: Caribbean Sea

Brunei

CAPITAL: Bandar Seri Begawan
POPULATION: 292,266
MAJOR LANGUAGES: Malay, English, and Chinese
AREA: 2,228 sq mi; 5,770 sq km
LEADING EXPORTS: crude oil and liquefied natural gas
CONTINENT: Asia

Bulgaria

CAPITAL: Sofia
POPULATION: 8,775,198
MAJOR LANGUAGE: Bulgarian
AREA: 42,824 sq mi; 110,910 sq km
LEADING EXPORTS: machinery and agricultural products
CONTINENT: Europe

Burkina Faso

CAPITAL: Ouagadougou
POPULATION: 10,422,828
MAJOR LANGUAGES: French (official) and Sudanic languages
AREA: 105,873 sq mi; 274,200 sq km
LEADING EXPORTS: cotton, gold, and animal products
CONTINENT: Africa

Burundi

CAPITAL: Bujumbura
POPULATION: 6,262,429
MAJOR LANGUAGES: Kirundi, French, and Swahili
AREA: 10,746 sq mi; 27,830 sq km
LEADING EXPORTS: coffee, tea, cotton, and hides and skins
CONTINENT: Africa

Cambodia

CAPITAL: Phnom Penh
POPULATION: 10,561,373
MAJOR LANGUAGES: Khmer and French
AREA: 69,902 sq mi; 181,040 sq km
LEADING EXPORTS: timber, rubber, soybeans, and sesame
CONTINENT: Asia

Cameroon

CAPITAL: Yaounde
POPULATION: 13,521,000
MAJOR LANGUAGES: 24 various languages, English, and French
AREA: 183,574 sq mi; 475,440 sq km
LEADING EXPORTS: petroleum products and lumber
CONTINENT: Africa

Canada

CAPITAL: Ottawa
POPULATION: 28,434,545
MAJOR LANGUAGES: English and French
AREA: 3,851,940 sq mi; 9,976,140 sq km
LEADING EXPORTS: newsprint, wood pulp, timber, and crude petroleum
CONTINENT: North America

Cape Verde

CAPITAL: Praia
POPULATION: 435,983
MAJOR LANGUAGES: Portuguese and Crioulo
AREA: 1,556 sq mi; 4,030 sq km
LEADING EXPORTS: fish, bananas, and hides and skins
CONTINENT: Africa

Cayman Islands

CAPITAL: George Town
POPULATION: 33,192
MAJOR LANGUAGE: English
AREA: 100 sq mi; 260 sq km
LEADING EXPORTS: turtle products and manufactured goods
LOCATION: Caribbean Sea

Central African Republic

CAPITAL: Bangui
POPULATION: 3,209,759
MAJOR LANGUAGES: French, Sangho, Arabic, Hunsa, and Swahili
AREA: 240,542 sq mi; 622,980 sq km
LEADING EXPORTS: diamonds, timber, cotton, coffee, and tobacco
CONTINENT: Africa

Chad

CAPITAL: N'Djamena
POPULATION: 5,586,505
MAJOR LANGUAGES: French, Arabic, Sara, Songo, and over 100 various languages and dialects
AREA: 495,772 sq mi; 1,284,000 sq km
LEADING EXPORTS: cotton, cattle, textiles, and fish
CONTINENT: Africa

Chile

CAPITAL: Santiago
POPULATION: 14,161,216
MAJOR LANGUAGE: Spanish
AREA: 292,269 sq mi; 756,950 sq km
LEADING EXPORTS: copper and other metals and minerals
CONTINENT: South America

China

CAPITAL: Beijing
POPULATION: 1,203,097,268
MAJOR LANGUAGES: Mandarin, Putonghua, Yue, Wu, Minbei, Minnan, Xiang, and Gan and Hakka dialects
AREA: 3,705,533 sq mi; 9,596,960 sq km
LEADING EXPORTS: textiles, garments, footwear, and toys
CONTINENT: Asia

Colombia

CAPITAL: Bogota
POPULATION: 36,200,251
MAJOR LANGUAGE: Spanish
AREA: 439,751 sq mi; 1,138,910 sq km
LEADING EXPORTS: petroleum, coffee, coal, and bananas
CONTINENT: South America

Comoros

CAPITAL: Moroni
POPULATION: 549,338
MAJOR LANGUAGES: Arabic, French, and Comoran
AREA: 838 sq mi; 2,170 sq km
LEADING EXPORTS: vanilla, ylang-ylang, cloves, and perfume oil
LOCATION: Indian Ocean

Congo

CAPITAL: Brazzaville
POPULATION: 2,504,996
MAJOR LANGUAGES: French, Lingala, Kikongo, and other languages
AREA: 132,051 sq mi; 342,000 sq km
LEADING EXPORTS: crude oil, lumber, plywood, sugar, and cocoa
CONTINENT: Africa

Cook Islands

CAPITAL: Avarua
POPULATION: 19,343
MAJOR LANGUAGES: English and Maori
AREA: 95 sq mi; 240 sq km
LEADING EXPORTS: copra, fresh and canned fruit, and clothing
LOCATION: Pacific Ocean

Costa Rica

CAPITAL: San José
POPULATION: 3,419,114
MAJOR LANGUAGES: Spanish and English
AREA: 19,730 sq mi; 51,100 sq km
LEADING EXPORTS: coffee, bananas, textiles, and sugar
CONTINENT: Central America

Côte d'Ivoire

CAPITAL: Yamoussoukro
POPULATION: 14,791,257
MAJOR LANGUAGES: French, Dioula, and 59 other dialects
AREA: 124,507 sq mi; 322,460 sq km
LEADING EXPORTS: cocoa, coffee, tropical woods, and petroleum
CONTINENT: Africa

Croatia

CAPITAL: Zagreb
POPULATION: 4,665,821
MAJOR LANGUAGE: Serbo-Croatian
AREA: 21,830 sq mi; 56,538 sq km
LEADING EXPORTS: machinery and transportation equipment
CONTINENT: Europe

Cuba

CAPITAL: Havana
POPULATION: 10,937,635
MAJOR LANGUAGE: Spanish
AREA: 42,805 sq mi; 110,860 sq km
LEADING EXPORTS: sugar, nickel, shellfish, and tobacco
LOCATION: Caribbean Sea

Cyprus

CAPITAL: Nicosia
POPULATION: 736,636
MAJOR LANGUAGES: Greek, Turkish, and English
AREA: 3,572 sq mi; 9,250 sq km
LEADING EXPORTS: citrus, potatoes, grapes, wines, and cement
LOCATION: Mediterranean Sea

Czech Republic

CAPITAL: Prague
POPULATION: 10,432,774
MAJOR LANGUAGES: Czech and Slovak
AREA: 30,388 sq mi; 78,703 sq km
LEADING EXPORTS: manufactured goods
CONTINENT: Europe

Denmark

CAPITAL: Copenhagen
POPULATION: 5,199,437
MAJOR LANGUAGES: Danish, Faroese, Greenlandic, and German
AREA: 16,630 sq mi; 43,070 sq km
LEADING EXPORTS: meat and meat products, and dairy products
CONTINENT: Europe

Djibouti
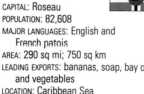
CAPITAL: Djibouti
POPULATION: 421,320
MAJOR LANGUAGES: French, Arabic, Somali, and Afar
AREA: 8,495 sq mi; 22,000 sq km
LEADING EXPORTS: hides and skins, and coffee (in transit)
CONTINENT: Africa

Dominica
CAPITAL: Roseau
POPULATION: 82,608
MAJOR LANGUAGES: English and French patois
AREA: 290 sq mi; 750 sq km
LEADING EXPORTS: bananas, soap, bay oil, and vegetables
LOCATION: Caribbean Sea

Dominican Republic
CAPITAL: Santo Domingo
POPULATION: 7,511,263
MAJOR LANGUAGE: Spanish
AREA: 18,815 sq mi; 48,730 sq km
LEADING EXPORTS: ferronickel, sugar, gold, coffee, and cocoa
LOCATION: Caribbean Sea

Ecuador
CAPITAL: Quito
POPULATION: 10,890,950
MAJOR LANGUAGES: Spanish, Quechua, and various languages
AREA: 109,487 sq mi; 283,560 sq km
LEADING EXPORTS: petroleum, bananas, shrimp, and cocoa
CONTINENT: South America

Egypt

CAPITAL: Cairo
POPULATION: 62,359,623
MAJOR LANGUAGES: Arabic, English, and French
AREA: 386,675 sq mi; 1,001,450 sq km
LEADING EXPORTS: crude oil and petroleum products
CONTINENT: Africa

El Salvador
CAPITAL: San Salvador
POPULATION: 5,870,481
MAJOR LANGUAGES: Spanish and Nahua
AREA: 8,124 sq mi; 21,040 sq km
LEADING EXPORTS: coffee, sugar cane, and shrimp
CONTINENT: Central America

Equatorial Guinea
CAPITAL: Malabo
POPULATION: 420,293
MAJOR LANGUAGES: Spanish, Pidgin English, Fang, Bubi, and Ibo
AREA: 10,831 sq mi; 28,050 sq km
LEADING EXPORTS: coffee, timber, and cocoa beans
CONTINENT: Africa

Eritrea
CAPITAL: Asmara
POPULATION: 3,578,709
MAJOR LANGUAGES: Tigre, Kunama, Cushitic dialects, Nora Bana, and Arabic
AREA: 46,844 sq mi; 121,320 sq km
LEADING EXPORTS: salt, hides, cement, and gum arabic
CONTINENT: Africa

Estonia
CAPITAL: Tallinn
POPULATION: 1,625,399
MAJOR LANGUAGES: Estonian, Latvian, Lithuanian, and Russian
AREA: 17,414 sq mi; 45,100 sq km
LEADING EXPORTS: textiles, food products, vehicles, and metals
CONTINENT: Europe

Ethiopia
CAPITAL: Addis Ababa
POPULATION: 55,979,018
MAJOR LANGUAGES: Amharic, Tigrinya, Orominga, Guaraginga, Somali, Arabic, English, and various languages
AREA: 435,201 sq mi; 1,127,127 sq km
LEADING EXPORTS: coffee, leather products, and gold
CONTINENT: Africa

Fiji
CAPITAL: Suva
POPULATION: 772,891
MAJOR LANGUAGES: English, Fijian, and Hindustani
AREA: 7,054 sq mi; 18,270 sq km
LEADING EXPORTS: sugar, clothing, gold, processed fish, and lumber
LOCATION: Pacific Ocean

Finland
CAPITAL: Helsinki
POPULATION: 5,085,206
MAJOR LANGUAGES: Finnish, Swedish, Lapp, and Russian
AREA: 130,132 sq mi; 337,030 sq km
LEADING EXPORTS: paper and pulp, machinery, and chemicals
CONTINENT: Europe

France
CAPITAL: Paris
POPULATION: 58,109,160
MAJOR LANGUAGES: French and regional dialects and languages
AREA: 211,217 sq mi; 547,030 sq km
LEADING EXPORTS: machinery and transportation equipment
CONTINENT: Europe

Gabon

CAPITAL: Libreville
POPULATION: 1,185,749
MAJOR LANGUAGES: French, Fang, Myene, Bateke, Bapounou/Eschira, and Bandjabi
AREA: 103,351 sq mi; 267,670 sq km
LEADING EXPORTS: crude oil, timber, manganese, and uranium
CONTINENT: Africa

The Gambia

CAPITAL: Banjul
POPULATION: 989,273
MAJOR LANGUAGES: English, Mandinka, Wolof, Fula, and various languages
AREA: 4,363 sq mi; 11,300 sq km
LEADING EXPORTS: peanuts and peanut products, and fish
CONTINENT: Africa

Georgia
CAPITAL: T'bilisi
POPULATION: 5,725,972
MAJOR LANGUAGES: Armenian, Azeri, Georgian, Russian, and various languages
AREA: 26,912 sq mi; 69,700 sq km
LEADING EXPORTS: citrus fruits, tea, and wine
CONTINENT: Asia

Germany
CAPITAL: Berlin
POPULATION: 81,337,541
MAJOR LANGUAGE: German
AREA: 137,808 sq mi; 356,910 sq km
LEADING EXPORTS: machines and machine tools, and chemicals
CONTINENT: Europe

Ghana

CAPITAL: Accra
POPULATION: 17,763,138
MAJOR LANGUAGES: English, Akan, Moshi-Dagomba, Ewe, Ga, and various languages
AREA: 92,104 sq mi; 238,540 sq km
LEADING EXPORTS: cocoa, gold, timber, tuna, and bauxite
CONTINENT: Africa

Greece

CAPITAL: Athens
POPULATION: 10,647,511
MAJOR LANGUAGES: Greek, English, and French
AREA: 50,944 sq mi; 131,940 sq km
LEADING EXPORTS: manufactured goods, foodstuffs, and fuels
CONTINENT: Europe

Grenada

CAPITAL: Saint George's
POPULATION: 94,486
MAJOR LANGUAGES: English and French patois
AREA: 131 sq mi; 340 sq km
LEADING EXPORTS: bananas, cocoa, nutmeg, and fruits and vegetables
LOCATION: Caribbean Sea

Guatemala
CAPITAL: Guatemala
POPULATION: 10,998,602
MAJOR LANGUAGES: Spanish, Quiche, Cakchiquel, Kekchi, and various languages and dialects
AREA: 42,044 sq mi; 108,890 sq km
LEADING EXPORTS: coffee, sugar, bananas, cardamom, and beef
CONTINENT: Central America

Guinea

CAPITAL: Conakry
POPULATION: 6,549,336
MAJOR LANGUAGES: French and various languages
AREA: 94,930 sq mi; 245,860 sq km
LEADING EXPORTS: bauxite, alumina, diamonds, gold, and coffee
CONTINENT: Africa

Guinea Bissau

CAPITAL: Bissau
POPULATION: 1,124,537
MAJOR LANGUAGES: Portuguese, Criolo, and various languages
AREA: 13,946 sq mi; 36,210 sq km
LEADING EXPORTS: cashews, fish, peanuts, and palm kernels
CONTINENT: Africa

Guyana

CAPITAL: Georgetown
POPULATION: 723,774
MAJOR LANGUAGES: English and various dialects
AREA: 83,003 sq mi; 214,970 sq km
LEADING EXPORTS: sugar, bauxite/alumina, rice, and shrimp
CONTINENT: South America

Haiti

CAPITAL: Port-au-Prince
POPULATION: 6,539,983
MAJOR LANGUAGES: French and Creole
AREA: 8,784 sq mi; 22,750 sq km
LEADING EXPORTS: light manufactures and coffee
LOCATION: Caribbean Sea

Holy See (Vatican City)

CAPITAL: Vatican City
POPULATION: 830
MAJOR LANGUAGES: Italian, Latin, and various languages
AREA: 17 sq mi; 44 sq km
LEADING EXPORTS: none
CONTINENT: Europe

Honduras

CAPITAL: Tegucigalpa
POPULATION: 5,549,743
MAJOR LANGUAGES: Spanish and various dialects
AREA: 43,280 sq mi; 112,090 sq km
LEADING EXPORTS: bananas, coffee, shrimp, lobsters, and minerals
CONTINENT: Central America

Hungary

CAPITAL: Budapest
POPULATION: 10,318,838
MAJOR LANGUAGES: Hungarian and various languages
AREA: 35,920 sq mi; 93,030 sq km
LEADING EXPORTS: raw materials and semi-finished goods
CONTINENT: Europe

Iceland

CAPITAL: Reykjavik
POPULATION: 265,998
MAJOR LANGUAGE: Icelandic
AREA: 39,770 sq mi; 103,000 sq km
LEADING EXPORTS: fish and fish products, and animal products
CONTINENT: Europe

India

CAPITAL: New Delhi
POPULATION: 936,545,814
MAJOR LANGUAGES: English, Hindi, Bengali, Telugu, Marathi, Tamil, Urdu, Gujarati, Malayam, Kannada, Oriya, Punjabi, Assamese, Kashmiri, Sindhi, Sanskrit, and Hindustani (all official)
AREA: 1,269,389 sq mi; 3,287,590 sq km
LEADING EXPORTS: clothing, and gems and jewelry
CONTINENT: Asia

Indonesia

CAPITAL: Jakarta
POPULATION: 203,583,886
MAJOR LANGUAGES: Bahasa Indonesia, English, Dutch, Javanese, and various dialects
AREA: 741,052 sq mi; 1,919,251 sq km
LEADING EXPORTS: manufactures, fuels, and foodstuffs
CONTINENT: Asia

Iran

CAPITAL: Tehran
POPULATION: 64,625,455
MAJOR LANGUAGES: Farsi (official) and Turkic languages
AREA: 634,562 sq mi; 1,643,452 sq km
LEADING EXPORTS: petroleum, carpets, fruit, nuts, and hides
CONTINENT: Asia

Iraq

CAPITAL: Baghdad
POPULATION: 20,643,769
MAJOR LANGUAGES: Arabic, Kurdish, Assyrian, and Armenian
AREA: 168,760 sq mi; 437,072 sq km
LEADING EXPORTS: crude oil and refined products, and fertilizers
CONTINENT: Asia

Ireland

CAPITAL: Dublin
POPULATION: 3,550,448
MAJOR LANGUAGES: Irish Gaelic and English
AREA: 27,136 sq mi; 70,280 sq km
LEADING EXPORTS: chemicals and data processing equipment
CONTINENT: Europe

Israel

CAPITAL: Jerusalem
POPULATION: 7,566,447
MAJOR LANGUAGES: Hebrew, Arabic, and English
AREA: 10,421 sq mi; 26,990 sq km
LEADING EXPORTS: machinery and equipment, and cut diamonds
CONTINENT: Asia

Italy

CAPITAL: Rome
POPULATION: 58,261,971
MAJOR LANGUAGES: Italian, German, French, and Slovene
AREA: 116,310 sq mi; 301,230 sq km
LEADING EXPORTS: metals, and textiles and clothing
CONTINENT: Europe

Jamaica

CAPITAL: Kingston
POPULATION: 2,574,291
MAJOR LANGUAGES: English and Creole
AREA: 4,243 sq mi; 10,990 sq km
LEADING EXPORTS: alumina, bauxite, sugar, bananas, and rum
LOCATION: Caribbean Sea

Japan

CAPITAL: Tokyo
POPULATION: 125,506,492
MAJOR LANGUAGE: Japanese
AREA: 145,888 sq mi; 377,835 sq km
LEADING EXPORTS: machinery, motor vehicles, and electronics
CONTINENT: Asia

Jordan

CAPITAL: Amman
POPULATION: 4,100,709
MAJOR LANGUAGES: Arabic and English
AREA: 34,447 sq mi; 89,213 sq km
LEADING EXPORTS: phosphates, fertilizers, and potash
CONTINENT: Asia

Kazakstan

CAPITAL: Almaty
POPULATION: 17,376,615
MAJOR LANGUAGES: Kazak and Russian
AREA: 1,049,191 sq mi; 2,717,300 sq km
LEADING EXPORTS: oil, and ferrous and nonferrous metals
CONTINENT: Asia

Kenya

CAPITAL: Nairobi
POPULATION: 28,817,227
MAJOR LANGUAGES: English, Swahili, and various languages
AREA: 224,970 sq mi; 582,650 sq km
LEADING EXPORTS: tea, coffee, and petroleum products
CONTINENT: Africa

Kiribati

CAPITAL: Tarawa
POPULATION: 79,386
MAJOR LANGUAGES: English and Gilbertese
AREA: 277 sq mi; 717 sq km
LEADING EXPORTS: copra, seaweed, and fish
LOCATION: Pacific Ocean

Korea, North

CAPITAL: P'yongyang
POPULATION: 23,486,550
MAJOR LANGUAGE: Korean
AREA: 46,542 sq mi; 120,540 sq km
LEADING EXPORTS: minerals and metallurgical products
CONTINENT: Asia

Korea, South

CAPITAL: Seoul
POPULATION: 45,553,882
MAJOR LANGUAGES: Korean and English
AREA: 38,025 sq mi; 98,480 sq km
LEADING EXPORTS: electronic and electrical equipment
CONTINENT: Asia

Kuwait

CAPITAL: Kuwait
POPULATION: 1,817,397
MAJOR LANGUAGES: Arabic and English
AREA: 6,881 sq mi; 17,820 sq km
LEADING EXPORT: oil
CONTINENT: Asia

Kyrgyzstan

CAPITAL: Bishkek
POPULATION: 4,769,877
MAJOR LANGUAGES: Kyrgyz and Russian
AREA: 76,644 sq mi; 198,500 sq km
LEADING EXPORTS: wool, chemicals, cotton, metals, and shoes
CONTINENT: Asia

Laos

CAPITAL: Vientiane
POPULATION: 4,837,237
MAJOR LANGUAGES: Lao, French, English, and various languages
AREA: 91,432 sq mi; 236,800 sq km
LEADING EXPORTS: electricity, wood products, coffee, and tin
CONTINENT: Asia

Latvia

CAPITAL: Riga
POPULATION: 2,762,899
MAJOR LANGUAGES: Lettish, Lithuanian, Russian, and various languages
AREA: 24,750 sq mi; 64,100 sq km
LEADING EXPORTS: oil products, timber, and ferrous metals
CONTINENT: Europe

Lebanon

CAPITAL: Beirut
POPULATION: 3,695,921
MAJOR LANGUAGES: Arabic, French, Armenian, and English
AREA: 4,016 sq mi; 10,400 sq km
LEADING EXPORTS: agricultural products, chemicals, and textiles
CONTINENT: Asia

Lesotho

CAPITAL: Maseru
POPULATION: 1,992,960
MAJOR LANGUAGES: Sesotho, English, Zulu, and Xhosa
AREA: 11,719 sq mi; 30,350 sq km
LEADING EXPORTS: wool, mohair, wheat, cattle, and peas
CONTINENT: Africa

Liberia

CAPITAL: Monrovia
POPULATION: 3,073,245
MAJOR LANGUAGES: English and Niger-Congo
AREA: 43,002 sq mi; 111,370 sq km
LEADING EXPORTS: iron ore, rubber, timber, and coffee
CONTINENT: Africa

Libya
CAPITAL: Tripoli
POPULATION: 5,248,401
MAJOR LANGUAGES: Arabic, Italian, and English
AREA: 679,385 sq mi; 1,759,540 sq km
LEADING EXPORTS: crude oil and refined petroleum products
CONTINENT: Africa

Liechtenstein

CAPITAL: Vaduz
POPULATION: 30,654
MAJOR LANGUAGES: German and Alemannic
AREA: 62 sq mi; 160 sq km
LEADING EXPORTS: small specialty machinery and dental products
CONTINENT: Europe

Lithuania
CAPITAL: Vilnius
POPULATION: 3,876,396
MAJOR LANGUAGES: Lithuanian, Polish, and Russian
AREA: 25,175 sq mi; 65,200 sq km
LEADING EXPORTS: electronics, petroleum products, and food
CONTINENT: Europe

Luxembourg
CAPITAL: Luxembourg
POPULATION: 404,660
MAJOR LANGUAGES: Luxembourgisch, German, French, and English
AREA: 998 sq mi; 2,586 sq km
LEADING EXPORTS: finished steel products and chemicals
CONTINENT: Europe

Macedonia

CAPITAL: Skopje
POPULATION: 2,159,503
MAJOR LANGUAGES: Macedonian, Albanian, Turkish, Serb, Gypsy, and various languages
AREA: 9,781 sq mi; 25,333 sq km
LEADING EXPORTS: manufactured goods and machinery
CONTINENT: Europe

Madagascar
CAPITAL: Antananarivo
POPULATION: 13,862,325
MAJOR LANGUAGES: French and Malagasy
AREA: 226,665 sq mi; 587,040 sq km
LEADING EXPORTS: coffee, vanilla, cloves, shellfish, and sugar
CONTINENT: Africa

Malawi
CAPITAL: Lilongwe
POPULATION: 9,808,384
MAJOR LANGUAGES: English, Chichewa, and various languages
AREA: 45,747 sq mi; 118,480 sq km
LEADING EXPORTS: tobacco, tea, sugar, coffee, and peanuts
CONTINENT: Africa

Malaysia

CAPITAL: Kuala Lumpur
POPULATION: 19,723,587
MAJOR LANGUAGES: Malay, English, Mandarin, Tamil, Chinese dialects, and various languages and dialects
AREA: 127,322 sq mi; 329,750 sq km
LEADING EXPORTS: electronic equipment
CONTINENT: Asia

Maldives
CAPITAL: Male
POPULATION: 261,310
MAJOR LANGUAGES: Divehi dialect and English
AREA: 116 sq mi; 300 sq km
LEADING EXPORTS: fish and clothing
CONTINENT: Asia

Mali
CAPITAL: Bamako
POPULATION: 9,375,132
MAJOR LANGUAGES: French, Bambara, and various languages
AREA: 478,783 sq mi; 1,240,000 sq km
LEADING EXPORTS: cotton, livestock, and gold
CONTINENT: Africa

Malta
CAPITAL: Valletta
POPULATION: 369,609
MAJOR LANGUAGES: Maltese and English
AREA: 124 sq mi; 320 sq km
LEADING EXPORTS: machinery and transportation equipment
CONTINENT: Europe

Marshall Islands

CAPITAL: Majuro
POPULATION: 56,157
MAJOR LANGUAGES: English, Marshallese dialects, and Japanese
AREA: 70 sq mi; 181.3 sq km
LEADING EXPORTS: coconut oil, fish, live animals, and trichus shells
LOCATION: Pacific Ocean

Mauritania
CAPITAL: Nouakchott
POPULATION: 2,263,202
MAJOR LANGUAGES: Hasaniya Arabic, Wolof, Pular, and Soninke
AREA: 397,969 sq mi; 1,030,700 sq km
LEADING EXPORTS: iron ore, and fish and fish products
CONTINENT: Africa

Mauritius
CAPITAL: Port Louis
POPULATION: 1,127,068
MAJOR LANGUAGES: English (official), Creole, French, Hindi, Urdu, Hakka, and Bojpoori
AREA: 718 sq mi; 1,860 sq km
LEADING EXPORTS: textiles, sugar, and light manufactures
LOCATION: Indian Ocean

Mayotte
CAPITAL: Mamoutzou
POPULATION: 97,088
MAJOR LANGUAGES: Mahorian and French
AREA: 145 sq mi; 375 sq km
LEADING EXPORTS: ylang-ylang and vanilla
CONTINENT: Africa

Mexico

CAPITAL: Mexico City
POPULATION: 93,985,848
MAJOR LANGUAGES: Spanish and Mayan dialects
AREA: 761,632 sq mi; 1,972,550 sq km
LEADING EXPORTS: crude oil, oil products, coffee, and silver
CONTINENT: North America

Micronesia

CAPITAL: Federated states of Kolonia (on the Island of Pohnpei)
*a new capital is being built about 10 km southwest in the Palikir Valley
POPULATION: 122,950
MAJOR LANGUAGES: English, Turkese, Pohnpeian, Yapese, and Kosrean
AREA: 271 sq mi; 702 sq km
LEADING EXPORTS: fish, copra, bananas, and black pepper
LOCATION: Pacific Ocean

Moldova

CAPITAL: Chisinau
POPULATION: 4,489,657
MAJOR LANGUAGES: Moldovan (official), Russian, and Gagauz dialect
AREA: 13,012 sq mi; 33,700 sq km
LEADING EXPORTS: foodstuffs, wine, and tobacco
CONTINENT: Europe

Monaco

CAPITAL: Monaco
POPULATION: 31,515
MAJOR LANGUAGES: French (official), English, Italian, and Monegasque
AREA: .73 sq mi; 1.9 sq km
LEADING EXPORTS: exports through France
CONTINENT: Europe

Mongolia

CAPITAL: Ulaanbaatar
POPULATION: 2,493,615
MAJOR LANGUAGES: Khalkha Mongol, Turkic, Russian, and Chinese
AREA: 604,270 sq mi; 1,565,000 sq km
LEADING EXPORTS: copper, livestock, animal products, and cashmere
CONTINENT: Asia

Morocco

CAPITAL: Rabat
POPULATION: 29,168,848
MAJOR LANGUAGES: Arabic (official), Berber dialects, and French
AREA: 172,420 sq mi; 446,550 sq km
LEADING EXPORTS: food and beverages
CONTINENT: Africa

Mozambique
CAPITAL: Maputo
POPULATION: 18,115,250
MAJOR LANGUAGES: Portuguese and various dialects
AREA: 309,506 sq mi; 801,590 sq km
LEADING EXPORTS: shrimp, cashews, cotton, sugar, copra, and citrus
CONTINENT: Africa

Myanmar (Burma)

CAPITAL: Rangoon
POPULATION: 45,103,809
MAJOR LANGUAGE: Burmese
AREA: 261,979 sq mi; 678,500 sq km
LEADING EXPORTS: pulses and beans, teak, rice, and hardwood
CONTINENT: Asia

Namibia
CAPITAL: Windhoek
POPULATION: 1,651,545
MAJOR LANGUAGES: English (official), Afrikaans, German, Oshivambo, Herero, Nama, and various languages
AREA: 318,707 sq mi; 825,418 sq km
LEADING EXPORTS: diamonds, copper, gold, zinc, and lead
CONTINENT: Africa

Nauru

CAPITAL: Government offices in Yaren District
POPULATION: 10,149
MAJOR LANGUAGES: Nauruan and English
AREA: 8 sq mi; 21 sq km
LEADING EXPORTS: phosphates
LOCATION: Pacific Ocean

Nepal

CAPITAL: Kathmandu
POPULATION: 21,560,869
MAJOR LANGUAGES: Nepali (official) and 20 various languages divided into numerous dialects
AREA: 54,365 sq mi; 140,800 sq km
LEADING EXPORTS: carpets, clothing, and leather goods
CONTINENT: Asia

Netherlands

CAPITAL: Amsterdam
POPULATION: 15,452,903
MAJOR LANGUAGE: Dutch
AREA: 14,414 sq mi; 37,330 sq km
LEADING EXPORTS: metal products and chemicals
CONTINENT: Europe

New Caledonia

CAPITAL: Noumea
POPULATION: 184,552
MAJOR LANGUAGES: French and 28 Melanesian-Polynesian dialects
AREA: 7,359 sq mi; 19,060 sq km
LEADING EXPORTS: nickel metal and nickel ore
LOCATION: Pacific Ocean

New Zealand

CAPITAL: Wellington
POPULATION: 3,407,277
MAJOR LANGUAGES: English and Maori
AREA: 103,741 sq mi; 268,680 sq km
LEADING EXPORTS: wool, lamb, mutton, beef, fish, and cheese
LOCATION: Pacific Ocean

Nicaragua

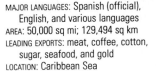

CAPITAL: Managua
POPULATION: 4,206,353
MAJOR LANGUAGES: Spanish (official), English, and various languages
AREA: 50,000 sq mi; 129,494 sq km
LEADING EXPORTS: meat, coffee, cotton, sugar, seafood, and gold
LOCATION: Caribbean Sea

Niger

CAPITAL: Niamey
POPULATION: 9,280,208
MAJOR LANGUAGES: French (official), Hausa, and Djerma
AREA: 489,208 sq mi; 1,267,000 sq km
LEADING EXPORTS: uranium ore and livestock products
CONTINENT: Africa

Nigeria

CAPITAL: Abuja
POPULATION: 101,232,251
MAJOR LANGUAGES: English (official), Hausa, Yoruba, Ibo, and Fulani
AREA: 356,682 sq mi; 923,770 sq km
LEADING EXPORTS: oil, cocoa, and rubber
CONTINENT: Africa

Niue

CAPITAL: (Free association with New Zealand)
POPULATION: 1,837
MAJOR LANGUAGES: Polynesian and English
AREA: 100 sq mi; 260 sq km
LEADING EXPORTS: canned coconut cream, copra, and honey
LOCATION: Pacific Ocean

Norway

CAPITAL: Oslo
POPULATION: 4,330,951
MAJOR LANGUAGES: Norwegian (official), Lapp, and Finnish
AREA: 125,186 sq mi; 324,220 sq km
LEADING EXPORTS: petroleum and petroleum products
CONTINENT: Europe

Oman

CAPITAL: Muscat
POPULATION: 2,125,089
MAJOR LANGUAGES: Arabic (official), English, Baluchi, Urdu, and Indian dialects
AREA: 82,034 sq mi; 212,460 sq km
LEADING EXPORTS: petroleum, re-exports, and fish
CONTINENT: Asia

Pakistan

CAPITAL: Islamabad
POPULATION: 131,541,920
MAJOR LANGUAGES: Urdu (official), English (official), Punjabi, Sindhi, Pashtu, Urdu, Balochi, and other languages
AREA: 310,414 sq mi; 803,940 sq km
LEADING EXPORTS: cotton, textiles, clothing, rice, and leather
CONTINENT: Asia

Palau

CAPITAL: Koror
POPULATION: 16,661
MAJOR LANGUAGES: English (official), Sonsorolese, Angaur, Japanese, Tobi, and Palauan
AREA: 177 sq mi; 458 sq km
LEADING EXPORTS: trochus, tuna, copra, and handicrafts
LOCATION: Pacific Ocean

Panama

CAPITAL: Panama
POPULATION: 2,680,903
MAJOR LANGUAGES: Spanish (official) and English
AREA: 30,194 sq mi; 78,200 sq km
LEADING EXPORTS: bananas, shrimp, sugar, clothing, and coffee
CONTINENT: Central America

Papua New Guinea

CAPITAL: Port Moresby
POPULATION: 4,294,750
MAJOR LANGUAGES: English, pidgin English, and Motu
AREA: 178,266 sq mi; 461,690 sq km
LEADING EXPORTS: gold, copper ore, oil, logs, and palm oil
LOCATION: Pacific Ocean

Paraguay

CAPITAL: Asuncion
POPULATION: 5,358,198
MAJOR LANGUAGES: Spanish (official) and Guarani
AREA: 157,052 sq mi; 406,750 sq km
LEADING EXPORTS: cotton, soybeans, timber, and vegetable oils
CONTINENT: South America

Peru

CAPITAL: Lima
POPULATION: 24,087,372
MAJOR LANGUAGES: Spanish (official), Quechua (official), and Aymara
AREA: 496,243 sq mi; 1,285,220 sq km
LEADING EXPORTS: copper, zinc, and fish meal
CONTINENT: South America

Philippines

CAPITAL: Manila
POPULATION: 73,265,584
MAJOR LANGUAGES: Pilipino and English (official)
AREA: 115,834 sq mi; 300,000 sq km
LEADING EXPORTS: electronics, textiles, and coconut products
CONTINENT: Asia

Poland

CAPITAL: Warsaw
POPULATION: 38,792,442
MAJOR LANGUAGE: Polish
AREA: 120,731 sq mi; 312,680 sq km
LEADING EXPORTS: intermediate goods
CONTINENT: Europe

Portugal

CAPITAL: Lisbon
POPULATION: 10,562,388
MAJOR LANGUAGE: Portuguese
AREA: 35,553 sq mi; 92,080 sq km
LEADING EXPORTS: clothing and footwear, and machinery
CONTINENT: Europe

Qatar

CAPITAL: Doha
POPULATION: 533,916
MAJOR LANGUAGES: Arabic (official) and English
AREA: 4,247 sq mi; 11,000 sq km
LEADING EXPORTS: petroleum products, steel, and fertilizers
CONTINENT: Asia

Romania

CAPITAL: Bucharest
POPULATION: 23,198,330
MAJOR LANGUAGES: Romanian, Hungarian, and German
AREA: 91,702 sq mi; 237,500 sq km
LEADING EXPORTS: metals and metal products, and mineral products
CONTINENT: Europe

Russia

CAPITAL: Moscow
POPULATION: 149,909,089
MAJOR LANGUAGES: Russian and various languages
AREA: 6,952,996 sq mi; 17,075,200 sq km
LEADING EXPORTS: petroleum and petroleum products
CONTINENT: Europe and Asia

Rwanda

CAPITAL: Kigali
POPULATION: 8,605,307
MAJOR LANGUAGES: Kinyarwanda (official), French (official), and Kiswahili
AREA: 10,170 sq mi; 26,340 sq km
LEADING EXPORTS: coffee, tea, cassiterite, and wolframite
CONTINENT: Africa

Saint Kitts and Nevis

CAPITAL: Basseterre
POPULATION: 40,992
MAJOR LANGUAGE: English
AREA: 104 sq mi; 269 sq km
LEADING EXPORTS: machinery, food, and electronics
LOCATION: Caribbean Sea

Saint Lucia

CAPITAL: Castries
POPULATION: 156,050
MAJOR LANGUAGES: English and French patois
AREA: 239 sq mi; 620 sq km
LEADING EXPORTS: bananas, clothing, cocoa, and vegetables
LOCATION: Caribbean Sea

Saint Vincent and the Grenadines

CAPITAL: Kingstown
POPULATION: 117,344
MAJOR LANGUAGES: English and French patois
AREA: 131 sq mi; 340 sq km
LEADING EXPORTS: bananas, and eddoes and dasheen (taro)
LOCATION: Caribbean Sea

San Marino

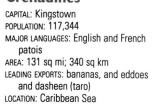

CAPITAL: San Marino
POPULATION: 24,313
MAJOR LANGUAGE: Italian
AREA: 23 sq mi; 60 sq km
LEADING EXPORTS: building stone, lime, wood, and chestnuts
CONTINENT: Europe

Sao Tome and Principe

CAPITAL: Sao Tome
POPULATION: 140,423
MAJOR LANGUAGE: Portuguese (official)
AREA: 371 sq mi; 960 sq km
LEADING EXPORTS: cocoa, copra, coffee, and palm oil
CONTINENT: Africa

Saudi Arabia

CAPITAL: Riyadh
POPULATION: 18,729,576
MAJOR LANGUAGE: Arabic
AREA: 757,011 sq mi; 1,960,582 sq km
LEADING EXPORTS: petroleum and petroleum products
CONTINENT: Asia

Senegal

CAPITAL: Dakar
POPULATION: 9,007,080
MAJOR LANGUAGES: French (official), Wolof, Pulaar, Diola, and Mandingo
AREA: 75,752 sq mi; 196,190 sq km
LEADING EXPORTS: fish, ground nuts, and petroleum products
CONTINENT: Africa

Serbia and Montenegro

CAPITAL: Belgrade
POPULATION: 11,101,833
MAJOR LANGUAGES: Serbo-Croatian and Albanian
AREA: 39,436 sq mi; 102,350 sq km
LEADING EXPORTS: none
CONTINENT: Europe

Seychelles

CAPITAL: Victoria
POPULATION: 72,709
MAJOR LANGUAGES: English (official), French (official), and Creole
AREA: 176 sq mi; 455 sq km
LEADING EXPORTS: fish, cinnamon bark, and copra
CONTINENT: Africa

Sierra Leone

CAPITAL: Freetown
POPULATION: 4,753,120
MAJOR LANGUAGES: English (official), Mende, Temne, and Krio
AREA: 27,700 sq mi; 71,740 sq km
LEADING EXPORTS: rutile, bauxite, diamonds, coffee, and cocoa
CONTINENT: Africa

Singapore

CAPITAL: Singapore
POPULATION: 2,890,468
MAJOR LANGUAGES: Chinese, Malay, Tamil, and English
AREA: 244 sq mi; 633 sq km
LEADING EXPORTS: computer equipment
CONTINENT: Asia

Slovakia

CAPITAL: Bratislava
POPULATION: 5,432,383
MAJOR LANGUAGES: Slovak and Hungarian
AREA: 18,860 sq mi; 48,845 sq km
LEADING EXPORTS: machinery and transportation equipment
CONTINENT: Europe

Slovenia

CAPITAL: Ljubljana
POPULATION: 2,051,522
MAJOR LANGUAGES: Slovenian, Serbo-Croatian, and various languages
AREA: 7,837 sq mi; 20,296 sq km
LEADING EXPORTS: machinery and transportation equipment
CONTINENT: Europe

Solomon Islands

CAPITAL: Honiara
POPULATION: 399,206
MAJOR LANGUAGES: Melanesian pidgin and English
AREA: 10,985 sq mi; 28,450 sq km
LEADING EXPORTS: fish, timber, palm oil, cocoa, and copra
LOCATION: Pacific Ocean

Somalia

CAPITAL: Mogadishu
POPULATION: 7,347,554
MAJOR LANGUAGES: Somali (official), Arabic, Italian, and English
AREA: 246,210 sq mi; 637,660 sq km
LEADING EXPORTS: bananas, live animals, fish, and hides
CONTINENT: Africa

South Africa

CAPITAL: Pretoria (administrative), Cape Town (legislative), Bloemfontein (judicial)
POPULATION: 45,095,459
MAJOR LANGUAGES: Afrikaans, English, Ndebele, Pedi, Sotho, Swazi, Tsonga, Tswana, Venda, Xhosa, and Zulu (all official)
AREA: 471,027 sq mi; 1,219,912 sq km
LEADING EXPORTS: gold, other minerals and metals, and food
CONTINENT: Africa

Spain

CAPITAL: Madrid
POPULATION: 39,404,348
MAJOR LANGUAGES: Spanish, Catalan, Galician, and Basque
AREA: 194,892 sq mi; 504,750 sq km
LEADING EXPORTS: cars and trucks, and semifinished goods
CONTINENT: Europe

Sri Lanka

CAPITAL: Colombo
POPULATION: 18,342,660
MAJOR LANGUAGES: Sinhala (official) and Tamil
AREA: 25,333 sq mi; 65,610 sq km
LEADING EXPORTS: garments and textiles, teas, and diamonds
CONTINENT: Asia

Sudan

CAPITAL: Khartoum
POPULATION: 30,120,420
MAJOR LANGUAGES: Arabic (official), Nubian, Ta Bedawie, Nilotic, Nilo-Hamitic, and Sudanic dialects
AREA: 967,532 sq mi; 2,505,810 sq km
LEADING EXPORTS: gum arabic, livestock/meat, and cotton
CONTINENT: Africa

Suriname

CAPITAL: Paramaribo
POPULATION: 429,544
MAJOR LANGUAGES: Dutch (official), English, Sranang, Tongo, Hindustani, and Japanese
AREA: 63,041 sq mi; 163,270 sq km
LEADING EXPORTS: alumina, aluminum, and shrimp and fish
CONTINENT: South America

Swaziland

CAPITAL: Mbabane
POPULATION: 966,977
MAJOR LANGUAGES: English (official) and SiSwati (official)
AREA: 6,641 sq mi; 17,360 sq km
LEADING EXPORTS: sugar, edible concentrates, and wood pulp
CONTINENT: Africa

Sweden

CAPITAL: Stockholm
POPULATION: 8,821,759
MAJOR LANGUAGES: Swedish, Lapp, and Finnish
AREA: 173,738 sq mi; 449,964 sq km
LEADING EXPORTS: machinery, motor vehicles, and paper products
CONTINENT: Europe

Switzerland

CAPITAL: Bern
POPULATION: 7,084,984
MAJOR LANGUAGES: German, French, Italian, Romansch, and various languages
AREA: 15,943 sq mi; 41,290 sq km
LEADING EXPORTS: machinery and equipment
CONTINENT: Europe

Syria

CAPITAL: Damascus
POPULATION: 15,451,917
MAJOR LANGUAGES: Arabic (official), Kurdish, Armenian, Aramaic, Circassian, and French
AREA: 71,501 sq mi; 185,180 sq km
LEADING EXPORTS: petroleum, textiles, cotton, and fruits
CONTINENT: Asia

Taiwan

CAPITAL: Taipei
POPULATION: 21,500,583
MAJOR LANGUAGES: Mandarin Chinese (official), Taiwanese, and Hakka dialects
AREA: 13,892 sq mi; 35,980 sq km
LEADING EXPORTS: electrical machinery and electronics
CONTINENT: Asia

Tajikistan

CAPITAL: Dushanbe
POPULATION: 6,155,474
MAJOR LANGUAGES: Tajik (official) and Russian
AREA: 55,253 sq mi; 143,100 sq km
LEADING EXPORTS: cotton, aluminum, fruits, and vegetable oil
CONTINENT: Asia

Tanzania

CAPITAL: Dar Es Salaam
POPULATION: 28,701,077
MAJOR LANGUAGES: Swahili, English, and various languages
AREA: 364,914 sq mi; 945,090 sq km
LEADING EXPORTS: coffee, cotton, tobacco, tea, and cashew nuts
CONTINENT: Africa

Thailand

CAPITAL: Bangkok
POPULATION: 60,271,300
MAJOR LANGUAGES: Thai and English
AREA: 198,463 sq mi; 511,770 sq km
LEADING EXPORTS: machinery and manufactures
CONTINENT: Asia

Togo

CAPITAL: Lome
POPULATION: 4,410,370
MAJOR LANGUAGES: French, Ewe and Mina, Dagomba, and Kabye
AREA: 21,927 sq mi; 56,790 sq km
LEADING EXPORTS: phosphates, cotton, cocoa, and coffee
CONTINENT: Africa

Tonga

CAPITAL: Nukualofa
POPULATION: 105,600
MAJOR LANGUAGES: Tongan and English
AREA: 289 sq mi; 748 sq km
LEADING EXPORTS: squash, vanilla, fish, root crops, and coconut oil
LOCATION: Pacific Ocean

Trinidad and Tobago

CAPITAL: Port-of-Spain
POPULATION: 1,271,159
MAJOR LANGUAGES: English, Hindu, French, and Spanish
AREA: 1,981 sq mi; 5,130 sq km
LEADING EXPORTS: petroleum and petroleum products
LOCATION: Caribbean Sea

Tunisia

CAPITAL: Tunis
POPULATION: 8,879,845
MAJOR LANGUAGES: Arabic and French
AREA: 63,172 sq mi; 163,610 sq km
LEADING EXPORTS: hydrocarbons and agricultural products
CONTINENT: Africa

Turkey

CAPITAL: Ankara
POPULATION: 63,405,526
MAJOR LANGUAGES: Turkish, Kurdish, and Arabic
AREA: 301,394 sq mi; 780,580 sq km
LEADING EXPORTS: manufactured products, and foodstuffs
CONTINENT: Europe and Asia

Turkmenistan

CAPITAL: Ashgabat
POPULATION: 4,075,316
MAJOR LANGUAGES: Turkmen, Russian, Uzbek, and various languages
AREA: 188,463 sq mi; 488,100 sq km
LEADING EXPORTS: natural gas, cotton, and petroleum products
CONTINENT: Asia

Tuvalu

CAPITAL: Fongafale, on Funafuti atoll
POPULATION: 9,991
MAJOR LANGUAGES: Tuvaluan and English
AREA: 10 sq mi; 26 sq km
LEADING EXPORT: copra
LOCATION: Pacific Ocean

Uganda

CAPITAL: Kampala
POPULATION: 19,573,262
MAJOR LANGUAGES: English, Luganda, Swahili, Bantu languages, and Nilotic languages
AREA: 91,139 sq mi; 236,040 sq km
LEADING EXPORTS: coffee, cotton, and tea
CONTINENT: Africa

Ukraine

CAPITAL: Kiev
POPULATION: 51,867,828
MAJOR LANGUAGES: Ukranian, Russian, Romanian, Polish, and Hungarian
AREA: 233,098 sq mi; 603,700 sq km
LEADING EXPORTS: coal, electric power, and metals
CONTINENT: Europe

United Arab Emirates

CAPITAL: Abu Dhabi
POPULATION: 2,924,594
MAJOR LANGUAGES: Arabic, Persian, English, Hindi, and Urdu
AREA: 29,183 sq mi; 75,581 sq km
LEADING EXPORTS: crude oil, natural gas, re-exports, and dried fish
CONTINENT: Asia

United Kingdom

CAPITAL: London
POPULATION: 58,295,119
MAJOR LANGUAGES: English, Welsh, and Scottish Gaelic
AREA: 94,529 sq mi; 244,820 sq km
LEADING EXPORTS: manufactured goods, machinery, and fuels
CONTINENT: Europe

United States

CAPITAL: Washington, D.C.
POPULATION: 263,814,032
MAJOR LANGUAGES: English and Spanish
AREA: 3,618,908 sq mi; 9,372,610 sq km
LEADING EXPORTS: capital goods and automobiles
CONTINENT: North America

Uruguay

CAPITAL: Montevideo
POPULATION: 3,222,716
MAJOR LANGUAGES: Spanish and Brazilero
AREA: 68,041 sq mi; 176,220 sq km
LEADING EXPORTS: wool and textile manufactures
CONTINENT: South America

Uzbekistan

CAPITAL: Tashkent
POPULATION: 23,089,261
MAJOR LANGUAGES: Uzbek, Russian, Tajik, various languages
AREA: 172,748 sq mi; 447,400 sq km
LEADING EXPORTS: cotton, gold, natural gas, and minerals
CONTINENT: Asia

Vanuatu

CAPITAL: Port-Vila
POPULATION: 173,648
MAJOR LANGUAGES: English, French, pidgin, and Bislama
AREA: 5,699 sq mi; 14,760 sq km
LEADING EXPORTS: copra, beef, cocoa, timber, and coffee
LOCATION: Pacific Ocean

Venezuela

CAPITAL: Caracas
POPULATION: 21,004,773
MAJOR LANGUAGES: Spanish and various languages
AREA: 352,156 sq mi; 912,050 sq km
LEADING EXPORTS: petroleum, bauxite and aluminum, and steel
CONTINENT: South America

Vietnam

CAPITAL: Hanoi
POPULATION: 74,393,324
MAJOR LANGUAGES: Vietnamese, French, Chinese, English, Khmer, and various languages
AREA: 127,248 sq mi; 329,560 sq km
LEADING EXPORTS: petroleum, rice, and agricultural products
CONTINENT: Asia

Western Samoa

CAPITAL: Apia
POPULATION: 209,360
MAJOR LANGUAGES: Samoan and English
AREA: 1,104 sq mi; 2,860 sq km
LEADING EXPORTS: coconut oil and cream, taro, copra, and cocoa
LOCATION: Pacific Ocean

Yemen

CAPITAL: Sanaa
POPULATION: 14,728,474
MAJOR LANGUAGE: Arabic
AREA: 203,857 sq mi; 527,970 sq km
LEADING EXPORTS: crude oil, cotton, coffee, hides, and vegetables
CONTINENT: Asia

Zaire

CAPITAL: Kinshasa
POPULATION: 44,060,636
MAJOR LANGUAGES: French, Lingala, Swahili, Kingwana, Kikongo, and Tshiluba
AREA: 905,599 sq mi; 2,345,410 sq km
LEADING EXPORTS: copper, coffee, diamonds, cobalt, and crude oil
CONTINENT: Africa

Zambia

CAPITAL: Lusaka
POPULATION: 9,445,723
MAJOR LANGUAGES: English (official) and about 70 various languages
AREA: 290,594 sq mi; 752,610 sq km
LEADING EXPORTS: copper, zinc, cobalt, lead, and tobacco
CONTINENT: Africa

Zimbabwe

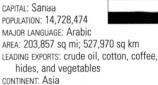

CAPITAL: Harare
POPULATION: 11,139,961
MAJOR LANGUAGES: English, Shona, and Sindebele
area: 150,809 sq mi; 390,580 sq km
LEADING EXPORTS: agricultural products and manufactures
CONTINENT: Africa

Glossary of Geographic Terms

basin
a depression in the surface of the land; some basins are filled with water

bay
a part of a sea or lake that extends into the land

butte
a small raised area of land with steep sides

▲ butte

canyon
a deep, narrow valley with steep sides; often has a stream flowing through it

cataract
a large waterfall; any strong flood or rush of water

delta
a triangular-shaped plain at the mouth of a river, formed when sediment is deposited by flowing water

flood plain
a broad plain on either side of a river, formed when sediment settles on the riverbanks

glacier
a huge, slow-moving mass of snow and ice

hill
an area that rises above surrounding land and has a rounded top; lower and usually less steep than a mountain

island
an area of land completely surrounded by water

isthmus
a narrow strip of land that connects two larger areas of land

mesa
a high, flat-topped landform with cliff-like sides; larger than a butte

mountain
an area that rises steeply at least 2,000 feet (300 m) above surrounding land; usually wide at the bottom and rising to a narrow peak or ridge

▶ glacier

◀ cataract

◀ delta

mountain pass
a gap between mountains

peninsula
an area of land almost completely surrounded by water and connected to the mainland by an isthmus

plain
a large area of flat or gently rolling land

plateau
a large, flat area that rises above the surrounding land; at least one side has a steep slope

river mouth
the point where a river enters a lake or sea

strait
a narrow stretch of water that connects two larger bodies of water

tributary
a river or stream that flows into a larger river

volcano
an opening in the Earth's surface through which molten rock, ashes, and gasses from the Earth's interior escape

▶ volcano

Gazetteer

A

Appalachian Mountains (37.20°N, 82°W) a mountain system in eastern North America, p. 11

Atlanta (33.45°N, 84.23°W) the capital of the state of Georgia, p. 93

B

Boston (42.15°N, 71.07°W) the capital of the state of Massachusetts, p. 87

C

Cariboo Mountains a mountain range in eastern British Columbia, Canada; a place where miners struck gold in the 1800s, p. 132

Chicago (41.49°N, 87.37°W) a major city in the state of Illinois, on Lake Michigan, p. 102

Cuyahoga River (41.22°N, 81.38°W) a river in northeastern Ohio, p. 57

D

Death Valley (36.30°N, 117°W) the hottest, driest region of North America, located in southeastern California, p. 11

Detroit (42.22°N, 83.10°W) a city in the state of Michigan, p. 103

F

Fraser River (51.30°N, 122°W) a major river of western North America, along the border between British Columbia and Alberta, p. 132

G

Grand Coulee Dam (47.58°N, 119.28°W) a dam on the Columbia River in the state of Washington, p. 23

Great Lakes

Great Lakes a group of five large lakes in central North America: Lakes Superior, Michigan, Huron, Erie, and Ontario, p. 13

I

Imperial Valley (33°N, 115.22°W) a valley in the Colorado Desert, extending from southeastern California to Mexico, p. 22

J

Jamestown the first permanent British settlement in North America, located in present-day Virginia; now a site of historic preservation, p. 36

L

Lake Erie the fourth largest of the five Great Lakes; forms part of the boundary between Canada and the United States, p. 57

M

Minneapolis–St. Paul (44.58°N, 93.15°W–44.57°N, 93.05°W) two cities in Minnesota; also called the Twin Cities, p. 104

Mississippi River (32°N, 91.30°W) a large river in the central United States flowing south from Minnesota to the Gulf of Mexico, p. 14

Montreal (45.30°N, 73.35°W) the largest city in the province of Quebec, Canada, p. 120

N

New York City (40.40°N, 73.58°W) a large city and port at the mouth of the Hudson River in the state of New York, p. 87

Niagara Falls (43.05°N, 79.05°W) a waterfall on the Niagara River between Ontario, Canada, and New York state; one of North America's most famous spectacles, p. 60

Nunavut a section of land in the Northwest Territories of Canada, granted by the government as Inuit "homeland," p. 78

O

Ontario (50.47°N, 88.50°W) the second-largest province in Canada, p. 52

P

Pacific Northwest the region in the northwestern United States that includes Oregon, Washington, and part of Idaho, p. 107

Pacific Rim the countries bordering on the Pacific Ocean, p. 134

Pennsylvania Colony a colony in America founded in 1680 by William Penn, who purchased land from the Native Americans, p. 36

Philadelphia (40°N, 75.13°W) a city and port in Pennsylvania, on the Delaware River, p. 87

Portland (45.31°N, 122.41°W) the largest city in the state of Oregon, p. 108

Q

Quebec (51.07°N, 70.25°W) a province in southeastern Canada, p. 51

Quebec City (46.49°N, 71.13°W) the capital city of the province of Quebec, Canada, p. 119

R

Regina (50.25°N, 104.39°W) the capital of the province of Saskatchewan, Canada, p. 129

Rocky Mountains (50°N, 114°W) the major mountain range in western North America, extending south from Alberta, Canada, through the western United States to Mexico, p. 10

S

San Jose (37.20°N, 121.54°W) a city in western California, p. 109

Saskatoon (52.07°N, 106.38°W) a city in the province of Saskatchewan, Canada, p. 129

Sierra Nevada Mountains a mountain range in California in the western United States, p. 107

St. Lawrence Lowlands a major agricultural region in the prairie provinces of Canada, p. 24

St. Lawrence River (48.24°N, 63.30°W) a river in eastern North America; the third-longest river in Canada, p. 12

St. Lawrence Seaway a navigable seaway from the Atlantic Ocean to the western end of the Great Lakes, maintained jointly by the United States and Canada, p. 60

St. Louis (38.39°N, 90.15°W) the largest city in Missouri, on the Mississippi River, p. 103

V

Vancouver (49.16°N, 123.06°W) a city in southwestern British Columbia, Canada, p. 16

Victoria (48.26°N, 123.23°W) the capital of British Columbia, Canada, p. 132

W

Washington, D.C. (38.50°N, 77°W) the capital city of the United States, located between Maryland and Virginia on the Potomac River, p. 98

Winnipeg (49.53°N, 97.09°W) the capital city of Manitoba, Canada, p. 16

Y

Yukon (63.16°N, 135.30°W) a territory in northwestern Canada, p. 53

Glossary

A

abolitionist a person who believed that enslaving people was wrong and who wanted to end the practice, p. 42

acid rain a rain containing acid chemicals harmful to plants and trees, formed when pollutants from cars and factories combine with moisture in the air, p. 58

agribusiness a large company that runs huge farms to produce, process, and distribute agricultural products, p. 22

alliance formal agreement to do business together, sometimes formed between governments, p. 38

alluvial deposited by water, relating to the fertile topsoil left by rivers after a flood, p. 22

amid in the middle of; within, p. 73

B

bilingual speaking two languages; having two official languages, p. 54

bison buffalo; a large animal something like an ox, p. 33

boomtown a settlement that springs up quickly, often to serve the needs of miners, p. 132

boycott a refusal to buy or use goods and services, p. 37

C

civil rights movement a large group of people who worked together in the United States beginning in the 1960s to end the segregation of African Americans and support equal rights for all minorities, p. 48

Civil War the war between the northern and southern states in the United States, which began in 1861 and ended in 1865, p. 42

clear-cutting a type of logging in which all the trees in an area are cut down, p. 59

Cold War a period of great tension between the United States and the former Soviet Union, which lasted for more than 40 years after World War II, p. 48

communism a system of government in which the government controls the means of production, determining what goods are to be made, how much workers will be paid, and how much items will cost, p. 48

commute to travel regularly to and from a place, particularly to and from a job, p. 87

complex complicated; not simple, p. 130

conservation preserving and protecting from loss, p. 105

Continental Divide the boundary that separates rivers flowing toward opposite sides of a continent; in North America, in the Rocky Mountains, p. 14

cooperative an organization managed by a group of people working together for a shared purpose, p. 128

corporate farm a large farm run by a corporation; may consist of many smaller farms once owned by families, p. 101

counter to answer in an opposite way, p. 109

crucial extremely important, p. 52

cultural diversity a wide variety of cultures, p. 69

cultural exchange a process in which different cultures share ideas and ways of doing things, p. 70

D

debate argument; disagreement expressed in words, p. 41

dense thick and crowded, p. 131

descendant child, grandchild, great-grandchild (and so on) of an ancestor, p. 121

dictator a person who rules a country completely and independently, p. 47

distinct clearly different; separate, p. 35

diverse very different, p. 35

dominion a self-governing area subject to Great Britain, for example, Canada and Australia prior to 1939, p. 53

drought long dry spell with no rain, p. 125

dwindle to become fewer in number, p. 100

E

economy a system for producing, distributing, consuming, and owning goods, services, and wealth, p. 8

enslave to force someone to become a slave, p. 35

ethnic group a group of people who share a language, a religion, a history, and cultural traditions, p. 71

expanse a wide open space or area, p. 22

F

fertile able to produce many crops, p. 11

forty-niner one of the first miners of the California Gold Rush of 1849, p. 107

fossil fuel a fuel formed over millions of years from animal and plant remains, includes coal, petroleum, and natural gas, p. 58

Francophone a person who speaks French as his or her first language, p. 121

free trade a trade with no tariffs or taxes on imported goods, p. 61

freshwater containing water that has no salt in it, p. 13

fugitive a runaway; someone who runs from danger, p. 41

fundamental basic; being the foundation on which something is built, p. 105

G

gangplank a movable bridge or walkway people cross to get on or off a ship, p. 91

geographic diversity a variety of landforms, climates, and vegetation, p. 70

glacier a large mass of ice that moves slowly over the land, formed over a long period of time from unmelted snow, p. 12

gunny sack a bag or sack made of burlap or other coarse materials, p. 99

H

habitat the area in which a plant or an animal naturally grows or lives, p. 108

haze foglike air, often caused by pollution, p. 58

Homestead Act a law passed in 1862 giving 160 acres (65 hectares) of land on the Midwestern plains to any adult willing to live on and farm it for five years, p. 45

hydroelectricity electric power produced by moving water, usually generated by releasing water from a dam across a river, p. 23

I

immigrant a person who moves to a new country in order to settle there, p. 40

immunity a natural resistance to disease, p. 126

indentured servant a person who, in exchange for benefits received, must work for a period of years to gain freedom, p. 35

indigenous originating in a certain place, p. 35

industrialization the process of building new industries in an area previously dominated by farming; the development of large industries, p. 96

Industrial Revolution the change from making goods by hand to making them by machine; the Industrial Revolution began in England in the 1700s and later spread to the United States and Europe, p. 40

interdependent dependent upon one other, p. 60

L

labor force the supply of workers, p. 45

lacrosse ballgame played by two teams with long rackets, p. 79

land bridge a bridge from one place to another formed by a narrow strip of land, p. 33

landmass a large area of land, p. 10

lock an enclosed section of a canal or river used to raise or lower a ship to another level, p. 13

Louisiana Purchase the sale of land in 1803 by France to the United States; all the land between the Mississippi River and the eastern slope of the Rocky Mountains, p. 38

lowlands lands that are lower than the surrounding land, p. 11

M

mammoth a huge animal something like an elephant, now extinct, p. 33

Manifest Destiny a belief that the United States had a right to own and rule all the land from the Atlantic Ocean to the Pacific Ocean, p. 40

mass transit a system of subways, buses, and commuter trains used to transport large numbers of people, p. 109

megalopolis a number of cities and suburbs that blend into one very large urban area, p. 87

migration movement of people from one country or region to another in order to make a new home, p. 33

missionary a person who tries to convert others to his or her religion, and who may offer health services or education, p. 35

mixed-crop farm a farm that grows several different kinds of crops, p. 100

N

NAFTA North American Free Trade Agreement, made in 1994 among Canada, the United States, and Mexico to establish mutual free trade, p. 61

navigate to travel; to figure out how to travel, p. 13

nomadic moving from one place to another frequently, p. 78

O

obstacle something that is in the way, p. 133

ore rock that contains valuable metal or minerals, p. 25

P

pastime recreation; activity that makes time pass pleasantly, p. 73

permafrost permanently frozen layer of ground below the top layer of soil, p. 19

petrochemical a substance, such as plastic, paint, or asphalt, that is made from petroleum, p. 95

plantation a large, one-crop farm with many workers, common in the southern colonies of the United States before the Civil War, p. 36

population density the average number of people per square mile or square kilometer, p. 88

prairie a region of flat or rolling land covered with tall grasses, p. 19

prejudice unfair judgment against someone made without reason, p. 121

prosperity a successful situation, especially with wealth, p. 39

province a political division of land in Canada, similar to a state in the United States, p. 19

Q

Quiet Revolution a peaceful change in the government of the Province of Quebec, Canada, in which the *Parti Québécois* won control of the legislature and made French the official language, p. 122

R

rain shadow an area on the side of a mountain away from the wind that receives little rainfall, p. 17

recession a downturn in business activity and economic prosperity, not as severe as a depression, p. 101

Reconstruction a plan for rebuilding the nation after the Civil War, included a period when the South was governed by the United States Army, p. 43

referendum a ballot or vote in which voters decide for or against a particular issue, p. 122

represent to speak for someone else and guard their interests, p. 37

reserve an area of land set aside by the Canadian government for indigenous peoples, p. 77

Revolutionary War the war in which the American colonies won their independence from Britain, fought from 1775 to 1781, p. 37

rural countrylike, not like a city, p. 96

S

segregate to set apart and force to use separate schools, housing, parks, and so on because of race or religion, p. 43

separatist in Canada, someone who wants the province of Quebec to break away from the rest of the country, p. 121

settlement house a community center for poor immigrants to the United States, for example, Jane Addams's Hull House in Chicago, p. 45

shield plateau; an area of high, mostly level land, p. 12

slum a usually crowded area of a city, often with poverty and poor housing, p. 44

sod top layer of soil covered with grass, p. 126

sparsely thinly; in a scattered, uncrowded way, p. 133

subway commuter train that travels underground, p. 87

Sun Belt the broad area of the United States that stretches from the southern Atlantic Coast to the coast of California; known for its warm weather, p. 97

T

tariff a fee charged on imported goods, p. 61

tenement an apartment house that is poorly built and crowded, p. 44

totem pole a tall, carved wooden pole containing tribe, clan, or family symbols, found among Native Americans of the Pacific Northwest, p. 130

tributary a river or stream that flows into a larger river, p. 14

tropics the area on the Earth between the $23\frac{1}{2}°$N and $23\frac{1}{2}°$S lines of latitude, where the climate is almost always hot, p. 17

tundra a cold, dry region covered with snow for more than half the year; a vast, treeless plain where the subsoil is frozen even in summer, p. 19

U

unique having no equal; the only one of its kind, p. 11

V

vast huge; enormous in size, p. 10

Index

The *italicized* page numbers refer to illustrations. The *m, c, p, t,* or *g* preceding the number refers to maps *(m)*, charts *(c)*, pictures *(p)*, tables *(t)*, or graphs *(g)*.

A

abolitionists, 41
Acadia, 51
acid rain, 58
Activity Shop: interdisciplinary, 66–67; lab, 30–31
Adams, Samuel, 37
Addams, Jane, 45
Africa, *m 163;* physical, 171; political, 170
African Americans: American civil rights movement and, 48–49; participation of, in the Civil War, 43; voting rights of, 39
agribusiness, 21
agriculture. *See* farming
air pollution, 58, *p 58,* 109. *See also* environmental issues
Alaska, 9, 10, 33; U.S. acquisition of, 46
Alberta: grain industry in, *p 61*
Ali, Muhammad, *p 93*
Allied Powers, 46
alluvial soil, 22
American Constitution. *See* Constitution: American
American Revolution, 37, *p 52,* 89
"America's breadbasket." *See* Midwest (U.S.)
Anaheim Mighty Ducks, 79
ancestry: most common U.S. and Canadian sources of, 7, *c 7*
Andereasen, Joseph, *p 74*
Anne of Green Gables, 78
Appalachian Mountains, 10, 29; coniferous forests in, 20
Arizona, 9
art: in Canada, *p 77, 78–79;* Inuit, *p 78;* student, 54; in New York City, 91; in the United States, 73–74
Asia, 33, *m 163;* physical, 172; political, 172
Atlanta, Georgia: cable television and, 97; and the 1996 Summer Olympic Games, 93
Atlantic Ocean, 18, 29, 56, 60
atomic bomb, 48
Atwood, Margaret, 78
Austin, Texas, 97
Australia, *m 163;* physical-political, *m 174*
Austria-Hungary, 46
authors: American, 35, 41–42, 74, 89; Canadian, 78
automobile industry: in Detroit, Michigan, 103
Azimuthal projection, 151

B

Battle of Quebec, 51, *p 51*
beavers: importance of, to French fur traders, 51; importance of, to native peoples of Canada, 50, *p 50*
Benét, Stephen Vincent, 84
Benjamin, Florence, 72
bicentennial: U.S., *p 49*
bilingualism: in Canada, 54, 76. *See also* Quebec
Billy the Kid, 73
bird watching. *See* forests: bird watching and

bison, 33
Black River Falls, Wisconsin, 99
bluegrass, 73
boll weevil, 94
Bond, Rebecca, 54
boomtowns. *See* Gold Rush: Canadian
border: Canadian and U.S., *p 56,* 59
Boston, Massachusetts, 89
boycott: American, of British goods, 37; by Mexican-American farmworkers, 109
Bressette, Thomas M., 77–78
British Columbia, 12; 118, *m 118;* Canadian Pacific Railway and, 133; Provincial Profile of, *m 131, c 131;* timber industry and, 25
British North American Act, 53
Broadway. *See* New York City: art in
Brooklyn Bridge, *p 90*
buffalo: European slaughter of, in Canada, 127
Burgess Shale, 12
burrowing owls, 127

C

Cajuns, 51
California, 11
Cambridge, Massachusetts, 89
Canada: British control of, 51–52; independence of, 54
"Canada's breadbasket." *See* Saskatchewan
Canadian Mounted Police, 133
Canadian Pacific Railway, *p 53,* 134
Canadian Shield, 12, 25, 29
cancer research: "Marathon of Hope" and, 79
Cape Canaveral, Florida, 97
Caribbean Sea, 35
Cariboo Mountains, 132
Carlotta, California, 21
Cartier, Jacques, 119–121
Cascade Mountains, 11
Cathedral-Basilica of Mary, Queen of the World, 123
cattle: and the Great Plains, 19
Central America, *m 160*
Central Plains, 11, 14
Central Powers, 46
Chamberland, Paul, 76
Charleston, South Carolina, 98
Chavez, Cesar, 109
Chemainus, British Columbia, *p 77*
Cherokee nation: Supreme Court case and, *m 39. See also* Native Americans; Sequoyah
Chesapeake Bay, 96
Cheyenne, *m 70. See also* Native Americans
Chicago, Illinois, 102–103, *p 102, p 144*
child labor, 45, 49
China, 10
Chinatown. *See* New York City: ethnic groups in
Chinese Americans, *p 72*
Chinese New Year, *p 72*
Chippewas, 77. *See also* Native Americans
Chukchees, 71. *See also* indigenous peoples

circle graphs, 81
civil rights movement, 48–49; and Mexican American farmworkers, 48
Civil War: African American soldiers in, *p 43;* causes of, 40–42; Reconstruction and, 43
Clark, William, 38
Clayoquot Sound, 59
clear-cutting, 59, *p 59. See also* logging industry
Cleveland, Ohio, *p 58;* and pollution of the Cuyahoga River, 57
climate: in Florida, 17; of the Midwest, 71; of the United States and Canada, 6, *m 6;* zones, 15–18. *See also* climate regions; Provincial Profiles; Regional Profiles
climate regions, 158, *g 158*
CN Tower, *p 54*
Coast Mountains, 12
Cold War, 48
colonies: early American, 36–37, *p 37*
Colorado River, 14
Columbia River, 14, 108; Grand Coulee Dam and, 23
Columbus, Christopher, 35
Comanches, *m 70. See also* Native Americans
combine harvester, *p 45*
Commonwealth of Nations, 55
communism, 48
commuters: New York City and, 87
compass: European explorers and, *p 35*
computer industry: in the South (U.S.), 97
concentration camps, 47
concept map, 81
Confederacy, 42
Confederate States of America. *See* Confederacy
Congressional Medal of Honor, *p 43*
coniferous forest, *m 18, c 159;* in mountain regions, 20
conservation: of forests, 59
Constitution: American, 37, 89
constitutional monarchy, 55
Continental Divide, 14
Cook, James, 131
Copland, Aaron, 73
corn: importance of, to European trade, 35
corporate farms, 101–102
cotton: importance of, to South's economy, 94–95; slaves and, 40–41
cotton gin, 40
Crown of Columbus, The, 35
Cuba, 46
cultural diversity, 69
cultural exchange, 70–71
culture: Canadian, 78–79; U.S., 73–74
Cuyahoga River, 57

D

Dallas, Texas, *p 96*
Death Valley, 11, 17
deciduous forest, *m 18,* 20, *c 159*
Declaration of Independence, 37, 89
Delaware River, 89

Acknowledgments

Program Development, Design, Illustration, and Production
Proof Positive/Farrowlyne Associates, Inc.

Cover Design
Olena Serbyn and Bruce Bond

Cover Photo
Jon Chomitz

Maps
GeoSystems Global Corp.

Text

35, From *The Crown of Columbus* by Louise Erdrich and Michael Dorris. Copyright © 1991 by Michael Dorris and Louise Erdrich. Reprinted by permission of HarperCollins Publishers, Inc. 44, From *How the Other Half Lives* by Jacob A. Riis. Copyright © 1971 by Dover Publications, Inc. Reprinted by permission. 69, 72 From *New Kids on the Block: Oral Histories of Immigrant Teens* by Janet Bode. Copyright © 1989 by Janet Bode. Published by Franklin Watts. 75, From *The Land and People of Canada* by Andrew H. Malcolm. Text copyrighted © 1992 by Andrew H. Malcolm. Reprinted with permission of HarperCollins Publishers, Inc. 78, From "Chippewas Push Claims for Land in Canada," by Clyde H. Farnsworth, *New York Times,* August 27, 1995. Copyright © 1995 by The New York Times Co. Reprinted by permission. 84, From *The Book of Americans* by Rosemary and Stephen Vincent Benét. Copyright © 1933 by Rosemary and Stephen Vincent Benét. Copyright © renewed 1961 by Rosemary Carr Benét. Reprinted by permission of Brandt & Brandt Literary Agents, Inc. 85, "The chief of the world", "Glooscap's wigwam", from *Whirlwind Is a Ghost Dancing* by Natalia Belting. Copyright © 1974 by Natalia Belting. Used by permission of Dutton Children's Books, a division of Penguin Books USA Inc. 95, From *Fannie Lou Hamer: From Sharecropping to Politics* by David Rubel. Copyright © 1990 by Silver Burdett Press, Simon & Schuster Elementary. Used by permission. 105, From *History of the United States* by Thomas V. DiBacco, Lorna C. Mason, and Christian G. Appy. Copyright © 1991 by Houghton Mifflin Company. Reprinted by permission. 114, From *Childtimes: A Three-Generation Memoir* by Eloise Greenfield and Lessie Jones Little. Copyright © 1979 by Eloise Greenfield and Lessie Jones Little. Reprinted by permission of HarperCollins Publishers, Inc. 123, From *Quebec, I Love You* by Miyuki Tanobe. Copyright © 1976 by Miyuki Tanobe, published by Tundra Books. Reprinted by permission.

Photo Research
Feldman & Associates, Inc.

Photos

1 T, © Rob Van Patten/The Image Bank, 1 M, © Andre Gallant/The Image Bank, 1 B, © Nancy Brown/The Image Bank, 4, © Mark Thayer, Boston, 7 M, © Andrea Pistolesi/The Image Bank, 7 B, © Eddie Hironaka/The Image Bank, 8, © John Edwards/Tony Stone Images, 9, © Olaf Soot/Tony Stone Images, 10, © Francis Lepine/Valan Photos, 11, © G. Brad Lewis/Tony Stone Images, 12, © Phillip Norton/Valan Photos, 13, © Thomas Kitchin/Tom Stack & Associates, 14, © Science VU/Visuals Unlimited, 15, © Donald Nausbaum/Tony Stone Images, 16 BL, © John Eastcott/Yva Momatiuk/Valan Photos, 16 BR, © D.S. Henderson/The Image Bank, 19, © Stephen Krasemann/Valan Photos, 20, © M. Julien/Valan Photos, 21, © Harald Sund/The Image Bank, 22, © Bruce Forster/Tony Stone Images, 24, © H. Armstrong Roberts, 25,

© Vince Streano/Tony Stone Images, 30, © Ronald E. Partis/Unicorn Stock Photos, 31 TL, TR, © David Young-Wolff/PhotoEdit, 33 T, B, © Steve McCutcheon/Visuals Unlimited, 34, © John Garrett/Tony Stone Images, 35, © Michael Holford/National Maritime Museum, 37, © The Bostonian Society/Old State House, 38, © The Granger Collection, 39, © The Granger Collection, 40, © Michael Keller/West Virginia State Museum, 42, © The Granger Collection, 43 T, © Corbis-Bettman, 43 M, © Seth Goltzer/William Gladstone/West Point Museum Collections, 44, © The Granger Collection, 45 BL, © The Granger Collection, 45 BR, © The Oakland Museum History Department, 46 M, © Library of Congress, 46 B, National Archives #111-SC-25026, 47, © The Granger Collection, 49, © UPI/Corbis-Bettman, 50, © John D. Cunningham/Visuals Unlimited, 51, © Library of Congress, 52, © The Granger Collection, 53, © Hulton Getty/Tony Stone Images, 54, Toronto and the CN Tower, by Rebecca Bond, age 10, of Ajax, Ontario, Canada, 55, © Winston Fraser/Fraser Photos, 56, © Phillip Norton/Valan Photos, 57 BL, © Audrey Gibson/Visuals Unlimited, 57 BR, © Cleveland Public Library/Photograph Collection, 59, © Rich Iwasaki/Tony Stone Images, 61, © Glen Allison/Tony Stone Images, 62, © Michael Newman/PhotoEdit, 66 ML, © SuperStock International, 66 MR, © Dennis MacDonald/PhotoEdit, 66 BL, © The Bettmann Archive/Corbis-Bettmann, 66 BR, © Ann Trulove/Unicorn Stock Photos, 68, © Robert Brenner/PhotoEdit, 69, © Michael Newman/PhotoEdit, 72, © Lawrence Migdale/Tony Stone Images, 73, © Paul Damien/Tony Stone Images, 74, Here's the Pitch, by Joseph Andereasen, age 11, USA. Courtesy of the International Children's Art Museum, 75, © Back From Abroad/The Image Bank, 76, © Val & Alan Wilkinson/Valan Photos, 77, © Dave G. Houser/Dave Houser Photography, 78, © J. Eastcott/Yva Momatiuk/Valan Photos, 79, © Elsa Hasch/AllSport USA, 85, © The Granger Collection, 87, © Wayne Eastep/Tony Stone Images, 90 TL, © Roy King/SuperStock International, 90 TR, © SuperStock International, 90 B, © Jon Ortner/Tony Stone Images, 91, © Charles Sykes/Visuals Unlimited, 92, © Peter Saloutos/Tony Stone Images, 93, © AFP/Corbis-Bettman, 95, © Andy Sacks/Tony Stone Images, 96, © Bob Thomason/Tony Stone Images, 97, © Everett Johnson/Tony Stone Images, 98, © Courtesy of U.S. Space Camp®/U.S. Space and Rocket Center, 99, © Inga Spence/Tom Stack & Associates, 102, © Gurmankin/Morina/Visuals Unlimited, 104, © Daniel Hummel/The Image Bank, 105, © Rosemary Calvert/Tony Stone Images, 107, © Robert C. Simpson/Valan Photos, 108, © Art Wolfe/Tony Stone Images, 109, © Barrie Rokeach/Rokeach Visual Photography, 110, © Stan Osolinski/Tony Stone Images, 115, © UPI/Corbis-Bettmann, 116, © The Granger Collection, 119, © Jean Bruneau/Valan Photos, 121, © Doris De Witt/Tony Stone Images, 122 TL, © Kennon Cooke/Valan Photos, 122 TM, © Reuters/Corbis-Bettman, 123, © John Edwards/Tony Stone Images, 124, © Jorgen Vogt/The Image Bank, 125, © Hulton Getty/Tony Stone Images, 127, © Albert Normandin/The Image Bank, 128, © George Hunter/Tony Stone Images, 129, © Wayne Shiels/Valan Photos, 130, © Aubrey Diem/Valan Photos, 132, © Alexander Alland Sr./Corbis-Bettmann, 133, © John Warden/Tony Stone Images, 134, © Gordon Fisher/Tony Stone Images, 135, © Barry Rowland/Tony Stone Images, 140, © Mark Thayer, Boston, 141, © David Young-Wolff/PhotoEdit, 143, © Mark Thayer, Boston, 144 T, © Steve Leonard/Tony Stone Images, 144 B, © Robert Frerck/Odyssey Productions, 145 T, © Wolfgang Kaehler/Wolfgang Kaehler Photography, 145 BL, © John Elk/Tony Stone Images, 145 BR, © Will & Deni McIntyre/Tony Stone Images, 155, © G. Brad Lewis/Tony Stone Images, 157, © Nigel Press/Tony Stone Images, 184 T, © A. & L. Sinibaldi/Tony Stone Images, 184 B, © John Beatty/Tony Stone Images, 185 T, © Hans Strand/Tony Stone Images, 185 BL, © Spencer Swanger/Tom Stack & Associates, 185 BR, © Paul Chesley/Tony Stone Images.